D1614286

CHRISTIAN DEMOCRACY IN EUROPE

CHRISTIAN DEMOCRACY IN EUROPE
A COMPARATIVE PERSPECTIVE

Edited by

David Hanley

Pinter Publishers
London & New York

Distributed exclusively in the USA & Canada by St Martin's Press

Pinter Publishers
25 Floral Street, Covent Garden, London, WC2E 9DS, United Kingdom
First published in Great Britain 1994

Distributed Exclusively in the USA and Canada by St Martin's Press,
Inc., Room 400, 175 Fifth Avenue, New York, NY10010, USA

British Library Cataloguing in Publication Data
A CIP catalogue record for this book is available from the British
Library

ISBN 1 85567 086 0

Library of Congress Cataloging-in-Publication Data

Christian democracy in Europe: a comparative perspective / edited by
    David Hanley.
        p.   cm.
    Includes bibliographical references and index.
    ISBN 1–85567–086–0
    1. Christian democratic parties – Europe.   2. Christian democracy
    – Europe.   I. Hanley, D. L. (David L.), 1944– .
JN94.A979C45 1994
324.24'082 – dc20   93–37728
                                                                            CIP

Typeset by Florencetype Ltd, Kewstoke, Avon
Printed and bound in Great Britain by Biddles Ltd of Guildford and King's Lynn

CONTENTS

LIST OF TABLES

LIST OF CONTRIBUTORS

David Broughton is Lecturer in Politics in the School of European Studies, University of Wales, Cardiff

Patrice Buffotot is Research Fellow in European and International Politics, University of Nanterre, France

Guido Dierickx is Dean of the Faculty of Social Sciences, University of Antwerp, Belgium

Mark Donovan is Lecturer in Politics, School of European Studies, University of Wales, Cardiff

Robert Elgie is Lecturer in Politics, Department of European Studies, University of Loughborough

David Hanley is Professor of European Studies, University of Wales, Cardiff

Lauri Karvonen is Lecturer in Political Science, Åbo Akademi, Finland

Joan Keating is Research Assistant in the School of Business and Economic Studies, University of Leeds

Kees van Kersbergen is Lecturer in Political Science, Free University of Amsterdam, Netherlands

Paul Lucardie is Director of the Centre for Documentation on Dutch Political Parties, University of Gröningen, Netherlands

John Madeley is Lecturer in Government, London School of Economics and Political Science

Wolfgang Müller is Professor of Political Science, University of Vienna, Austria

Hans-Martien ten Napel is Lecturer in Political Science, University of Leiden, Netherlands

Barbara Steininger is Lecturer in Political Science, University of Vienna, Austria

LIST OF ACRONYMS

ACLI	Association of Catholic Workers
ACW	Algemeen Christelijk Werkersverbond
AGALEV	(Flemish Ecologists)
ARP	(Calvinist) Anti-Revolutionary Party
BB	Boerenbund (Farmers' League)
BDA	(Federation of German Employers)
CD	Centre Démocrate
CDA	Christian Democratic Appeal
CDI	Christian Democrat International
CDP	Centre Démocratie et Progrès
CDS	Centre des Démocrates Sociaux
CDU-CSU	Christian Democratic Union/Christian Social Union
CEPIC	Centre Politique des Indépendants et Cadres Chrétiens
CEPESS	Centre d'Etudes Politiques, Economiques et Sociales
CEUCD	Central European Union of Christian Democrats
CFE-1	Conventional Forces in Europe
CHU	(Dutch Reformed) Christian Historical Union
CISL	(Italian trade union confederation)
CLN	Committee for National Liberation
COREL	Committee for Electoral Reform
CPP	Christian People's Party
CSCE	Conference on Security and Co-operation in Europe
CSG	Catholic Social Guild
CSP	Christlich Soziale Partei (Christian Social Party – forerunner of ÖVP)
CV	Cartellverband der katholischen österreichischen Studentenverbindungen (Catholic student fraternity)
CVP	Christelijke Volkspartij (Christian People's Party)
DC	Démocratie Chrétienne
DC	(Italian Christian Democratic Party)
DGB	(main German industrial trade union federation)
ECDU	European Christian Democratic Union
EDU	European Democratic Union
EPC	European Political Co-operation
EPP	European People's Party

FDF	Front Démocratique des Francophones
FDP	Free Democrat Party (German liberals)
FG	Fine Gael
FN	Front National
FPÖ	Freiheitliche Partei Österreichs
IDU	International Democratic Union
IRBM	Intermediate Range Ballistic Missiles
KDS	Kristen Demokratisk Samling
KVP	(Catholic People's Party)
MOC	Mouvement Ouvrier Chrétien
MR	Mouvement Réformateur
MRA	Moral Rearmament
MRP	Mouvement Républicain Populaire
NCMV	National Christelijk Middenstandsverbond
ND	Nea Demokratia
NEI	Nouvelles Equipes Internationales
OCDA	Organisation of Christian Democrats in America
ÖGB	(trade union congress)
ÖVP	Österreichische Volkspartei (Austrian People's Party)
PB	Parti van de Berger (Citizen's Party)
PCI	(Italian Communist Party)
PDP	Partido Democratico Popular
PP	Partido Popular
PPE	Parti Populaire Européen
PPI	Parti Populare Italiano (Italian Popular Party)
PR	Parti Républicain
PS	Parti Socialiste
PSC	Parti Social Chrétien
PvdA	(Dutch Social Democrats)
PVV	Partij voor Vrijheid en Vooruitgang (Dutch Liberal Party)
RDC	Rassemblement du Centre
RPR	Rassemblement pour la République
RW	Rassemblement Wallon
SDI	Strategic Defense Initiative
SDP	(British) Social Democratic Party
SI	Socialist International
SKL	Suomen Kristillinen Liitto
SP	Socialist Party
SPD	Sozialdemokratische Partei Deutschlands
SPÖ	Sozialistische Partei Österreichs
UDB	Union Démocratique Belge
UDC	Union du Centre
UDF	(Confederation of French centre-right parties)

VU   Volksunie (Flemish nationalist party)
VVD   Volkspartij voor Vrijheid en Democratie ([Conservative]
          Liberal Party)

ACKNOWLEDGEMENTS

This project began as part of the 1992 Joint Sessions of the European Consortium for Political Research, held in Limerick. I am most grateful to the Organising Committee for providing such a good setting for our discussions and to all the contributors for their prompt delivery of manuscripts and their readiness to respond to editorial suggestions. My task as editor has been lightened by the generous help of my colleagues David Broughton and Mark Donovan, as well as by the invaluable aid of Anne James and the secretarial team of the School of European Studies.

David Hanley
University of Wales, College of Cardiff

INTRODUCTION: CHRISTIAN DEMOCRACY AS A POLITICAL PHENOMENON

David Hanley

It is customary when introducing a work on a familiar topic to justify the new contribution by referring to the inadequacies of the existing literature. In the case of Christian Democracy (CD), however, one has to talk less in terms of inadequacy than of non-existence. Considering the weight of this movement in the politics of contemporary Europe, it is astonishing how little academic attention it actually attracts. Scholars remain grateful for the pioneering work of Michael Fogarty (1957); Ronald Irving's (1973, 1979) lucid studies of the French variant and his comparative work on the bigger parties; the exploratory work of Mayeur (1980); and the concise introduction by Letamendia (1977). Most of these, however, already date from the 1970s or before. Hugues Portelli and his collaborators have drawn our attention to the international aspects of the movement in a work that ranges far beyond Europe (Portelli and Jansen, 1986), and Roberto Papini (1988) has enlarged our knowledge of the historical development of the movement. John Whyte's work on the wider question of Catholicism and politics contributes some suggestive comparative insights (Whyte, 1981). Scholars close to the movement have themselves contributed useful work, much of it in outlets close to one or other of the CD parties and hence perhaps less well known than it might otherwise be (Clemens, 1989; Jansen, 1989; Becker and Klepsch, 1990). Some of the most recent work is patchy both in coverage and quality (Caciagli et al., 1992). But there is still a gap in terms of detailed studies of big national parties, not to mention work on more specialised areas such as comparative ideological or policy studies. The international dimension of the movement has also received relatively little attention, in comparison with its rapid recent growth (Pridham and Pridham, 1979; Pridham, 1982).

This omission is all the more astonishing when we examine the salience of the CD movement. In 1993 it governs (usually in partnership) Italy and the Benelux countries (in all of which it has long been the natural party of government), France, Germany and Greece. Recently it has shared power in Portugal and Ireland. Its attraction for the UK Conservatives is such that for some time they have been assiduously seeking membership of the CD group in the European Parliament. One can only explain the lack of academic attention to the CD movement by concluding that governing parties have become boring for political scientists, an assertion that is supported *a contrario* by the fate meted out to social democratic parties. Widely held to be in crisis – gravely so in the view of some – these parties have at the very least been struggling to hang on to their vote in most of Europe and in a number of cases they have lost office for long periods (Lemke and Marks, 1992). Yet these parties attract far more study. It would be interesting to make a bibliometric comparison between studies of Social Democracy and Christian Democracy undertaken over the last twenty years; it would be a safe bet that the former would win by a mile.

Recent developments in Europe have all, however, pointed to an increasing role for Christian Democracy. Within EC institutions, it is clear that the CD groups are a major force behind integrationist drives such as the push for monetary and political union, often abetted most closely by their social democratic rivals. Outside the EC, the CD movement has seen a dramatic upswing in previously unpromising territory such as Scandinavia. In Eastern Europe with the breakdown of communist rule and the (temporary?) discrediting of social democracy by association with Stalinist excesses, CD parties have emerged or in some cases re-emerged into positions of prominence or governmental authority; the Czech lands, Slovakia, Hungary, Slovenia and Croatia are obvious examples. The international organisations of the CD movement are striving to incorporate and encourage these new forces. Despite all this activity, the overall CD profile still remains remarkably low compared to that of its social democratic rival.

Even allowing for the rich ideological dimension of social democracy and its fascinatingly arcane structural problems such as its factionalism, there is a stark imbalance here that needs to be rectified.

The present volume aims to help fill what is clearly a very large gap. It falls into several distinct parts. The first seeks to identify more specifically the whole phenomenon of Christian Democracy. Every chapter in the volume, however, runs up against this fundamental problem of definition at some point, whatever the starting point of the individual author's investigation. Indeed if there were one single lesson to be derived from this whole exercise it would be that Christian Democracy is in many ways an elusive and shifting phenomenon, albeit probably susceptible of a slightly tighter definition than some of its rivals, conservatism for example.

Having set down a number of hypotheses about the 'essence' of the movement, the volume then addresses the ways in which this identity is manifested. Clearly the action of large, successful CD parties is the most obvious manifestation, and the second part of the book is thus devoted to the study of such parties. Much of the CD presence in Europe however is secured, and not always on the periphery, by smaller forces. Some of these have declined from positions of power, others have never reached such exalted positions. Others again may be at the start of a rising curve, however astonishing this might seem in an age reputedly destined for inevitable secularisation. In general, such forces are little known, and the third part of the volume seeks to rectify this omission. Finally, we turn our attention beyond the boundaries of the nation state which have implicitly dominated most of the previous chapters, in order to explore the international dimension of Christian Democracy, examining in particular its attempts to build a transnational party and its dilemmas with regard to the defence and security of Europe. We thus cover a wide range of ground in our attempt to pin down the CD movement; but it is to the initial problem of definition that we must now return.

Most political scientists if asked would probably say that Christian Democracy is a form of party that belongs among the moderate conservatives, the centre right or some such anodine formula (Layton-Henry, 1982; Laver, Gallagher and Mair, 1992). If pressed further, respondents might claim that it does have a recognisable doctrine based on Catholic social thought (Maritain and Mounier would probably be mentioned at this point) and a commitment to cultural pluralism. To this might be added a policy style that characteristically contains a fairly generous type of welfarism and, in the domain of foreign affairs, an unswerving attachment to European federalism and an uncritical Atlanticism.

Like all caricatures, such a portrait of today's Christian Democracy would contain some truth, but it would also err by exaggeration and omission. CD parties do indeed cover a wide range of political opinion and practice, as this volume makes clear. But like all members of the different political families within the modern world, they have basic features in common (Seiler, 1980). It is notoriously difficult to define ideal types; thus what follows is an approach to conceptualising the common identity of CD parties.

Such parties can only be understood historically. Arising in the latter half of the nineteenth century, they were essentially parties of religious, that is Catholic defence. Usually they were linked to Catholic social movements, though the relationship between the two by no means automatically favoured the development of political parties, as Mayeur points out (1980, p. 10). While their social thought was generally anti-capitalist, it was often derived from organicist or corporatist modes of thinking, the relationship of which to modern electoral democracy was not always evident; to call these early religious parties Christian Democratic is thus premature. The structures and the performance of such parties varied considerably from one country to another, depending on such factors as the attitudes of conservative forces, the degree of division or unity among Catholics and the policies of government (anti-clerical or pluralist) (Whyte, 1981). But it can be said that by 1914 such forces were generally in favour of parliamentary democracy (albeit with some significant exceptions, especially outside Western Europe) and social policies built on welfarist principles, while remaining vigilant about the defence of Catholic prerogatives and institutions, especially schools. It seems clear that these parties deriving from a religious impulse were qualitatively distinct both from liberal and socialist rivals (both secularist in orientation) and from conservative groupings (which may well have appealed to religion, but only as an adjunct to other criteria, be they order, tradition, hierarchy or self-interest).

The movement towards political modernisation brought these parties ever more explicitly into the democratic framework. The disastrous experience of fascism was decisive in removing lingering doubts about the need for full democracy among the parties of religious defence, and by the end of World War II such parties could legitmately be called Christian Democratic. But as the clerical/anti-clerical antagonism softened and Catholics negotiated their place within political regimes, and as the protective network of the welfare state became generalised, the identity of such parties became more blurred. This was even more the case as they became essential members of government coalitions in much of Europe. Many analysts believe that this loss of identity has gone so far as to render these parties almost indistinguishable from contemporary conservatism. Even a sympathiser like Mayeur (1980, p. 236) holds that 'in Belgium, the Netherlands, Germany, Austria and Italy . . . they have taken the place of the conservative parties'. Layton-Henry (1982, p. 17) agrees that 'they can be identified as conservatives of the pragmatic and reformist tradition'.

Such verdicts are too severe. It is true that in the 1990s the differences between established political families seem to have been reduced everywhere; one has only to think of the huge ideological recentring undertaken by Social Democracy in recent times (Paterson and Gillespie, 1993). Nevertheless within this reduced ideological space, Christian Democrats are as anxious as any of their rivals to preserve their identity and they have a clear basis on which to do this.

All political parties have long memories of where they came from. Christian Democrats remain conscious of their religious origins first and foremost; they are in politics to express a Christian vision of humankind and its destiny. This vision has implications at both doctrinal and behavioural levels.

The most articulate version of CD doctrine is that of personalism, a term to which Christian Democrats from the Low Countries usually append the prefix 'social'. Personalism sees society as composed not of indviduals (as in the liberal paradigm), but persons. The person is an outgoing, fundamentally sociable being, whose destiny is realised not in competition (again as with liberalism) but more through insertion into different types of community, be it neighbourhood, church, family or nation. This type of thought is instinctively solidaristic and as such always potentially anti-capitalist; it is surely the most lasting legacy of older Catholic social doctrine and it is qualitatively distinct from liberalism or conservatism. Acceptance of the 'social market' may have dulled the original impulse behind such solidaristic thinking, but it is still there within the internal debates of most CD parties, a testimony to the distinctiveness of this type of politics. Other allegedly distinct features of CD doctrine, such as belief in an integrated Europe, are much poorer guides to the specificity of CD politics, not least because they are nowadays so widely shared by other families, especially liberals and social democrats. It is this specifically solidaristic impulse which translates so readily into the type of pro-welfare policies associated with CD parties.

If doctrine and policy are one pole of CD consistency, the behaviour of the CD electorate is another. We know that there is a distinct type of CD voter (Broughton, 1992). Older than average, with a high rate of religious observance, fairly classless in sociological terms (though with a tendency for the middle classes and rural populations to be over-represented), these voters are increasingly pro-European and strongly pro-welfare in policy terms. But they are also deeply attached to traditional Christian morality and to the protection of material Catholic interests such as schools or hospitals, as has long been argued (Seiler, 1980). Here is clear evidence for the religious orientation of these voters. It would also be interesting to know how many of them have been influenced by membership of some kind of voluntary organisation with a link to religion. This is one of the reasons for the rise of CD parties in the first place; it seems fair to postulate that the continuing distinctiveness of a CD identity will depend to a large extent on the ability of such organisations to survive. The whole area of the voluntary sector and its relation to actual CD political parties is an ill-understood phenomenon, however, and more research is urgently needed on this topic.

If there are ideological and behavioural signs of a distinct CD identity, it may be asked which parties qualify for the label. The assumption behind such a question is often that many members of the CD International cannot in fact be classified in this way. This is a dangerous way to approach the problem. It is pointless to draw up a scale where zero represents an ultra-conservative party and ten a pure CD archetype and then try to place existing parties along the scale. Even so, this exercise is quite often undertaken in an implicit way, with the parties of the Low Countries nearer the ten mark and the Christian Democratic Union/Christian Social Union (CDU/CSU) scoring nearer to zero.

Some parties have always had a more explicit ideology and a stronger infrastructure within civil society. But even within these, there has always been a tension between those who were in politics to pursue a Christian vision and those more concerned with preserving the social order, provided it accommodated certain religious demands. CD parties have always been polarised between the principled and the minimalists. What has happened is that this tension has become stronger, with the advantage going increasingly to the pragmatists or minimalists. There are many reasons for this, and it is beyond the scope of this introduction to cover them. But the growing movement towards secularisation and the apparent success of the 'social market' (essentially sufficient state intervention to mitigate the social effects of unbridled competition) would seem to have undermined the position of the principled Christian Democrats.

This does not mean however that there are no more dilemmas or choices for CD parties to make or that the pragmatists have triumphed completely. It certainly does not mean that CD parties have become indistinguishable from conservative parties. The conclusion to this volume sets out an agenda for continuing conflict, which will revolve around the question: what is the purpose of CD parties in today's world? We may for the moment retain an image of a distinct political movement, which the succeeding chapters attempt to elaborate more fully.

The contributions by Guido Dierickx and Kees van Kersbergen add considerable nuances to this portrait. Dierickx attempts to distil the essence of CD ideology from recent statements in Belgium and the Netherlands, and he does so by setting them against the other major ideologies of today, including the great rival, Social Democracy. By focusing on the concept of social personalism, he suggests an ideology that is both solidaristic (opening out onto progressive social policies) yet at the same time developmental, one that is modernising in ways that its rivals are not. This demonstration of the nature of CD ideology is supported by an examination of CD attitudes to a wide range of policy issues. Approaching the problem of CD identity from a different angle, that of policy style, van Kersbergen reaches similar conclusions. The movement's essential function is to balance competing social interests within the state sphere, a task which it accomplishes mainly through the application of social policy. What is characteristic about such policy however is its family orientation, the family being seen as an ideal tool of social regulation. Kersbergen shows a logical structure to CD thought in which concepts of family, property, and guaranteed welfare and social rights buttress each other to maintain a system which accepts natural inequalities, the better to mitigate their effects by social intervention. This Gramscian or Poulantzian view of the way in which class tensions are defused through the 'black box' of the state enriches considerably the received views about CD doctrines of solidarism, without invalidating the ethical impulse behind them.

Another general interpretation of the nature of Christian Democracy is found in the first chapter of the second part of the book, which deals with CD parties that have played major roles in governing their countries. Starting from their analysis of the CD parties in the Low Countries, Paul Lucardie and Hans-Martien ten Napel accept that CD is a flexible and useful tool of political and social modernisation, but ask if it has not been so successful in its task as to be in danger of losing its identity. They see the CD experience in the Low Countries as the start of a drift among leading parties towards a neo-liberal orientation in policy and ideology at the expense of the more traditional personalist slant. This liberal drift may be seen as a factor in the continuing high success rate of parties like the CDU/CSU, the implication being that such parties do better because they appeal more openly to neo-liberal or even conservative standpoints and do not bother overmuch with personalist trimmings. In particular the liberal drift is seen as having helped enlarge parties' audiences beyond the initial hard core of believing or practising Christians, who are nowadays a commodity in declining supply.

This criticism regarding the loss of doctrinal specificity and moves towards some soggy but popular 'centrist' ground could just as easily be levelled at social democratic rivals of course, and there is some truth in both accusations. But there are severe implications for the consistency of the CD movement. CD theorists were always quite savage towards liberalism, not just because of its secularist tendencies but also because of its complacent views as to the beneficial effects of market capitalism; some of the more radical ones found liberalism more of an enemy than Marxism

(Mounier, 1949). Such analysis confirms that there are indeed two polarities within the movement, with a very principled reading of Christian Democracy (found especially in some smaller states) confronting a much looser, pragmatic interpretation aimed more at securing power and achieving results.

Much of the book then engages the very nature of the CD movement, offering a number of hypotheses. After this attempt to pin down the identity of Christian Democracy, attention turns to its protagonists. A number of chapters focus first, as was mentioned, on the major parties with a prominent record in government. While each is to a certain extent unique, care is taken to bring out the similarities between these parties. Analysis is undertaken of their development, structures, ideological and policy stances and their record in office, particularly when, as is almost inevitably the case, they are coalition partners.

CD parties are not all dominant, however, and one of the aims of this volume is to consider the role of 'lesser brethren', especially as there are sometimes more lessons to be learned here than from the study of more prominent actors. Lauri Karvonen's comparative study of the rising CD movements in Scandinavia reveals some paradoxes. Much of their recent success would appear to be due to a protest vote, which combines economic resentment and dissatisfaction with the political class in general with an older fund of conservative protest articulated around moral or cultural issues. In fact these parties would appear to have drawn the sort of vote that normally goes to more populist parties further south. Only time will tell whether this agglomeration of different types of support can become a more lasting phenomenon or whether it is simply a flash in the pan.

The French and British cases reveal deeper dimensions of the CD movement. Scholars have suggested historical reasons for the consistent failure of the 'eldest daughter of the Church' to sustain a viable CD movement (Dreyfus, 1988). Robert Elgie's chapter reminds us that in fact the French movement in its different incarnations has been quite powerful since World War II, only to lose this hard-won position relatively quickly and apparently forever. What his study reveals is a factor present in much of the volume, namely the power of institutional constraints, in particular the electoral system. Much of the difficulty which the French CDS has in simply existing as an autonomous force can be traced to the tyranny of the majority ballot.

Institutional constraints also underlie the little-known story of the failure of a CD tradition to take root in Britain. Even if we suppose that the tradition can only have started from a minority base (Catholics), it was bound to run into the power of established institutions (the Labour and to some extent the Liberal parties) as well as the strongly entrenched class divisions (often with ethnic underpinnings) within British Catholicism, which proved harder to overcome than on the Continent. Joan Keating's study thus differs from all the others in that it analyses not an autonomous and self-conscious movement but rather a series of groups trying to influence established and more significant movements. Nevertheless, some of the difficulties encountered in Britain have been similar to those experienced in more promising contexts.

Heavily implicit in most studies of Christian Democracy has been the supposition that it is a Catholic movement. The chapters by Lauri Karvonen and John Madeley remind us that Protestant variants continue to flourish in the north of Europe. The Norwegian case study goes deeper to reveal that within Protestantism itself there is more than one strand. Madeley shows that the Calvinist tradition involves a particular view of the relationship between state and individual, and indeed between the latter and his/her church. In contrast to the Lutheran tradition with its view of minimal need for political commitment on behalf of the individual (whose relationship is directly with God, omitting intermediaries such as church and state apparatuses) the Calvinist or Pietist attitude to politics is more activist. No longer content to rely on the state to ensure the conditions for the propagation of religion, it appeals to Christians to mobilise politically against a rising tide of secularism which the state and its allies in the established churches cannot or will not combat. Such a basis for mobilisation is of course compatible with the defence of other interests of a cultural or peripheral nature. But it is highly original, and it represents a very different style of Christian politics from that practised in the Benelux states or Germany. Is it therefore meaningful to speak of their all being part of the same CD family? Or should we think in terms of a particular Nordic sub-species, the more so because, as Karvonen shows, the CD parties in Scandinavia do in any case relate so closely to each other?

Despite the universal claims of Christian churches, they and the parties which claim the Christian label operate in the arena of the nation state. It would be facile to believe that they are immune to national factors. The Belgian case with its minimal levels of contact between French- and Dutch-speaking parties (who were all in the one party less than two decades ago) is proof enough of this. Yet more than any other political family, the CD parties have striven explicitly for some kind of supranational identity; one would be tempted to say that perhaps the one thing they really share with liberals is a tangible discomfort in the face of raw nationalism. This is not simply a function of membership (in most cases) of churches with universalist pretensions but relates to a world view posited fundamentally on mutual understanding and reciprocity between individuals and groups. CD manifestoes like to speak, unselfconsciously, of 'making strangers into friends'. Christian Democrats recognise that humankind fulfils itself in different kinds of communities, one of which may well be the nation, alongside the family or voluntary associations. But equally they know the fine line that often separates genuine identification with one's nation from unwarrantable pride and chauvinism. Hence their longstanding attachment to European integration as a means of overcoming nationalism. It should be pointed out however that some have expressed doubts as to whether this supranational commitment extends readily to embrace those of non-European and particularly Islamic culture.

Two contributions to this volume examine this supranational dimension. What they find is that the reality sometimes belies the promises. The

European Peoples' Party (EPP) thus appears in David Hanley's study as something of a misnomer. In no way could it be seen as a transnational mass party; rather it is a privileged forum for collaboration between like-minded elites of similar social background, which enables a considerable amount of co-ordination to take place within the decision-making processes inside EC institutions. But these elites are still national politicians first and foremost, operating in their own states. The most that can be said is that the EPP is better placed than other transnational groupings to take advantage of moves towards greater political integration, especially if this were to involve greater power for the European Parliament. But this agenda remains fraught with difficulties.

On a less visible level the EPP helps give identity and cohesion to the CD family by fulfilling the classic function of party Internationals, acting as a gatekeeper and bestowing legitimacy on prospective entrants. It is suggested that even this apparently simple task is an invidious one, quite simply because it involves making a definition of the nature of the movement. Not for the first time in this book, a tension emerges between the principled wing of the movement with a strict definition (arguably applicable only to a handful of parties) and a less principled version which prefers numbers to quality and has often endorsed dual membership of the Conservative as well as the CD International. The strange case of the candidacy of the UK Conservatives (arguably one of those parties in Europe least qualified for membership of the EPP) illustrates this tension neatly.

In addition to its integrationist stances on European unity, the CD movement has long been known for the coherence of its views on security policy. The Cold War which saw the flowering of most of the CD parties as parties of government also saw them develop an Atlanticist orthodoxy. Always fearful of a potential Soviet threat, they were the most enthusiastic supporters of NATO, never wavering over stressful issues such as the adoption of flexible response or the installation of the Cruise and Pershing missiles in the early 1980s. If CD parties called for talks on arms, missile or troop reductions, then such appeals were always couched in pragmatic language. The American presence in Europe was seen as essential and, more tacitly, American primacy in the Alliance was accepted. This was even true of the French Centre des Démocrates Sociaux (CDS), who thus swam against the tide of defence orthodoxy set in motion by de Gaulle.

The end of the Cold War and the emergence of possible new threats on the southern flank of Europe on the one hand, coupled with increasing pressure from within the USA for reduced involvement in Europe on the other, have meant a reappraisal of CD strategic thinking. These pressures have reinforced longstanding latent tendencies within the movement. For as Patrice Buffotot shows, CD efforts today aim at creating a 'European pillar' of the Atlantic Alliance. Some CD politicians would see this as a first step towards European self-sufficiency in defence matters, others more as a necessary reinforcement of an Alliance that is probably still an inescapable necessity. But both shades of opinion are determined to push the EC much more towards common action on defence and security matters. Thus it is that CD parties have pressed for the reinforcement of the Political Co-operation mechanism and indeed for the creation of a Defence and Security Commissioner and Defence and Security Councils of Ministers. As ever, the European Parliament is to be closely associated with such developments. In fact CD federalism finds another string to its bow in the defence and security issue. The Maastricht treaty only gave the beginnings of satisfaction here, and we may clearly expect pressure for more integrated defence and security policy coordination from Christian Democrats in the future. There remains, as Buffotot shows, in addition to resistance from possible partners (the UK Conservatives, for instance) considerable uncertainty as to which institutions should be privileged in furthering the integrationist process (the EP, WEU, the EC Council, etc.).

These considerations of the international profile of the CD movement complete the survey undertaken here. The picture that emerges is of a movement that is very wide ranging in the strength and achievement of its members. Yet there is undoubtedly a very high degree of cohesion across national boundaries; the fact is that all these actors have common origins and a common political culture; they share many policy options and they have a distinct style. The internal cohesion of the movement is subject to tension; but such is the fate of all political movements, and the Christian Democrats' cohesiveness is arguably much higher than that of the rival/partner social democracy. CD parties are certainly key players in the European political system of today, and this volume will have achieved its aims if readers come away with a greater awareness of their origins, policies and likely development in the future.

References

Becker, W. and Klepsch, E. (eds), 1990, *Zur Geschichte der christlich-demokratischen Bewegung in Europa*, Knoth, Melle.
Broughton, D., 1992, The Christian Democratic voter: a four-country comparison, paper presented to ECPR Joint Sessions, Limerick.
Caciagli, M. et al., 1992, *Christian Democracy in Europe*, Institut de Ciencias Politiques i Socials, Barcelona.
Clemens, C., 1989, *Christian Democracy: the different dimensions of a modern movement*, EPP, Brussels.
Dreyfus, F.-G., 1988, *Histoire de la démocratie chrétienne en France*, Albin Michel, Paris.
Fogarty, M., 1957, *Christian Democracy in Western Europe, 1820–1953*, Routledge and Kegan Paul, London.
Irving, R., 1973, *Christian Democracy in France*, Allen & Unwin, London.
Irving, R., 1979, *The Christian Democratic parties of Western Europe*, Allen & Unwin, London.
Jansen, T. (ed.), 1989, *Efforts to define a Christian Democratic doctrine*, EPP, Brussels.
Laver, M., Gallagher, M. and Mair, P., 1992, *Representative government in Western Europe*, McGraw Hill, New York.
Layton-Henry, Z., 1982, *Conservative politics in Western Europe*, Macmillan, London.
Lemke, C. & Marks, G. (eds), 1992, *The crisis of socialism in Western Europe*, Duke University Press, Durham & London.

Letamendia, P., 1977, *La Démocratie chrétienne*, Presses Universitaires de France, Paris.

Mayeur, J.-M., 1980, *Des partis catholiques à la démocratie chrétienne*, Colin, Paris.

Mounier, E., 1949, *Le personnalisme et la révolution au XXe. siècle*, Seuil, Paris.

Papini, R., 1988, *L'Internationale démocrate-chrétienne, 1925–86*, Cerf, Paris.

Paterson, W. and Gillespie, R. (eds), 1993, Rethinking Social Democracy in Western Europe, *West European Politics* 16 (1).

Portelli, H. and Jansen, T. (eds), 1986, *La démocratie chrétienne: force internationale*, Institut de Politique Internationale et Européenne, Nanterre.

Pridham, G., 1982, Christian Democrats, Conservatives and transnational party cooperation in the European Community: centre forward or centre right?, in Layton-Henry, pp. 318–46.

Pridham, G. and Pridham, P., 1979, Transnational parties in the European Community I: the party groups in the European Parliament, in Henig, S (ed.), *Political Parties in the European Community*, Allen & Unwin, London.

Seiler, D.-L., 1980, *Partis et familles politiques*, Presses Universitaires de France, Paris.

Whyte, J., 1981, *Catholics in Western democracies: a study in political behaviour*, Gill & MacMillan, Dublin.

THE NATURE OF CHRISTIAN DEMOCRACY

1

CHRISTIAN DEMOCRACY AND ITS IDEOLOGICAL RIVALS: AN EMPIRICAL COMPARISON IN THE LOW COUNTRIES

Guido Dierickx

Some methodological reflections

Systematic comparisons of political ideologies are a rarity in academic literature. This striking deficiency can partially be explained by the poor conceptual apparatus provided by earlier generations of analysts. Every attempt at comparison must therefore begin by proposing its own concepts and definitions.

An ideology is a systematised set of opinions, meaning that the opinions have been hierarchically ordered to some degree. Among the opinions we can then distinguish at least two levels: principles and applications, or final and intermediary objectives. The ideological principles function as premises from which applications can be derived for specific issues. But they also function as final objectives which can be reached only via the realisation of one or several intermediary objectives. The terms 'principles' and 'applications' emphasise the logical structure of the ideological system, the terms 'final' and 'intermediary' focus on the phases of its realisation. In this chapter we will mainly consider the latter typology.

Most political ideologies include more than opinions about the objectives of political action. A fully developed ideology has opinions about all major phases and aspects of the political decision-making process: objectives, problems, and issues of power and conflict. It may be the case that rival ideologies only disagree about a few of these opinions. In that case, the majority of their opinions become less relevant for comparative purposes. We could argue that the five major political ideologies in Belgium do indeed differ on all counts, i.e. on their final objectives, on their problem definitions, and on their perception of power and conflict. In this discussion, however, we can elaborate only on the contrasts with regard to their problem definitions and final objectives.

To begin with we shall try to meet a first requirement of a good comparison, symmetry. The ideologies will be compared on the basis of comparable opinions, drawn from the historical (or diachronical) structure of ideologies. We shall first compare them with regard to their most salient problem definition, then with regard to their final objectives. We shall conclude with a comparison of their opinions about several salient issues.

A comparison of ideologies can only be a comparison of ideal-typical ideologies. Belgium is well suited for comparative purposes since it features no less than five distinctive ideologies which all succeeded in recruiting a considerable and more or less stable following: liberalism, socialism, social-personalism, ecologism and nationalism. The latter two seem to be missing, at least for the time being, within the Dutch ideological space.

Ideologies are variable and fluid entities. The analyst must reduce this variability to an ideal type. But how can we define this type? There is probably no final answer to this question. However, two criteria should clearly be respected.

First, the ideal type should be close to the average of all existing manifestations of the ideology, especially to those that have authority and political impact. The most important sources for the following analysis are official documents issued by the parties. Fortunately, both the Francophone and the Flemish Christian Democrats devoted a recent party congress to their ideology, the Parti Social Chrétien (PSC) in 1983 and the Christelijke Volkspartij (CVP) in 1986. The Dutch Christian Democratic Appeal (CDA) seems to rely less on congresses than on its intellectually powerful study centre. The major document issued by this Weten-schappelijk Instituut voor het CDA is a full-length book *Publieke Gerechtigheid* (1990). After careful checking we were satisfied that these Belgian congress documents and the Dutch publication were indeed representative of their respective party ideologies. Moreover, they are being recommended as such by their respective party headquarters.

Second, the ideal types should be formulated so as to stress the differences between ideologies more than the similarities. Ideological dissimilarities are at the origin of many political conflicts, and political conflicts are the lifeblood of democratic decision-making. Therefore, ideological differences are what the political game is all about. Where an outsider would observe only ideological convergence, the insiders would stress the remaining differences. The comparativist sides with the insiders in order to make his comparison more striking. In so doing, however, he tends to locate the political ideologies at the periphery of the ideological space, or at least at an exaggerated distance from its centre.

Both criteria are at odds with each other. The first one tends to stress the convergence of ideologies by ignoring the ideological radicals, while the second tends to stress their divergence in order to increase the clarity of the comparisons. As a result the reader is presented with an ideological space in which the different ideologies occupy a clearer position than in the real political world.

Problem definitions

What are the most salient problems as seen by our political ideologies? It is safe to say that both the Liberal and the Socialist ideologies view the socio-economic problems as fundamental for the development of society. They have been largely successful in claiming a priority for these issues. Christian Democrats, Nationalists and Ecologists, on the other hand, are inclined to question these priorities. For the Christian Democrats philosophical, ethical and, in a broader sense, cultural issues are paramount, while for the Nationalist linguistic and cultural issues are the most salient. The Ecologists display a more diffuse salience pattern since this party does not originate in a clear-cut subcultural opposition in society. It is obvious, though, that this ideology opposes the prime status given to socio-economic issues in the traditional sense.

This elementary fact suggests a hypothesis which will prove extremely useful. The difference in issue salience stems from different evaluations of the societal upheavals in the nineteenth century. The fathers of sociology described this massive social change as a shift from *Gemeinschaft* ('community') to *Gesellschaft* ('society'). To our surprise these traditional concepts prove more useful to compare our five ideologies than the more current distinction between left and right.

Nationalism, ecologism and, to a degree, Christian Democracy, are *Gemeinschaft* ideologies. They question the evolution of our society toward a large-scale and impersonal *Gesellschaft*, and they try to save as much as possible of the old *Gemeinschaft*. They do have rather different types of *Gemeinschaft* in mind and this will show in the differences between their final objectives. But their problem definitions are similar, if not identical.

The socio-linguistic interest of the Nationalists originates in a concern about the disintegration of national bonds. It can no doubt be argued that nationalism became a utopia no earlier than the period of romanticism and that it hardly ever existed in reality, except at a limited local level. Nationalism, in the final analysis, is a social construction of reality that wishes to provide individuals with a large-scale frame for cultural reintegration ('the nation') in a society subject to the disintegration of more local *Gemeinschafts*.

The Ecologists are likewise worried about the disintegration caused by the extensiveness and the impersonality of our (post-)industrial society. Certainly in Flanders the 'small is beautiful' theme is as important as the ecological theme strictly speaking. But this party aims at a different kind of social reintegration than the Nationalists. Neither language nor national heritage are deemed to produce integration, but rather the local community.

The most outspoken *Gesellschaft* ideology is, of course, that of the liberal parties. Their ideological ancestors were the most vocal advocates of modernisation. From the period of Enlightenment on they have striven to emancipate the individuals from the bonds of the old, traditional *Gemeinschaft*, from the Church, the village, the family. Their problem was not weak integration but strong, confining, oppressing integration. In the new *Gesellschaft* the individual would find sufficient possibilities of integration, thanks to the structures of the market, the city, the free associations.

Social democracy also belongs to the *Gesellschaft* ideologies. Socialists concede that the integration of individuals in the new *Gesellschaft* proves to be a problematic process. But they do not regret the disintegration of the old *Gemeinschaft* and they do not want to replace it with a new one. On the contrary, they think that the emancipation of the individuals, especially of the workers, has not yet been completed, and should be further pursued. Because of their common aversion to any lack of emancipation of the individual, social democrats and liberals have long been natural fellow travellers. In Belgium the Socialists split off from the Liberal Party only in the late nineteenth century. Because, however, the Liberals thought that with the emancipation of the middle classes the emancipation effort was largely completed, a clash with the Socialists was inevitable. This clash came to dominate the political arena, but its dominance should not obscure the fact that both ideologies are strongly related.

The Christian Democrats occupy a middle ground between *Gesellschaft* and *Gemeinschaft* ideologies. Originally their main concern was with what they regarded as the disintegration of the religious and ethical community. This disintegration went together with modernisation as influenced by anticlericalism and secularism. But was this disintegration an essential and inevitable part of the new *Gesellschaft*? Here the forefathers of Christian Democracy disagreed, causing a split in the Catholic party in Belgium and between Protestant parties in the Netherlands. In Belgium the more progressive Catholics asserted that the new *Gesellschaft* offered some real opportunities for renewed religious and philosophical integration. The quantitative losses of the Church could be compensated by qualitative gains. In particular the Catholics have made great efforts to establish new types of *Gemeinschaft* within the modern *Gesellschaft*. But their idea of a good *Gemeinschaft* is quite different from that of Nationalists and Ecologists as we shall see.

Final objectives: *Gesellschaft* ideologies

The spokesmen for ideologies tend to formulate their principles and final objectives more in expressive than in instrumental terms. Their phrasing of their ideology aims more at the gathering of a following than at spelling out what exactly they intend to do about the future of their society. This makes the enterprise of discovering the true (i.e. instrumental) ideology a difficult one. This is even more so where parties are not forced to translate their verbal statements into political practice, and where they are not forced to balance the objectives against the means, the potential gains against the costs. This hermeneutic problem is compounded when the student has to read the ideological documents of opposition parties (such as the Ecologists). What they say cannot be compared to what they actually do in office. In what follows we will try to uncover the latent, instrumental objectives by taking into account both verbal statements and political practice.

It is common wisdom that there are basically only three political objectives in a democratic system: liberty, equality and solidarity. However simplistic this statement may sound, it at least suggests a useful working hypothesis. The Liberals have a first claim on liberty, the Socialists on equality, the Christian Democrats and the Nationalists on solidarity. These parties do not focus exclusively on these central principles, but their priorities are nevertheless clear. All ideologies feel compelled to add supporting principles to their somewhat vague central principle in order to avoid misunderstandings and obscurities.

Liberty is a good example of such a vague principle. It can be invoked more readily to suggest what one does not want than to specify what one does want. The Flemish Liberals have therefore resorted to supporting principles such as responsibility, equality of opportunity, and pluralism. This liberty can be seen as a given whenever it is not blocked by external constraints. It is not a liberty which still has to be acquired and to be developed. The only suggestion that this liberty has to be developed toward a more or less specific finality is to be found in a vague reference to the need–satisfaction hierarchy of Maslow. Generally Liberals consider liberty as something to be cherished and to be protected, not as something to be developed and to be steered.

If this liberty does not have a specific finality, one does have to stress its consequences. Free individuals are supposed to be responsible individuals and to initiate all kinds of historical processes, as entrepreneurs in the free market and as citizens in the democratic system.

If liberty and responsibility are qualities of individuals, what does this tell us about the social aspects of human life? No specific finality should be imposed on the individual's liberty from the outside and certainly not from above, i.e. from the government. Liberals are true optimists. The good society will follow from the liberty of individuals striving for their own good, whatever that may be.

It is true, of course, that the Liberals of recent years have looked for safeguards against the potentially perverse consequences of this liberty. They find these safeguards in supporting principles such as equality of opportunity and pluralism. Both want individuals not to hinder each other in the exercise of their liberty. Equality of opportunity is meant to do away with power differences at the outset of the exercise of liberty, whereas pluralism is supposed to avert the temptation to use power in the course of the exercise of liberty. Both principles are to some extent a burden on individual freedom. But by redefining this cost as a value the Liberals believe that this burden will be borne more easily.

Socialists are also heirs to the ideas of the Enlightenment and thus optimists who want to steer individual and collective history to a modest degree only. Their correction of history is based on the principle of equality (and not on the principle of liberty), not because they reject the liberal principle but because they think the era of liberty has not yet dawned. The Liberals have underestimated the external constraints on human liberty, especially the constraints stemming from power relations and from socio-economic inequalities. To do away with this inequality is the main objective of socialist political action.

Socialists, then, tend to stress the forces that oppose the emancipation of individuals. Inequality is based on power and is being reproduced by power processes. They conclude that equality should not be limited to an equality of opportunity but should be extended to an equality of results. Indeed, the competition processes are biased by power differentials, even if equality of opportunity exists at the start of that competition. Equality of results intends to correct those power biases in the economic and in the political market-place.

Because Socialists realise that the restoration of equality must lead to conflict, they have supplemented their final objective with secondary objectives of a tactical nature. They have called for solidarity but this solidarity is one among the underprivileged, among the workers, and is destined to combat the capitalists. It does not extend to people who are not their potential coalition partners in class conflict.

More recently, democratic socialism has displayed more humanistic trends, after questioning the exclusive priority of socio-economic equality. The traditional Liberals have viewed liberty as the necessary and the sufficient condition for human progress. The traditional Socialists have viewed equality in the same light. Once equality had been established the individuals could be left to their own spontaneous development. The Belgian socialist Hendrik De Man replied that such development could not be left to its own inertia and that it should be subjected to active policy-making. However, the impact of his ideas has been less than complete. The latent individualism of the socialist ideology has not been converted into something resembling the personalism of Belgian Christian Democracy. But it cannot be denied that De Man struck a new chord in socialist thought. The present Socialists are more concerned with the unintended effects of bureaucratic intervention because this intervention tends to reduce the citizenry to a set of individuals. At times, socialist spokesmen can be heard expressing a longing for a new spirituality distinct from socialist ideology. The resolve to keep religious philosophies away from public life has, however, not yet weakened to any great degree.

Final objectives: *Gemeinschaft* ideologies

Solidarity is the obvious remedy for all those who regret the societal trend of *Vergesellschaftung*. But the use of solidarity as a final (and not as a supporting) objective can be specified in various ways. All *Gemeinschaft* ideologies agree, however, that solidarity is somehow a criterion for assessing the validity of the development of the individual.

Overall the Ecologists, especially the Flemish Ecologists (AGALEV), form the most radical *Gemeinschaft* party. The solidarity they propose is principally the solidarity of a small-scale loosely organized community with immediate, permanent and strongly affective interpersonal relationships. The resemblance with traditional anarchism is striking. Like the anarchists, the Ecologists not only loathe large-scale economic structures but also large-scale political structures. Both structures do indeed strengthen the social distance (and the hierarchy) between human beings. In the ideal *Gemeinschaft* these social distances will be greatly reduced. Possibly economic performance will be weaker as well. But similar to the old anarchists, the new ones are ready to bear this cost of their reduced economic and political capacities.

Not surprisingly the Ecologists support their solidarity objective with principles such as 'small is beautiful', equality and non-violence. These are all qualities of family, neighbourhood and village communities in their utopian form. Actually our Ecologists are somewhat milder than their anarchist predecessors. Their parties accept a number of achievements of the present economic and political Gesellschaft. But further economic growth is not a must. They attach a high ecological and, let us not forget, social and cultural price tag to a further *Vergesellschaftung*.

Nationalist parties attract a considerable and permanent following only in Flanders. But their brand of solidarity is interesting for comparative purposes as it extends to all the members of the socio-linguistic community. This is a solidarity on a larger scale than the anarchistic variety. It is destined to bridge all distances and oppositions between the members of the same socio-linguistic nation. One would expect the nationalist ideology to elaborate these points by proposing a number of supporting objectives. But the moderate nationalists of the Volksunie have not developed an articulate ideology of their own on most of the socio-economic and philosophical issues on the political agenda. They have more often than not adopted centrist positions, akin to those of the CVP, on socio-economic matters. This is an understandable strategy since either these issues are not very salient to them or the party is divided on them.

On one set of issues the Volksunie has been careful to articulate a position of its own. Earlier nationalist tendencies have been tempted to seek external enemies in order to promote internal solidarity. These tactics are not completely alien to the Volksunie but in principle its nationalism is kept on the right track by the supporting objective of non-violence. The party is in favour of confederal political structures which would ensure the convivium of the nations in Belgium, in Europe and in the entire world. Solidarity within the nation and mutual respect between nations, is how the moderate nationalists hope to reconstruct the world.

In recent years, a more radical nationalist party has come to the forefront in Flanders, and to a lesser extent, in Wallonia. The Vlaams Blok can be compared to the Front National in France in that it wants to safeguard the national cultural heritage by following a logic of exclusion, mainly of Islamic and African immigrants. Here the principle of non-violence, at least of verbal non-violence, is abandoned in order to attack the enemies from without. But there are also enemies from within: the leftist who does not care about the moral fibre of the nation, the economic and political elites who do not care about the daily life of ordinary people.

We will maintain that the Christian Democratic parties in both Belgium and the Netherlands belong to the family of the *Gemeinschaft* ideologies. Yet they are undoubtedly the most moderate members of this family. Indeed, when the Belgian Christian Democrats still defined themselves as personalists, it was easy to mistake them for another variety of individualists. But even that personalism stressed the finality of human development much more than individualism ever did. How this finality had to be specified was left to Christian anthropology and ethics, to which the Christian Democratic party freely referred. The emphasis on very precise policy options with regard to private life, the family, culture and education, left little to the imagination.

More recently (1986) the Flemish CVP has redefined its ideology as 'social-personalism', instead of 'personalism', in order to distance itself explicitly from all kinds of individualism. The emphasis on the development of the personality has remained but its finality is now, more than before, the solidarity with other people. It is fair to say that solidarity is now the final objective of the CVP and that this solidarity consists first of all in the quality of interpersonal relationships. Personalism and solidarity are each other's complement and condition. Hence the concept of 'social-personalism'. The ideal of the social-personalist is friendship between human beings who were once strangers and enemies to each other.

Social-personalism is therefore different from other *Gemeinschaft* ideologies. It is less concerned with the impersonality of the *Gesellschaft* than green anarchism. The *Gesellschaft* allows us to meet strangers with whom we can develop new, solidary relationships. The *Gesellschaft* precedes the *Gemeinschaft* and is its necessary condition. It follows that the social-personalists do not look forward to dismembering the large-scale *Gesellschaft* into smaller *Gemeinschaft* units. They dream instead of mastering the complexities of the *Gesellschaft* with the help of adequate, mostly cultural policies. The *Gesellschaft* is a challenge to the social-personalist and not just a perversion of human society.

The social-personalist is equally reticent towards nationalism because the latter imposes limits on the aspirations toward interpersonal solidarities. Why should a person let his solidarities be confined to the members of his own nation only?

The concept of 'social-personalism' was coined by the Flemish Christian Democrats in 1986. It is striking that their Francophone counterparts implemented a similar correction to the original 'personalism' through a completely independent process of ideological reflection, without however using exactly the same terms (1983). It is safe to say that the Francophones would have had no reticence in adopting the same final objectives, personalism coupled with solidarity, and the same supporting objectives, responsibility and stewardship. In fact they chose various sets of principles at different times. Two principles reappear always: 'liberté' and 'solidarité'. If the PSC stressed the principles of liberty and responsibility (i.e. the call on individuals to commit themselves completely to the tasks at hand, without leaving the initiative to agencies such as the state), this difference was due to the fact that Wallonia, at the time of their ideological congress, faced a major economic crisis and the apparent failure of the welfare state. In 1986, on the other hand, the CVP stressed stewardship, a term they borrowed from the Dutch CDA and from the Pastoral Letters of the American bishops, since Flanders at the time had become sensitised to the ecological problem and had witnessed a stunning breakthrough by the Green party.

The Dutch CDA originated in 1975, from the federation of two Calvinistic parties, the Anti-Revolutionary Party (ARP) and the Dutch Reformed Christian Historical Union (CHU), and one Catholic party, the Catholic People's Party (KVP). For the Calvinistic partners in the new party to use the term of personalism would have had an appearance of shallow humanism. Man was not created to work at his own development but to further justice, i.e. to co-operate with God's creation of human society. It may not be obvious to everyone what was intended by this 'justice' but one thing at least was clear: there was a challenge to be responded to. Therefore the concept of personalism is not mentioned and responsibility becomes a final objective instead. This final objective squares well with the CDA fascination with the 'deresponsibilisation' of individuals in the bureaucratic welfare state. To cope with this problem the response should come from a restoration of associational initiatives. In this emphasis on associational life the solidarity principle manifests itself together with the responsibility principle (actually 'differentiated responsibility'). So the CDA has opted for a set of four principles which is only slightly different from that proposed by the CVP, namely justice, differentiated responsibility, solidarity and stewardship. The implementation of these principles shows that the CDA has a close ideological relationship to CVP and PSC.

In what follows we investigate the application of the social-personalistic principles to issues in important policy areas. These policy areas can be ordered in concentric circles around the citizen, ranging from the most individual to the most public aspects of his life experience, and starting with the area of family life and ending with international relations. We will, however, limit our discussion to four of these policy areas (i.e. family policy, cultural policy, economic policy and social policy). In each of these domains the analysis will focus on a single issue. We intend to show that social personalism is perfectly able to take a position which is different from that of its ideological rivals. Of course it has been obvious to all observers that Christian Democrats were able to do so in the more 'personalised' policy matters where ethical considerations loom large. But a closer inspection reveals that the same ability to take a specific stand can be found in more 'public' policy domains.

The family

The salience of family policies is undoubtedly much higher among Christian Democrats than among their political rivals. *Gesellschaft* ideologies tend to privatise these issues. Most *Gemeinschaft* ideologies do not

care very much either because other types of community are more important to them than the family.

The Christian Democrats view the (core) family as a privileged opportunity to implement their social-personalistic principles. They want the
citizens to adapt their private lives to demanding interpersonal relationships. Family life, especially the traditional family life of a married couple
with several children, is a first embodiment of such relationships and a
good training for analogous relationships in other sectors of society.

The Christian Democrats perceive the family as having intrinsic and not
only instrumental value. They wish to subsidise the having of children
because of the right of the child and not for the purpose of (vertical)
redistribution, which is of more concern to the socialists. Where CVP, PSC
and CDA would like to entrust more health care and other social service
duties to the family, they do so not just to alleviate the burden of the state
bureaucracy or of the Ministry of Finance, or to improve the quality of the
service rendered to the aged, the young and the sick (though this too is a
major consideration), but first and foremost because they hope to strengthen the family. The contemporary family is weakened by the loss of social
functionality. Adding to the functionality of the family might therefore be
a somewhat paradoxical but nevertheless sound policy from a social-
personalistic point of view.

The most striking illustration of the priority of the family in the Christian
Democratic tradition is, of course, their opposition to moral permissiveness in private matters. To a considerable degree this opposition is inspired
by the idea that this permissiveness is wrecking the commitments needed
for proper family life.

The Liberals, on the other hand, are more disposed to follow the trend
to greater permissiveness. They do not agree that anything goes but they
are willing to abide by whatever norms society would agree on. They do
not oppose moral permissiveness but they do oppose moral disorder.

Cultural policies

Cultural policy-making can only have modest ambitions in a democracy.
The freedoms of opinion, of speech and of association require that cultural
matters be kept out of the grasp of government. Nevertheless there are
several domains of cultural policy-making which are not left to the private
sector and which can be the focus of fierce ideological debates. Education
is one such policy.

The *Gesellschaft* ideologies especially are not eager to expand further
the agenda of active cultural policy-making. Individualism has great faith
in the cultural creativity of individual citizens. Both Liberals and Socialists
have traditionally insisted on the privatisation of (religious) world views.
The optimism of the Socialists lags behind that of the Liberals though.
More and more Socialists want a cultural programme to complete their
socio-economic ideology.

Culture, as they realise, is more than the suprastructure of history. It should function as a solid ethical and spiritual infrastructure for the socio-economic and political layers of society, especially when in the words of a Flemish Socialist leader, 'this society is characterised by materialism, loneliness, anguish and spiritual alienation'. These voices would certainly strike a sensitive chord among social-personalists but among their fellow Socialists they are as yet rather lonely voices in the desert.

Cultural options become manifest in education policies more than any-where else. This is certainly the case in Belgium where a free, overwhelm-ingly Catholic school system exists alongside state (and local authority) school systems and where the competition between these has not yet settled into a pattern of stable equilibrium.

For the Liberals, who abandoned their traditional anti-clericalism in 1961, the education system is no longer an instrument to spread a philo-sophical message. They still consider themselves as the natural advocates of the 'official' school systems. But they have retreated to caring for educational procedures and for educational quality control. They are thus willing to leave the content of education to the decisions of the consumers. In this they show no worry that the consumers will turn out to be sensitive only to the economic functions of education and to the requirements of the labour market and of economic development.

Not sharing the optimism of the Liberals, the Socialists are unwilling to leave the education system to the inertia of market forces. The education system is an instrument to combat cultural and social injustices in a society which, left to itself, is unjust. For this reason they have favoured the comprehensive school reform (which should improve the situation of the socially deprived) and the state school system (because the Catholic schools undermine class solidarity). The choice of the consumers should not carry too much weight.

They also feel little sympathy for the present situation of 'external pluralism' between the school systems. They would like to replace it with a single system of internally pluralistic schools, thus eliminating the homo-geneously Catholic schools. Christian Democrats suspect them of still yearning for a single state school system with a neutral (or rather anti-religious) inspiration.

The *Gemeinschaft* ideologies are more likely to impose a philosophical function on the school system. And indeed occasionally both the Flemish Greens and the Flemish Nationalists display such inclinations. AGALEV has stated on at least one occasion that it wants schools to be judged on principles such as non-violence, grassroots democracy, social justice and ecological awareness. The Volksunie wishes the educational system to maintain Flemish cultural identity in Europe. But for strategic reasons both parties refrain from stressing the overtly cultural and philosophical potential of the educational system. First one should get rid of the present ideological (Catholic) colouring of most schools. Both therefore favour internally pluralistic schools. These are less threatening to local, i.e. Flemish community building.

The Christian Democrats are the only partisans of external pluralism. This position certainly has a strategic component. The present external pluralism is based on philosophical choice and leaves much room for Catholic initiatives. But principles play a role too. Social-personalists think that schools have the task of creating and communicating philosophical and religious meaning. In Catholic schools this task is taken seriously, at least to some extent. For the time being the performance of the other schools is less convincing in this respect. But maybe one day these may do better than their status of dull neutrality has allowed them to in the past. Anyway, the Catholic schools have proved to be the best bet until now. That they also have served the Catholic cause in society is unlikely to irritate a party which, after all, consists almost entirely of Catholics.

Economic policies

Most issues within the economic policy area pit the leftist against the rightist *Gesellschaft* ideologies, with the *Gemeinschaft* ideologies generally occupying the centre of the political arena. But even then the Christian Democrats frequently succeed in taking a distinct position. Since it is not possible to discuss more than one issue here we shall limit ourselves to the issue of workers participation. How should labour, capital and management co-operate in contemporary enterprises which require a very strong division of labour and of responsibilities?

The positions of the traditional left and right are well known. The Socialists are inclined to advocate self-management by the workers as an expression of the supremacy of labour over capital. If, for practical reasons, this were not feasible, and if negotiations on an equal footing were possible, Socialists insist on negotiations at the national level rather than at the local level. At the national level the unions are, more often than not, in a stronger bargaining position, and class solidarity among workers is less likely to be disrupted.

The Liberals reject the idea of self-management by the workers. The entrepreneurs should be able and willing to keep their firms in good shape and must therefore conserve full authority and full economic benefits. The co-operation of the workers can and should be ensured by some kind of profit-sharing. More generally, everything should be done to foster harmonious human relations between the various segments of the enterprise (in order to defuse the latent conflict between the capitalists and the workers, as the critics of the left would add). At the same time negotiations should be held at the local level so as to adapt the wages to the market position of the individual firm (and to avoid that cross-sectorial class solidarity which would disrupt the natural market mechanisms).

The Ecologists have not yet developed very stable ideas about these matters. Their ideal is that of small co-operatives where the quality of human work can be guaranteed against the strain of fragmentation and alienation. This ideal allows them to avoid tackling the issue of the organisation of labour in large-scale enterprises. Where the Greens occasionally do express themselves on the issue they appear to come out in favour of self-management in a wider sense. They would welcome experiments with a board of directors manned by the employees, the consumers and the local community (but not by the capital owners). Public ownership is a necessary, if not a sufficient, condition for any service to the community. In socio-economic matters the Ecologists frequently appear to take positions to the left of the present Socialists. They seem to be moved by a profound distrust of the elite, of 'the rich and the powerful'. Here the populist theme of their ideology shows up once again.

As expected the social-personalists choose a centrist position and come out in favour of co-management. This position implies that workers and entrepreneurs should meet in an institutionalised negotiation process and that care should be taken not to confront weak individual workers with strong individual entrepreneurs. Negotiations should be held between equal partners since the possession of labour should carry as much weight as the possession of capital in the management of the firm. However, the social-personalists do not want the negotiations to occur only on a national, centralised level. Centralised negotiations are necessary but only to set the framework for more decentralised negotiations.

One could wonder whether the Christian Democrats can link this position to their social-personalist principles. We believe they can. The Dutch CDA certainly would stress the fact that co-management allows both workers and managers to take up their specific responsibilities in an occupational sector which is threatened by an extreme division of labour and thus by a process of deresponsibilisation. The Belgian CVP and PSC would put somewhat more emphasis on the necessity to restore the human quality of work. Work, when it is fragmented, anonymous and alienated from its end product, contributes very little to the development of human personality and is therefore not up to the standards set by the principle of personalism.

Social policies

Probably the most sensitive issue in the field of social policy-making is social inequality or 'relative social deprivation'. To what extent should the government take advantage of its taxation and social security policies to implement a strategy of vertical redistribution? This is indeed a question to which the five political ideologies under scrutiny here respond in very different ways.

This is also a question which can be dealt with rather succinctly since the basic positions of the Liberals and the Socialists are well known. The Liberals stick to the principle of equality of opportunity and the Socialists still manifest a fondness for the principle of equality of results. The difference between both boils down to the perception of the inequalities as being individually deserved and socially functional, or individually undeserved and socially dysfunctional.

As a matter of fact the Belgian Ecologists appear as more radically leftist than the Belgian Socialists. Not only do they want to tackle both absolute and relative deprivation in society. They also are the only ones to condemn excessive wealth in strongly moralistic terms. As a consequence they demand more equality with respect to income and to property. They are thus alone in entertaining the possibility of progressive and sizeable taxes on inheritances and property. On the other hand, everyone should be entitled to a basic income higher than the present one, without conditions with regard to race, nationality or occupational performance. Such radicalism must surprise even the Socialists. Whether green generosity could finance green egalitarianism will be questioned by many opponents. But it is a fact that such egalitarianism is not out of place in an ideology which stresses solidarity and closeness in small communities.

The Nationalists of the Volksunie are not opposed to social policies with an element of vertical income redistribution. But they hedge this commitment by pointing to several functional necessities. One should not put at risk the health of the economic infrastructure nor the growth of the economic system. Yes, there should be a minimum guaranteed income, independent of performance in the work force. But the professional income should be tangibly higher. Theirs is a centrist position with a keen feeling for the functions of inequality.

The Dutch Christian Democrats have, to this observer at least, not dwelt extensively on the issue of inequality. Perhaps they are fascinated by their principle of responsibility at the expense of their principle of solidarity. Or perhaps they lack a powerful union pressure group in their ranks to make them come to terms with this issue. The Belgian, and more particularly the Flemish, Christian Democrats do have a strong union wing and do display a clearer position. But this position is often misread as a mere centrist and compromising one. The Flemish Christian Democrats intend to combat inequalities without being egalitarian. What do they mean by such a puzzling statement?

First they point to the fact that in society not only economic but also political and cultural goods are being distributed. Cultural goods should be communicated but not be 'redistributed'. It does not make sense to tackle cultural inequalities by denying the culturally privileged the possibility of further developing their abilities. A policy of combating inequalities through levelling does not square well with the personalism of the Christian Democrats.

But this caveat is no excuse for disregarding the problem of socio-economic inequality. In their congress of 1986 they stated: 'Inequality is a difference between human beings that is being used to create distances and to elevate some and humiliate others. It is a difference which leads to the abuse of power and to the corrosion of solidarity between human beings.' There exist then economic 'differences' that need not be problematic. Social-personalists think that the development of individuals does not depend on the equality of their economic possessions. But thanks to the principle of solidarity they are sensitive to economic disparities which are used to bring about power disparities and power abuses. This occurs all too frequently. The social-personalists therefore go beyond the principle of equality of opportunity. The citizen is not free to use his wealth at will, even if this wealth has been gained according to the tenets of official justice. Actually this wealth has often been gained through the abuse of power and not through services rendered to society.

This vantage point requires a precise and patient analysis of the many social processes that create disparities and inequalities in society. This intellectually appealing programme is very difficult to implement and creates a host of practical problems. Which groups suffering from 'relative deprivation' deserve our attention most? In 1986 the Christian Democrats specified that 'priority will be given to inequalities which threaten to become hereditary or permanent, which lead from bad to worse, or which create further inequalities'. But most politicians are actually unable to come up with the analysis that is required here. They will necessarily be guided (and misguided) by more or less judicious, more or less accidental feelings of compassion. As a result Christian Democrat politicians tend to intervene in favour of various deprived groups, without distinguishing between priorities.

Conclusion

Christian Democratic ideologies show a remarkable affinity with each other, even where they have, for several generations, gone through separate developments. There are different emphases, of course, between the Belgian and the Dutch versions of Christian Democracy. Both are an expression of (social) personalism but the concept of personalism actually applies better to the Belgian than to the Dutch (especially the Calvinistic) variety of Christian Democracy.

It is certainly not correct to say that this difference of emphasis has no consequences for the options taken with regard to specific issues. But however real this distinction may be, it still allows us to draw a clear line between social-personalism and all the other political ideologies in the Low Countries. Contrary to common wisdom Christian Democracy has been able to formulate an ideology of its own not on a few but on many issues.

The chapter proposes a simple model for the comparison of these five ideologies. Its main feature is that it locates them in a two-dimensional ideological space in which the most important dimension is not the opposition between left and right but that between *Gesellschaft* and *Gemeinschaft*. Both Liberals and Socialists are at the *Gesellschaft* end of the dimension, Nationalism and Ecologism (a misnomer!) at the *Gemeinschaft* end, and Social Personalism somewhere in the middle but more to the *Gemeinschaft* end.

Of course, the left–right dimension discriminates very successfully between Liberals and Socialists, with the *Gemeinschaft* ideologies in its centre. A further analysis would be compelled to propose a third dimension to discriminate between the *Gemeinschaft* ideologies. But for our purpose we felt satisfied with a qualitative distinction.

A final caveat is in order. Ideology, as defined here, does prepare decision-making. But there can be quite a distance between ideology and actual policies. In the case of governing parties, such as the CVP, the PSC, and the CDA, the distance may at times be considerable indeed.

References

Anon (1976), *CDA van Woudschoten tot Hoogeveen*, Stichting Kader- en Vormingswerk ARP, the Hague.
Anon (1978), *Grondslag en Politiek Handelen, Rapport van de CDA-commissie Grondslag en Politiek Handelen*, the Hague.
Anon (1979), *Manifest van Kortrijk*. Handvest van het Modern Liberalisme.
Anon (1983), *Actes du Congres de Mouscron PSC*, Les Editions de l'Arbre de Vie, Bruxelles.
Anon (1983), *Samen Sterk voor Vrede en Werk. SP-alternatief*.
Anon (1986), *Geloof, Hoop en Toekomst. Manifest en congresresoluties Christelijke Volkspartij*, Brussel.
Anon (1989), *De SP in Actie. Resultaten, nieuwe uitdagingen*. Discussienota Politiek Congres 21–22 oktober 1989, Antwerpen.
Anon (1990), *Parlons pour Construire*, Centre de Perfectionnement des Cadres Politiques, Bruxelles.
Anon (1991), *Programme Electoral. Parti Socialiste*, Brussel.
Anon (n.d.), *De Vlaamse Vrij Demokraat*, Vlaams-Nationaal Studiecentrum, Brussel.
Anon (n.d.), *Met Christendemocratische Overtuiging*, Discussietekst, IPOVO-CVP, Brussel.
Dierickx, G. (1989), Het ideologisch CVP-Congres van 1986: een terugblik, *Nieuw Tijdschrift voor Politiek*, blz. 22–54.
Dierickx, G. (red.) (1986), *CVP, waar is uw geloof? De identiteit van de Vlaamse Christen-Democraten*, DNB/IPOVO, Antwerpen/Brussel.
Spitaels, Guy (1990), *Le Projet Socialiste*. Texte proposé aux congressistes de la Convention-Forum, Ottignies/Louvain-la-Neuve, 24–25 novembre.
Van den Wijngaert, M. (1976), *Ontstaan en Stichting van de CVP–PSC: de lange weg naar het kerstprogramma*, DNB/IPOVO, Brussel/Antwerpen.
Van Putten, J. (1990), *Politieke Stromingen* (3rd edn), Het Spectrum, Utrecht.
Werkgroep Ekonomie AGALEV (1984), *Op Mensenmaat, een groene kijk op ekonomie*. vzw Ploeg, Brussel.
Wetenschappelijk Instituut voor het CDA (1990), *Publieke Gerechtigheid*, Bohn Stafleu Van Loghum, Houten.

2

THE DISTINCTIVENESS OF CHRISTIAN DEMOCRACY

Kees van Kersbergen

What is Christian Democracy? Is it a distinctive political movement? Here I suggest an affirmative answer to the latter question by developing responses to a number of arguments *against* distinctiveness that can be found in literature on political parties. So far I have located three refutations of the thesis of distinctiveness. The first argument holds that Christian Democracy is no more than a variety of conservatism, one that perhaps pays slightly more attention to religious matters and issues of morality. The second claim is that Christian Democracy lacks distinctiveness because it is fundamentally a movement of the centre (or the middle). The third and related contention is that the specificity of Christian Democracy is thwarted by its being enshrined in catch-all parties.

In my view, however, none of these arguments convincingly invalidates the plausibility of the thesis of distinctiveness. First, I present a brief outline of possible arguments against the proposition that Christian Democracy is a distinctive political phenomenon. Following these accounts, I will formulate immediate rejoinders. These counter-arguments are then elaborated in the second part. There I argue that Christian Democracy is distinct from its competitors by virtue of its specific model of social and economic policy and because religion accords the movement an unparalleled opportunity to adapt to changing circumstances. In the conclusion I try to establish the extent to which Christian Democracy might retain its idiosyncratic character and relevance even with conditions of the declining political significance of Christianity as a religion in Western Europe.

Christian Democracy equals conservatism

The hypothesis I wish to test then, is that Christian Democracy is a distinctive political phenomenon. At first sight, this may seem a trivial statement, but if one took the trouble of surveying a few textbooks on comparative politics, comparative government or comparative political sociology, one would find that such distinctiveness is typically denied. Christian Democracy is usually interpreted as being simply a variant of conservatism or located on the centre-right.

One textbook, for instance, teaches students that 'support for the Church is so important among conservatives that in some countries they include the term *Christian* in their name' (Steiner, 1986, p. 30, original emphasis). Another more recent textbook categorises Christian Democracy as a member of the party family of the centre-right. The difference between conservatism and Christian Democracy would primarily relate to the fact that the latter 'temper mainstream conservatism with a defence of religious values', while the former are differentiated by 'a more strident antisocialist rhetoric as well as by the absence of traditional links with organised religion' (Gallagher et al., 1992, p. 70). Students of comparative political sociology, on the other hand, will have to put up with the assertion that 'in many cases it is difficult to distinguish conservative parties from Christian Democratic parties' (Lane and Ersson, 1991, p. 108). Mény, too, has difficulties delineating conservatism and Christian Democracy. He argues that 'Christian Democrats and conservatives may find themselves in agreement in a number of respects: pessimism as to human nature, attachment to the right of property, to non-extremist groups, and to the authority of those legitimately invested with it (heads of families, etc.)' (Mény, 1990, p. 50).

It may indeed be the case that there are many similarities between conservatism and Christian Democracy. The question, however, is whether it would not be possible to produce an equally valid list of similarities between the Christian Democratic and, say, the social democratic or liberal images of society? I would therefore claim that those who refute distinctiveness by pointing to the resemblance between conservatism and Christian Democracy, still face the task of showing that no such analogy exists between Christian Democracy and other political ideologies, notably social democracy and liberalism.

Christian Democracy as a phenomenon of the centre

From a cursory look at these textbooks the following picture emerges: at best Christian Democracy can be understood as some disguised form of conservatism. A slightly more refined picture, however, can also be found, especially among students of Christian Democracy per se. In contrast to what one might call the 'distinctiveness thesis', the refutation of distinctiveness here stems from the prevailing observation that Christian Democracy is fundamentally a phenomenon of the political centre. Students of Christian Democracy tend to agree that their object of analysis tends to be in between something, to occupy some position in the middle, to inhabit some abstractly defined political centre. And such a centre is perceived alternately as an aspect of party systems, in ideological terms or with reference to policy styles, outcomes or output. The centre argument holds that Christian Democracy shares features of both the right and the left.

Christian Democracy is 'no more than a manifestation of the eternal search for a middle way between liberalism and collectivism, between capitalism and communism, with a bias in favour of capitalism and liberalism' (Irving, 1979, p. xviii). If there is one characteristic feature of Christian Democratic ideology, it comprises the 'forthright rejection of the extreme doctrines put forward by capitalism on the one hand and Marxism on the other. Both represent forms of materialism that run counter to the unswerving teaching of the Church' (Mény, 1990, p. 51). Christian Democratic movements and parties are 'only soundings of the time and change with historical changes. There is nothing like a programme in the sense of the *Communist Manifesto*, based as it is on belief in a foreseeable historical process' (Maier, 1969, p. 10). Natural Law is also important, which 'offers Christian Democracy precisely that broad basis, which permits it to have as many variations in the structures of its everyday politics as there are national and confessional forms of Christian parties' (Maier, 1969, p. 11). It is a movement operating in the centre and it seems to have no basic theory of its own; rather it prefers to plagiarise elements of liberal, conservative and socialist thought at will in order to blend these into a hotchpotch of ideology. Christian Democracy and conservatism may not be precisely identical, but they do share the conviction that private property constitutes an inviolable right, that communism is an abhorrent movement, and that the state should be confined and carefully watched in terms of its interventionist zeal. 'But Christian Democrats reject the tenets of nineteenth century liberalism: they accept the necessity for the state to protect the weak in society and to guide the economy, and they favour concertation, i.e., consultation between government, industry, the trade unions and other interest groups' (Irving, 1979, p. xxi).

It seems clear where Christian Democratic originality lies: 'The parties, especially, draw material from all the corners of the political universe, and criticise and rework it into a pattern in which each element finds its place in the perspective of the rest' (Fogarty, 1957, p. 18). Liberal individualism appears as personalism in Christian Democratic discourse. The self in the theory of personalism is something more than an individual, because its metaphysics not only accounts for the individual in his or her social ambience, but also stresses religious aspects as indispensable and manifest facets of the inextricable human identity. Socialist or social democratic collectivism surfaces as the Christian Democratic philosophy of solidarism, emphasising that the collectivity exists to assist and complete the person rather than the other way around. Collectivism is also transformed into a specific version of pluralism, which holds that society consists of a multiplicity of institutions of which the state is only one, albeit pivotal arrangement. Conservative traditionalism emerges in Christian Democratic political theory as 'an appreciation of the time factor, of the difficulties of successful change, and of the importance of smooth, continuous development' (Fogarty, 1957, p. 18).

Christian Democratic parties conceive of themselves as popular or people's parties in a specific ideological, anti-liberal sense. They would rather address a people organised in associations and professions than atomised and therefore superficial individuals (Mayeur, 1980, p. 7). Perhaps bourgeois, conservative and Christian Democratic movements are interchangeable entities (Van Veen, 1983). In that case one would hardly have to question the possible differences between these movements. And yet the self-identification of Christian Democracy as basically operating in the centre of the political spectrum seems to a large extent justified (Von Beyme, 1985, p. 96).

All theorists, therefore, tend to have some spatial metaphor for depicting Christian Democracy as occupying a conditional centre of the party system in common or of the politico-ideological spectrum in general. Adjectives such as centre, middle, popular appear to point in the same direction. Christian Democracy cannot be defined as a movement with a well-defined, fully fledged ideology. It cannot be pinned down to some point on a right–left continuum either, but it rather occupies some grey, happy medium. Unlike liberalism and socialism, Christian Democracy appears to lack a political and social theory of its own. It is habitually defined in negative terms; it is neither socialist nor liberal, but shares some elements of both political movements. It carefully manoeuvres between the Scylla and Charybdis of capitalism and socialism.

The argument is therefore clear: Christian Democracy cannot be specified on its own terms, because it does not have any. It is fundamentally opportunistic and pragmatic, and therefore indistinct. A counterclaim might be that such an understanding of the phenomenon of Christian Democracy is inadequate, for it is grounded within two implicit assumptions that appear difficult to justify. The first contends that, because the centre of politics can indeed be specified theoretically and empirically in an unambiguous manner, a centre position of Christian Democracy equals a position in between at least two other relevant actors within the political system. The second maintains that a position of go-between, that is, a political stance that could be described as middle-of-the-road, cannot possibly be the consequence of distinctive principles and strategies. Those who deny Christian Democratic distinctiveness on the basis of what one might call the centre argument, would therefore still have to show: (a) what is meant by the centre of politics; (b) that such a centre can be located empirically; (c) that centrist strategies and policies are not predicated upon distinctive precepts.

Christian Democracy as a catch-all party

The concept of the catch-all party (Kirchheimer, 1966) is widely held to be applicable to Christian Democratic parties in particular (Von Beyme, 1985, p. 93). Indeed, Christian Democratic parties have readily labelled themselves as people's parties, indicating that they provided a home for a variety of classes, groups and strata within the national community.

The quintessence of the catch-all argument is that the pre-war mass integration parties that were primarily the political representatives of particular social groups or religious segments converted themselves in the

1950s and 1960s into so-called real people's parties. These parties gave up their old aim of integrating the masses into the political system and into bourgeois society in order to replace it with the sole aim of winning as many votes as possible during electoral competition with other similar parties. A new type of party arose that disposed of its old ideological heritage for the sake of potentially better electoral results. What emerged was a party that is only distinctive in one respect: its yearning for votes.

There are two arguments underpinning the assertion that Kircheimer's catch-all concept is not applicable to Christian Democracy. First, Christian Democracy is not just a political party, but a political movement. This implies that, in much the same manner in which social democracy must be interpreted with reference to the social democratic labour movement as a whole (Esping-Andersen and van Kersbergen, 1992), Christian Democratic parties cannot be properly analysed outside the context of the Christian Democratic movement as a whole. The parties have to a large extent been the political representatives or counterparts of associated societal organisations and institutions. Therefore, Christian Democracy not only faces the logic of electoral competition, but has to deal with organisational and institutional logics too (see chapter 5).

Second, how should one interpret the role of religion in electoral competition? Can this be done unambiguously? It seems to me that religion as an electoral magnet is very much like a real magnet: it has the disposition to both attract and repel. Strictly speaking, then, having religion as an electoral asset means that Christian Democracy can never become a full-blown catch-all party.

The thesis that the Christian Democratic ideology excludes the non-believer might be exaggerated. Yet there may equally be some truth in the idea that the party faces an electoral trade-off between the support of religious and non-religious voters. My argument would be that those who would refute Christian Democratic distinctiveness by referring to the catch-all nature of the party would have to show both that the Christian Democratic movement has mutated to such an extent that the organisational and other links between the political party and the associated organisations have slackened considerably, and that, in effect, the label Christian has hardly any significance.

In order to substantiate the claim of distinctiveness it appears that I would have to show (a) that Christian Democracy is not covert conservatism, (b) that centrism does not necessarily exclude the possibility of idiosyncrasy, and (c) that the concept of a catch-all party is not unambiguously applicable to Christian Democracy.

Elements of distinctiveness

Social conservatism

Scattered throughout the literature referred to above one can, in fact, find clues as to what it is that might establish a constitutional difference between Christian Democracy and conservatism. Mény, in spite of his emphasis on the correspondence between the two, argues that for Christian Democrats 'the spiritual comes before the material and economics should be put to the service of mankind. It is on this basis that the Christian Democrats disassociate themselves from the conservatives, for whom social interests take second place to the dictates of the economy' (Mény, 1990, p. 51).

Gallagher et al., notwithstanding their understanding of Christian Democracy as belonging to the party family of the centre-right, claim that 'Christian parties can easily be distinguished form secular conservative parties . . . because their popular base, their social concerns, and their reluctance to promote policies which might lead to social conflict have always inclined them (the Catholic parties in particular) toward a more centrist, pro-welfare programme' (Gallagher et al., 1992, p. 73).

Apparently, Christian Democratic distinctiveness has something to do with social doctrine, or as one author put it: 'All Christian Democrats began with a belief that a middle way could be found between capitalism and socialism in the spirit of the Catholic social doctrine and the social encyclicals' (Von Beyme, 1985, p. 94). It is the social concern of Christian Democrats that distinguishes them from conservatives and hints at some common ground with social democracy.

Principles and pragmatism

I have argued that the understanding of Christian Democracy as a phenomenon of the centre, as essentially pragmatic and opportunistic, is erroneous. It is grounded upon the incorrect supposition that a position of go-between cannot possibly be the consequence of distinctive political principles. Nevertheless, such principles do exist (Irving, 1979). First, there are Christian precepts comprising an adherence to elementary human rights. Second, the commitment to liberal democracy and liberal democratic values is part and parcel of the Christian Democratic legacy. Finally, integration or societal accommodation is the principal constituent of Christian Democratic distinctiveness, 'in the dual sense of a commitment to class reconciliation . . . and to transnational reconciliation' (Irving, 1979, pp. xviii–xix).

The key concepts for understanding Christian Democracy are integration, (class) compromise, accommodation and pluralism. It is precisely the ceaseless attempt at integrating and reconciling a plurality of societal groups with possibly opposed interests that makes Christian Democracy distinctive. Christian Democracy voices, translates, codifies and restructures societal conflict within itself in the attempt to arbitrate and accommodate societal discord. Socialism and liberalism – at least in Christian Democratic interpretation – tend to be the political articulations of opposing poles of societal difference, disagreement and conflict. Class reconciliation and co-operation lie at the heart of what defines Christian Democracy as distinctive.

Both pragmatism and opportunism are effects – perhaps even necessary effects – of the properties of integration, reconciliation, accommodation and pluralism. The *differentia specifica* of Christian Democracy implies that the movement is always in principle (by virtue and by necessity of its self-imposed political position) bipolar (or rather multi-dimensional), flexible and in possession of a highly developed capacity to adapt in its task of formulating a compromise between antagonistic interests. Christian Democracy is in this sense the embodiment of societal accommodation, or at least aspires to become so. It is quite likely that it is this property of the movement which makes it so hard to pin down. For, obviously, it is not at all clear which societal truce holds at what particular time. Moreover, it is peculiar to Christian Democracy that the movement is internally divided into factions or wings. Surely, many a political movement shares such characteristics, but it is only Christian Democracy that tends to establish organisational links with, for instance, both the labour movement and the organisations of employers. The central concepts of the Christian Democratic ideology not only reflect bipolarity, multi-dimensionality and flexibility, but above all facilitate the co-existence of such a plurality of views and interests. Therefore, what is commonly described as the movement's main weakness is, in fact, its greatest strength.

If there exists a bias in favour of capitalism and liberalism as Irving (1979) has argued, such an inclination must be understood as a contingent outcome and not as some sort of eternal feature. It might hold under certain historical conditions. What really matters is the actual balance of power within the movement and, as far as the movement mirrors society, within the national community. Whatever the bias in the explicit formulation of an accord, a plurality of interests will always be present.

I would claim that this insight is also critical for appreciating the differences between Christian Democracies in Western Europe. Variation most likely occurs as a consequence of variation in the structuring of the accommodation of interests within the movements. If these considerations are correct then an analysis of the conditions under which Christian Democracies operate becomes more imperative than mere abstract discussions in terms of resemblances and positions in the political spectrum. In addition, one would have to speak in terms of both similarity and difference. It seems that the more Christian Democracy depends on the structural and historical conditions on which it acts, the less it makes sense to view the phenomenon as historically and cross-nationally distinct.

Catch-allism 1: votes and dilemmas

The thesis so far, therefore, is that (a) Christian Democracy is more articulate than conservatism on matters of social concern, and (b) that the centre-position of Christian Democracy is based upon distinctive principles. Nevertheless, it might still be the case that Christian Democracy dilutes its ideological inheritance under the pressure of electoral competition. To what extent is Christian Democracy a catch-all movement producing parties that are only distinctive in terms of their electoral appetite?

I have argued that, strictly speaking, having religion as an electoral asset implies that Christian Democracy can never become a full-blown catch-all party. However, there is something peculiar here. Appealing to religion or confession may result in scaring away non-religious voters or at least voters with a different creed. In a nation where, say, 30 to 40 per cent of the population are proclaimed members of the Catholic Church, a party that exclusively tries to mobilise the Catholic voters *qua* Catholics can never hope to win a parliamentary majority. Broadening the attractiveness to non-religious voters or to members of different creeds runs the risk of weakening Catholic support. Christian Democracy might then encounter a dilemma quite similar to that of social democracy. Paraphrasing Przeworski (1985) the trade-off could be expressed as follows: when Christian Democratic parties direct their efforts to mobilising the support of non-religious allies, they find it increasingly difficult to recruit and maintain the support of the religiously inspired voters.

Such a dilemma, however, would be primarily relevant under conditions of the continuing salience of religion as an electoral mobiliser, that is, under conditions of marginal or constrained secularisation. It implies that if Christian Democratic parties can be argued to be catch-all parties at all, the thesis would only gain significance in the late 1960s and early 1970s, when the process of secularisation started to affect political affiliation in a more profound way. In other words, a theory of Christian Democratic distinctiveness has to consider both the political salience of religion and the aftermath of secularisation.

Nevertheless, with respect to religious politics, the analysis in terms of a possible dilemma is only one limited way of scrutinising the effect of religious appeal under the constraints of the logic of electoral competition. It focuses exclusively on the negative pole of the magnet of electoral appeal. The one-sided attention tends to obscure the positive pole: religion as a vehicle of general political appeal. Christian Democracy has always had strong integrative capacities by virtue of its (religiously inspired) political ideology. Precisely because Christian Democracy possessed religion as a catalyst of political articulation it was able to avoid the dilemma and the associated electoral trade-off which has haunted social democracy. One of the main differences between social democracy and Christian Democracy with respect to the topic of political democracy and electoral competition is of course that the former's vehicle for mass support was the appeal to class as a principal base for political articulation, while the latter employed religious appeal to cross-cut class cleavages. Crucial is the ability to 'attract or approach voters who are concerned with a different basic issue, namely the decision against the class war and in favour of co-operation and class integration' (Von Beyme, 1985, p. 93).

What seems threatening for social democracy appears beneficial for Christian Democracy. And what is a trade-off in social democratic politics may involve a pay-off for Christian Democracy. Diluting the ideological salience of class is precisely what Christian Democracy would have to do in order to promote class compromise and reconciliation. By stressing the inter-class character of the movement Christian Democracy manages to attract voters by appealing to catholicity understood in its literal sense.

If social democracy is 'a movement that seeks to build class unity and mobilise power via national legislation' (Esping-Andersen, 1985, p. 10), then Christian Democracy could be defined as a political movement that seeks to establish cross-class compromise via a policy mix which gives capitalism a human face and social policy a capitalist criterion and foundation. Christian Democracy's choice or problem, therefore, has never been whether to seek support exclusively in one class or to rely on multi- or even non-class forces, but rather how to formulate and implement a feasible mediation between the various layers of society, whether these be class or defined some other way. Anticipating somewhat the argument presented below, the idea immediately arises that the search for a workable political mediation between various interests is not necessarily contingent upon an explicit religious ideology. It may very well be that Christian Democracy manages to maintain its ability to compromise and its coalitional potential, even under conditions of lasting secularisation. In contrast to Kirchheimer, one could then argue that catch-allism in the case of Christian Democracy is not so much an effect of the transformation of Western European party systems and of the growing intensity of electoral competition, but rather the manifestation of the very nature of these parties. Christian Democracy was a catch-all party *avant la lettre*.

Catch-allism 2: social policy performance

It seems that in the case of Christian Democracy the catch-all thesis as it was originally formulated by Kirchheimer is difficult to maintain. Schmidt (1985), however, has argued that the catch-all thesis can be developed in a somewhat different direction. Rather than focusing on the input-side of the political system it may make sense to look at the output of governments. Questions on the nature and content of government policies in Western democracies could be rephrased in a catch-all way: to what extent do different parties in government pursue different policies? Or to what extent do the contents of policies converge during the regimes of different parties (Schmidt, 1980; 1982)?

Although the Christian Democratic parties of continental Western Europe are in several respects very close to Kirchheimer's ideal, the finding is that these parties have distinctive profiles within their pragmatic, opportunistic and reformist tradition. Under conditions of economic prosperity Christian Democratic parties are said to produce a Christian Democratic surplus in social and economic intervention by the state, which comes very near to the surplus produced by social democracy (Schmidt, 1985, p. 389; Keman, 1988). In social policy Christian Democracy can be a big spender too. In this sense it is more akin to social democracy than to conservatism. On Schmidt's account Christian Democrats readily intervene in the economy, in spite of their political rhetoric which sometimes appears to prescribe the opposite.

However, behind this façade of a high level of social expenditure – which could easily compete with the social democratic level – lies a qualitatively important difference with social democracy. Christian Democratic governments tend to combine a high level of social and economic intervention with axiomatic preconditions that are tailored to market dynamics, the upholding of incentives and the growth or strengthening of private property (Schmidt, 1985, p. 390). It is here that the catch-all thesis becomes relevant for understanding this mix of welfare state and capitalist economy. The logic of electoral competition forces Christian Democratic parties to moderate the conflicts between capital and labour in order to attract voters from the ranks of workers more easily. At the same time these parties try to stabilise other social and cultural cleavages that are beneficial to them. Christian Democrats tend to choose those issues which appear to be particularly apt at mitigating traditional socio-economic cleavages and keep socio-cultural lines of conflict stable (Schmidt, 1985, p. 390). It is because of this logic that Christian Democratic parties formulate and implement a social and economic policy, which on the one hand can encourage affluence for both workers and employers alike, and on the other hand is able to reinforce status differentials.

Social capitalism

Christian Democracy has its own model of social policy, which significantly and systematically differs from both the liberal and the social democratic model of social policy and which establishes Christian Democratic distinctiveness *vis-à-vis* conservatism. The concept of social capitalism can be adopted from Hartwich (1970) in order to describe this Christian Democratic model.

There exists an unequivocal link between this idea of social capitalism and other facets of distinctiveness identified above: the continuous attempt at integrating and reconciling a plurality of societal groups with possibly opposed interests. Social capitalism has been the model with which Christian Democracy tried to establish cross-class appeal, and religion was its vehicle. Religion as the vehicle for mobilising support for social capitalism did not risk particularism and the consequent trade-off tendencies both at the level of societal organisation and of electoral competition. Religious appeal is in principle universal in the sense that it attracts all people who share a common religion, creed or simply a cultural heritage that was strongly influenced by Christendom, whether they be capitalists or workers, men or women, old or young, black or white and whether they live in a town or in the countryside. Religion cuts across class and acts to unite different social groups, a fundamental condition for the establishment of social capitalism.

The dilemma for Christian Democracy is therefore different from the one that social democracy faced. Christian Democrats find it easier to cope with the class dilemma. Although they appear to face the same dilemma as social democrats, resulting from the need to create a broad social base of support consisting of various social and economic groups, religion, in fact, helps to solve this dilemma.

The logic of electoral competition structures the nature and the policy content of Christian Democracy in a specific way. It forces Christian Democracy as a *Mittelstandspartei* to attempt to moderate societal cleavages – and in particular the antagonism between labour and capital – in order to attract voters from all social layers and especially from the working class. At the same time Christian Democracy tries to stabilise the political and ideological importance of religious cleavages as well as other conflicts that appear to have beneficial effects on Christian Democratic support. The strategy of Christian Democracy works via policy. It is the Christian Democratic model of social capitalism that must be understood as an attempt to build bridges between the various social, economic and cultural groups within a society. At the same time, this model allows for a reinforcement of occupational, economic and social status differentials. In contrast to the social democratic model of welfare state development, Christian Democracy's model cannot be understood as an attempt to create universal solidarity, but rather as a means to moderate societal cleavages while reinforcing social groups and group identities. Social capitalism tries to capture the best of both worlds. Crucial in this regard is the attempt to dilute the salience of class as the basis of political articulation and mobilisation.

To sum up then, Christian Democracy is confronted with two dilemmas, and attempts to solve the one with the other. The first is a dilemma comparable to that of social democracy, namely needing to secure the support of more classes while, in seeking this cross-class support, risking the declining support of one of them. The second dilemma exists in using Christian ideological appeal (appeal to religious belief or the Christian religion more generally) in order to establish this cross-class compromise, while running the risk of losing non-religious support. Religious appeal may be interpreted as a means of establishing cross-class support for the model of social capitalism by diluting the general ideological salience of class, while upholding societal differences. Doing this, however, may have the effect of scaring away the non-religious vote, especially in periods when the general ideological and political salience of religion is declining. Social capitalism has been the model through which Christian Democracy has tried to integrate labour demands into the formulation and implementation of social and economic policy without scaring away the support of the bourgeois political forces, and through which it has tried – in a more general sense – to build bridges between various social, economic and cultural groups within society. Religion has been a powerful and crucial vehicle for establishing cross-class support for social capitalism under the constraints of the logic of electoral competition.

Social capitalism, then, synthesises a basic commitment to capitalist market relations and a readiness to correct its detrimental effects. Social policy is primarily conceived of as a safety net. It helps those who are threatened with being crushed by market forces. The Christian Democratic model of social policy would differ from the social democratic model. On the one hand it would be reluctant to accord a strong interventionist capacity to the state to change the social outcomes of market relations, and on the other hand it would rather attach social rights to the family or groups than extend citizenship. It would differ from the liberal model in its refusal to view the individual as the basic unit of society, and in the fact that it does accord the state a certain stabilising role, albeit only in the function of tackling shortfalls in both the market and the family.

Social capitalism is the specific arrangement between market, state and family by which resources produced in the private economy are channelled into families that fail to secure adequate income by themselves. The state assists those who fail to help themselves in the performance of their natural duty. My claim, then, is that Christian Democracy is a distinctive political phenomenon and that what is distinctive about the movement concerns a religiously inspired model of social reform which is both social and capitalist (van Kersbergen, 1991).

Conclusion: secularisation, adaptation and the dynamics of the Christian Democratic alternative

Rather than presenting a summary of my argument so far, I would like to discuss the paradox of the persisting attractiveness of Christian Democracy in an increasingly secular world. I try to provide arguments in favour of the thesis that this is indeed a paradox. I start from three premises:

(a) The increasing pressure of political competition in the post-war era was affected, among other things, by the ongoing secularisation that moderated significant religious cleavages within societies (Schmidt, 1985).
(b) 'The transformation of the social structure presents parties with a necessity to adapt to maintain their electoral strength.' (Lane and Ersson, 1991, p. 112)
(c) Christian Democracy still is a political movement with an unparalleled ability to adapt to changing circumstances.

If Christian Democracy could previously reconcile a plurality of interests within its own ranks on the basis of the integrative capacity of religion, one would expect that this facilty would be exhausted when the political significance of religion decreases. Secularisation, therefore, should lead to the collapse of the Christian Democratic compromise. Although the Christian Democratic movements of Western Europe have disintegrated to some extent and although the parties have lost considerable support in the 1980s, Christian Democracy has not decomposed at all. How can the tenacity of Christian Democracy under conditions of continuing secularisation be explained?

Of all the possible and plausible explanations of this paradox I wish to concentrate solely on that which deals with secularisation. Probably the most common perspective argues that secularisation is fundamentally the decline of the categorical impact of religion on human conduct; it is the 'growing tendency of mankind to do without religion' (Chadwick, 1976). Secularisation concerns the increasing powerlessness of organised religion in temporal affairs coupled with the decreasing plausibility of the religious interpretation of the world (Martin, 1978). It is the process 'by which sectors of society and culture are removed from the domination of religious institutions and symbols' and it 'manifests itself in the evacuation by the Christian churches of areas previously under their control or influence' (Berger, 1990, p. 107).

Such a one-dimensional view of secularisation, however, tends to disregard what I see as other crucial facets of the seemingly declining momentum of the Christian religion in Western nations. One could study secularisation from another angle and suggest that it also represents the condensation or transference of religious morality into secular ethics. Secularisation may be looked upon as comprising a transformation of religious contents into worldly substance; Christian values are increasingly represented in secular terms. One cannot view secularisation solely as a process of religious diminution or as the dwindling of the presence of the church in society. It should also be taken to refer to a process of assimilation and translation of a basically religious system of values into a secular ethic. What is at stake here is the adjustment of religious idealism to worldly affairs and interests. One way of thinking about the transformation of religious values is trying to see it as a process of absorption by, assimilation to, or perhaps even complete transformation into, a worldly ethical system.

As a consequence of this process of transformation, the original Christian contents of some of the central values of worldly belief systems are increasingly difficult to discern. Christian values, in a way, condense into their secular state. This aspect of secularisation makes the open religious influence on politics vanish and supplants it by a 'diffuse moralism throughout society' (Mead, 1983, pp. 52–3). Modern Western society is still continuously shaped by its own religious heritage, but in a manner which is increasingly imperceptible. In other words, 'there may not only be secularisation of consciousness within the traditional religious institutions but also a continuation of more or less traditional motifs of religious consciousness outside their previous institutional contexts' (Berger, 1990, p. 109). Phrased like this, however, we ultimately end up with the thesis that Christianity is intimately interwoven with the character of contemporary society. Such an assertion might perhaps be true, but at the same time it is trivial. We might be left with the banality of pantheism.

If one accepts that the distinctiveness of Christian Democracy is embodied in a specific integrative theory of capitalism and in a peculiar view of its reform, one could and should be more specific. One could ask which crucial values embodied in social policy one can think of as basically originating in Christian ethics. One argument might be that the 'materialisation' of religious values has culminated in what might be called a form of implicit Christianity (Kaufmann, 1988). The idea of fundamental and universal human rights can be traced back to the Christian principle of the equality of all human beings before God on the basis of the creation of man in God's image (Kaufmann, 1988, p. 74) and redemption by Jesus Christ. This universal ethic of Christianity is embodied in the increasing opportunities to take part in the institutions of society. The materialisation of this ethical element in the institutions of the welfare state, for instance, has by now lost its Christian component, but it is still operational. The welfare state, one might say, is an implicitly Christian form of societal inclusion.

One could also think of social policy as fundamentally comprising a theological dimension (Mead, 1983), in the sense that the Christian obligation to give produces a religious side to the public provision of benefits. Formally, the distinction between state and church, for instance, may be clear; but mainly traditional religious values affect social policy. This theological dimension of social policy becomes visible when governments try to cut social spending. The difficulty of substantially doing so may have to do with 'a theological imbalance: it is simply much easier to justify giving things to the needy than not giving them in the light of the religious ideas that, directly or indirectly, have shaped Western notions of the social good. Policy-makers may not think of themselves as religious, but they are products of a culture which for centuries has respected Biblical images of what it means to do good to others' (Mead, 1983, p. 54). Whatever the strength of the rational, analytical arguments in favour of restraint, 'none of these answers the religious case for welfare or collectivism on its own ground. A policy of restraint, whatever its other merits, must still be culpable in terms of a moral tradition commanding unlimited provision for the poor' (Mead, 1983, p. 54). Such a specification appears to make sense empirically and may account for some of the fundamentally moral discourses on social policy in terms of obligations, responsibility and care in relation to retrenchment policies, for instance in the Netherlands (van Kersbergen and Becker, 1988, p. 495).

Christian Democrats grasp very well that secularisation is not a one-dimensional process. Rather than viewing the transformation of Christian ethics into a worldly morality as hampering the possibilities for Christian democratic politics, they deem this multi-dimensional evolution of the social structure an important condition for further mobilisation. The natural adaptability of Christian Democracy remains unaltered, provided that it is realised that religion has accorded Christian Democracy an integrative capacity, that Christian morals are now more generally diffused outside the traditional institutions of religion, and that the search for harmony and stability is far from over in a world where conflicts of interests remain at the heart of politics.

Thus, the chairman of the Belgian CVP has argued that the Christian Democratic ideology is more lasting than the competing systems of values of socialism, communism and liberalism. This is because (a) only Christian Democracy has acknowledged the radical multi-dimensionality of the person, (b) only Christian Democracy has cherished the idea of reconciliation unequivocally, and (c) the search for harmony and stability has become second nature for the movement (van Rompuy, 1991, pp. 26–7). And by the same token, Leo Tindemans argued that right-minded and socially responsible people could now easily define themselves as Christian Democrats without God. The point is well articulated by Tindemans himself:

Ancient Rome provides us with strong images of a clear preoccupation with the young, strong and healthy man who was not poor and who did not consider himself as restrained by any code of morality. The greatness of Christianity is precisely that the sick, the weak and the old were regarded as worthy people too and that in this spirit one attempted to change the morality of society: to make it more humane, Christian. (Tindemans, 1991, p. 148).

In other words, Christian Democrats claim that the maturation of compassion in society is the actualisation of the spirit of Christianity. Therefore, those who are ready to defend and to help expand human dignity, human rights, compassion, public justice and morality are ready to defend and express the Christian message. They are, in fact, Christian Democrats, even if they do not believe in God. In the Christian Democratic image of society and humankind, Christianity is universal even in the absence of religion. Secularisation might be a threat to the churches or to organised religion in general, but it is neither imperatively a danger for Christian values nor necessarily an obstacle to the enduring attractiveness of the Christian Democratic alternative.

Christian Democrats, then, will (and do) disavow Fukuyama's claim that we have reached the end of history with the ultimate victory of liberal democracy (Fukuyama, 1992; see also van Stokkom, 1991). The argument is that the fall of totalitarianism, and its communist form in particular, has not necessarily proven the superiority of liberal democracy, but – at least in Eastern Europe – has created a moral vacuum in which Western (Christian) ethics seek their place once again. Rather than the end of history, we are about to enter a phase of history in which we will witness the strength and superiority of a thoroughly, albeit perhaps by now implicitly, Christian and European culture of tolerance and compassion (Zijderveld, 1990; Salemink, 1991). Such is the message that we will hear from Christian Democrats in the next ten years or so.

References

Berger, P. L., 1990, *The sacred canopy. Elements of a sociological theory of religion*, Doubleday, New York.
Chadwick, O., 1976, *The secularisation of the European mind in the nineteenth century*, Cambridge University Press, Cambridge.
Esping-Andersen, G., 1985, *Politics against markets. The social democratic road to power*, Princeton University Press, Princeton NJ.
Esping-Andersen, G. and K. van Kersbergen, 1992, Contemporary research on social democracy, *Annual review of sociology*, 18: 187–208.
Fogarty, M. P., 1957, *Christian Democracy in Western Europe 1820–1953*, Routledge & Kegan Paul, London.

Fukuyama, F., 1992, *The end of history and the last man*, Free Press, New York; Maxwell Macmillan, Toronto.

Gallagher, M., M. Laver and P. Mair, 1992, *Representative government in Western Europe*, McGraw-Hill, New York.

Hartwich, H.-H., 1970, *Sozialstaatspostulat und gesellschaftlicher Status Quo*, Westdeutscher Verlag, Köln and Opladen.

Irving, R. E. M., 1979, *The Christian Democratic parties of Western Europe*, Allen & Unwin, London.

Kaufmann, F.-X., 1988, Christentum und Wohlfahrtsstaat, *Zeitschrift für Sozialreform*, 34(2): 65–89.

Keman, H., 1988, *The development toward surplus welfare: social democratic politics and policies in advanced capitalist democracies (1965–1984)*, CT Press, Amsterdam.

Kirchheimer, O., 1966, The transformation of the western European party systems, in J. LaPalombara and M. Weiner (ed), *Political parties and political development*, Princeton University Press, Princeton NJ, pp. 177–201.

Lane, J.-E. and S. O. Ersson, 1991, *Politics and society in Western Europe*, Sage, London.

Maier, H., 1969, *Revolution and church. The early history of christian democracy, 1789–1901*, University of Notre Dame Press, Notre Dame and London.

Martin, D., 1978, *A general theory of secularisation*, Blackwell, Oxford.

Mayeur, J. M., 1980, *Des partis catholiques à la démocratie chrétienne. XIXe–XXe Siècles*, Colin, Paris.

Mead, L. M., 1983, Religion and the welfare state, R. F. Tomasson (ed.), *The welfare state, 1883–1983. Comparative social research*, Jai Press, Greenwich, Conn. and London, pp. 50–65.

Mény, Y., 1990, *Government and politics in Western Europe. Britain, France, Italy, West Germany*, OUP, Oxford.

Przeworski, A., 1985, *Capitalism and social democracy*, Cambridge University Press, Cambridge.

Salemink, T. A. M., 1991, Christen-democraten en het 'einde van de geschiedenis', in B. van Stokkom (ed.), *Voorbij de ideologie? Zingeving en politiek na Fukuyama's 'einde van de geschiedenis'*, Gooi en Sticht/Stichting Thomas More Academie, Baarn, pp. 139–55.

Schmidt, M. G., 1980, *CDU und SPD an der Regierung. Ein Vergleich ihrer Politik in den Ländern*, Campus, Frankfurt and New York.

Schmidt, M. G., 1982, *Wohlfahrtsstaatliche Politik unter bürgerlichen und sozialdemokratischen Regierungen*, Campus, Frankfurt and New York.

Schmidt, M. G., 1985, Allerweltsparteien in Westeuropa? Ein Beitrag zu Kirchheimers These vom Wandel des westeuropäischen Parteiensystems, *Leviathan* 3: 376–98.

Steiner, J., 1986, *European democracies*, Longman, New York and London.

Tindemans, L., 1991, De opdracht van de christen-democratie als politieke beweging in de komende tien jaar, CDA/Wetenschappelijk Instituut voor het CDA, *De betekenis van de christen-democratische politieke overtuiging voor de komende tien jaar in europese context*, Bohn Stafleu Van Loghum, Houten: 144–9.

Van Kersbergen, K., 1991, *Social capitalism. A study of christian democracy and the post-war settlement of the welfare state*, Dissertation, EUI, Florence, Italy.

Van Kersbergen, K. and U. Becker, 1988, The Netherlands: a passive social democratic welfare state in a christian democratic ruled society, *Journal of social policy*, 17(4): 477–99.

Van Rompuy, H., 1991, Het christen-democratisch mensbeeld, CDA/ Wetenschappelijk Institut voor het CDA, *De betekenis van de christen- democratische politieke overtuiging voor de komende tien jaar in europese context*, Bohn Stafleu Van Loghum, Houten: 25–31.

Van Stokkom, B., 1991, *Voorbij de ideologie?* Gooien Sticht/Stichting Thomas More Academie, Baarn.

Van Veen, H.-J. (ed.), 1983, *Christlich-demokratische und konservative Parteien in Westeuropa*, Shöningh, Paderborn.

Von Beyme, K., 1985, *Political Parties in Western Europe*, Gower, Aldershot.

Zijderveld, A. C., 1990, Van oude en nieuwe christenen. Cultuur en religie en het CDA, *Christen-democratische verkenningen*, 9: 366–72.

PART II
THE MAJOR ACTORS

3

BETWEEN CONFESSIONALISM AND LIBERAL CONSERVATISM: THE CHRISTIAN DEMOCRATIC PARTIES OF BELGIUM AND THE NETHERLANDS

Paul Lucardie and Hans-Martien ten Napel

Though the kingdoms of Belgium and The Netherlands share a common history of only fifteen years (1815–30), they are nevertheless comparable in many respects. A skilful historian could certainly write a comparative history of both countries (Kossmann, 1978). Yet one should not exaggerate the similarities. Even though the Reformation reached the southern parts of the Low Countries (now in Belgium) earlier than the northern parts, it had a much greater impact in the latter area. The Dutch republic in the north gained independence from the Habsburg Empire about 200 years earlier than the southern provinces. The Industrial Revolution affected Belgium earlier than The Netherlands, which remained more dependent on agriculture as well as on trade and commerce. Dutch is spoken in both countries, but almost half of Belgium speaks another official language (41 per cent French, 1 per cent German), whereas only 3 per cent of its northern neighbour speaks another language (Frisian). These differences have had an impact on the party systems of the two countries. Even so, their parties can be compared, especially the Christian Democratic parties which have developed closer ties in recent years.

According to Horner (1981), the Christian Democratic parties of the Low Countries are still confessional parties (*Konfessionsparteien*), whereas their sister parties in Germany and Italy are evolving towards liberal-conservative catch-all parties (*Volksparteien*). In this chapter Horner's thesis will be used to structure our survey of the historical origins and development, organisation, electorate, ideology and government records of the three parties. In each section, the two Belgian parties and the Dutch party will be treated separately.

Historical origins and development

Belgium

Although the Catholics in Belgium held their first national political congress in the town of Mechelen as early as 1863, they started organising themselves more seriously as a political party only when the Liberals introduced a law threatening the independence of Catholic schools in 1879 (Irving, 1979, p. 169; de Winter, 1992, p. 32).

The Catholic Party held an absolute majority in the Chamber of Representatives from 1884 until the introduction of universal suffrage in 1919 and it remained the predominant political force in Belgium until World War II. It soon came to consist of several socio-economic factions, usually called *standen* (estates) (Gerard, 1985, pp. 53–282). By 1919 there were four such *standen*: the conservative Verbond der Katholieke Verenigingen en Kringen, the working class Werkersverbond, the farmers' Boerenbond and the middle class Middenstandbond.

In the interwar period the *standen* gradually became more important than the party organisation itself. It was not possible to join the Catholic Party directly, but only by being a member of one of its factions. In addition, there was no common political programme, only loose collaboration at election time. In 1936, however, an important reorganisation took place, leading to a more unified party organisation with a Flemish wing (Katholieke Vlaamse Volkspartij) and a Walloon wing (Parti Catholique Social) and individual membership (Gerard, 1985, pp. 283–509).

After World War II the *Christelijke Volkspartij* (Christian People's Party, CVP) replaced the Catholic Party (van den Wijngaert, 1976: de Groof, 1977; Vandeputte, 1991). Although from the very beginning this party also had two wings, a Flemish and a Walloon one, for well over twenty years it managed to maintain a unitary structure. In 1968, however, the party split along linguistic lines over the issue of the division of the Catholic University of Louvain. (The Socialists and the Liberals were also to split in the 1970s). Initially some common structures – for example, a national president, national headquarters and a secretariat – were retained, but after a while even these organs either became inoperative or were also split (de Winter, 1992, pp. 32–3, 37–8). Today, one of the very few remnants of the old unitary party is its research centre, the Centre d'Etudes Politiques, Economique et Sociales (CEPESS).

From the beginning, Belgian Christian Democrats have been very much involved in efforts to establish international co-operation between Christian Democratic parties. Thus, for example, in 1947 not only the Nouvelles Equipes Internationales (NEI) was founded in Chaudfontaine (Belgium), but also a Belgian Christian Democrat, Jules Soyeur, became its first secretary general. From 1950 until 1965, moreover, two other prominent (founding) members of the CVP, Auguste Edmond de Schrijver and Theo Lefèvre, were presidents of the NEI. Finally, Leo Tindemans served from 1965 until 1974 as the first secretary general of the European

Christian Democratic Union (ECDU), and from 1976 until 1985 as the first president of the European People's Party (EPP).

The Netherlands

Because of the traditional *verzuiling* (pillarisation) of Dutch society and politics – which implied separate organisations for Calvinists and Catholics in every area – a unitary Christian Democratic party was only formed in 1980. In that year, three confessional parties, which had formed a federation in 1975, merged into the Christian Democratic Appeal (CDA) (ten Napel, 1992; Verkuil, 1992). The Calvinist Anti-Revolutionary Party (ARP), the predominantly Dutch Reformed Christian Historical Union (CHU) and the Catholic People's Party (KVP) had worked more or less closely together in parliament and in government since the late nineteenth century.

From the introduction of proportional representation in 1917, until 1967, the three religious parties together controlled an absolute majority in the Dutch Lower House (Tweede Kamer). In the 1960s and 1970s, the hold of the CHU and the KVP upon their respective Protestant and Catholic electorates decreased dramatically, while the ARP had already suffered considerable losses during the 1948–67 period. The electoral decline contributed to the decision of the three parties initially to federate and then to merge. The merger was facilitated, however, first by ideological rapprochement between the parties and second by ecumenical processes within the Protestant and Catholic churches.

In 1977 the federated Christian Democrats received a slightly higher vote than the three separate parties had received at the previous election. At the 1981 and 1982 parliamentary elections the CDA again suffered some losses. In this period the party was divided, not only into confessional groups but also into left and right wings. Only with great difficulty did it define its position on salient issues like the modernisation of nuclear arms in Western Europe. Yet by 1986, the CDA had overcome these difficulties, closed its ranks and moved from a defensive to a more expansive strategy (van Holsteyn and Irwin, 1988). As a result, it increased its share of the popular vote by more than 5 per cent. At the most recent elections, in 1989, it managed to maintain that level of support, possibly also because of the popularity of its experienced leader, Prime Minister Ruud Lubbers.

The Party organisation and its network

Belgium

In 1945, the newly formed CVP seemed eager to terminate the traditional links which had existed between the Catholic Party and the Catholic Church. Yet, some public support has been given to the CVP by the Catholic Church in the post-war period, most notably by Cardinal Van

Roey, who also openly condemned attempts to create a *travailliste* (left-wing Catholic) Union Démocratique Belge (UDB) in 1944 (Dewachter, 1987, p. 357). Moreover, on both the royal question and the school issue, the CVP and the Church turned out to be very much on the same side. It could be argued, therefore, that not until Vatican II did real changes occur in this respect (Dewachter, 1987, pp. 344–6). However, even with no research data available as yet (Billiet, 1987, p. 299), it is probably safe to assume that there are still numerous, if more informal, links between the Catholic Church and the Flemish and Walloon Christian Democratic Parties.

More or less the same holds true for the links between the CVP and the Catholic social organisations. To be sure, in 1945 the CVP organised itself on the basis of individual membership instead of indirect membership through the *standen*. But it could not, of course, abolish the *standen*. Of these only the conservative Verbond der Katholieke Verenigingen en Kringen actually disappeared. Meanwhile, the General Christian Workers Association (Algemeen Christeljk Werkersverbond, ACW), the National Christian Middle Class Association (Nationaal Christelijk Middenstands-verbond, NCMV), and the Farmers' League (Boerenbond, BB) have proved increasingly influential at all levels of the CVP. At the parliamentary level, for example, the share of the so-called *sans familles* (those CVP parliamentarians who were not backed by any of the organisations mentioned above) decreased in the 1946–81 period, from 36 per cent to 7 per cent. During this same period the CVP parliamentarians affiliated with the Farmers' League have been able to maintain their share of the seats (21 per cent in 1946, against 18 per cent in 1981) despite the decline of the agricultural sector. The members affiliated with the Middle Class Association have made a minor gain (11 per cent in 1946 against 18 per cent in 1981) and the Workers' Association increased its share from 32 per cent in 1946 to 50 per cent in 1981 (Dewachter, 1987, p. 340; see also Smits, 1982). At the ministerial level, 41.1 per cent of the 168 CVP Cabinet members between 1958 and 1985 were affiliated with the ACW, 16.4 per cent with the NCWV, 14 per cent with the BB, while a surprisingly high percentage of 28.6 were *sans familles* (de Winter, 1992, p. 43).

Within the Walloon Christian Democratic Party, factionalism is institutionalised to a lesser degree. Although a number of deputies from the Parti Social Chrétien (PSC) have in practice been close to it, the French-speaking Catholic farmers' organisation (Alliance Agricole) is not formally recognised by the party as a *stand*. The organisation of French-speaking Catholic Workers (MOC: *Mouvement Ouvrier Chrétien*), which used to seek exclusive political representation by the PSC, in 1971 decided also to recognise parliamentarians of rival parties – notably federalist Francophone movements such as the Front Démocratique des Franco-phones (FDF) in Brussels and the Rassemblement Wallon (RW) in Wallonia – as its representatives. Since then, those sections of the MOC which focus on the PSC form the so-called Démocratie Chrétienne (DC). Finally, relations between the PSC and the organisation of the Catholic middle classes in Wallonia (CEPIC: Centre Politique des Indépendants et

Cadres Chrétiens) are not as close as they used to be, especially after a group of deputies from the PSC left the CEPIC to form – together with some previously *sans familles* – the Rassemblement du Centre (RDC) in the early 1980s. In 1981, the *sans familles* accounted for 47 per cent of the PSC seats in the House and the Senate (up from 42 per cent in 1974), the DC for 32 per cent (down from 38 per cent in 1974), while the CEPIC representation remained slightly above 20 per cent in this period (Smits, 1982; Dewachter, 1987, p. 34). Of all the PSC ministers and secretaries of state in the 1971–85 period, 39.3 per cent belonged to the CEPIC, 37.5 per cent to the DC, while only 23.2 per cent were *sans familles* (de Winter, 1992, p. 43–4).

Table 3.1 Membership and electorate of the CVP and the PSC

Year	Membership		Electorate		Membership ratio (%)	
	CVP	PSC	CVP	PSC	CVP	PSC
1968	114.843	30.900	1.154.682	488.335	9.9	6.3
1971	100.517	45.998	1.156.678	473.626	8.7	9.7
1974	114.369	47.422	1.222.646	478.209	9.4	9.9
1977	124.730	56.298	1.460.757	545.055	8.5	10.3
1978	125.027	61.049	1.447.131	560.540	8.6	10.6
1981	124.473	55.333	1.165.239	398.342	10.7	13.9
1985	114.716	42.372	1.291.244	482.254	8.8	8.8
1987	139.575	42.838	1.195.839	491.839	11.7	8.7
1991	131.719*	43.322*	1.036.043	476.740	12.7	9.1

Note: *Membership of 1990

Sources: Deschouwer, 1992, pp. 127, 132 (membership ratio calculated by present authors); Verminck, 1991, p. 536; Vos, 1992, p. 464

As far as membership of the Christian Democratic parties in Belgium is concerned, in 1990 the CVP had 131.719 members, up from 114.843 in 1968. In the same year, the PSC had 43.322 members, up from 30.900 in 1968 (see Table 3.1). The Parti Socialiste (PS) still has by far the highest membership ratio of all Belgian political parties, with around 18 per cent of its voters being party members in 1989. The membership ratios of the CVP and the PSC, at present 12.7 and 9.1 per cent respectively, lie around the national average of almost 10 per cent in 1989 (Deschouwer and Koole, 1992, p. 340).

As is the case with the other political parties in Belgium, which, like Italy, is often characterised as a *particratie*, the national party chairmen of the CVP and the PSC are not only in charge of the daily political leadership of their parties, but they also have a preponderant impact on political decision-making in general. Thus, for example, they meet weekly with 'their' ministers, and sometimes also 'their' parliamentary leaders, to discuss the cabinet agenda. The CVP and the PSC differ, however, in the way in which their national party presidents are selected. Whereas in the CVP the highest decision-making body of the party – the national party congress – officially elects the chairman upon recommendation of the national party council, in the PSC he or she has been chosen through a direct and secret vote by all members of the party since the late 1960s (de Winter, 1992, pp. 35–7).

Despite their predominant position in the Belgian political system, there is still relatively little legal recognition of parties. Partly as a result of this, no details are known about their finances, except that since 1971 the party groups have received parliamentary grants, and that in 1989 a bill was passed to organise the financing of Belgian political parties by the state on the condition that they reduced their campaign expenditures (Deschouwer, 1992, p. 123).

The Netherlands

Through their Calvinist and Catholic pillars, the ARP, CHU and KVP used to control Dutch society to a large extent. During the heyday of pillarisation both the Catholic and Calvinist churches contributed significantly to the political power of the KVP and the ARP respectively (Luykx, 1991). Since the late 1960s these pillars have started to crumble (Lijphart, 1975; Daalder, 1987). It would be mistaken, however, to believe that all pillar organisations have now disappeared.

In some cases, Calvinist and Catholic organisations have merged or evolved into Christian organisations: the Christian Federation of Employers, the Christian Federation of Small Businessmen and the Christian National Federation of Trade Unions. Other socio-economic groups, such as farmers, have maintained separate Protestant and Catholic organisations. These socio-economic organisations meet about four times a year with the leaders of the CDA in a Convention of Christian Social Organisations. Moreover, most schools in the Netherlands are still denominational (and funded by the state); so are hospitals, homes for the elderly, welfare organisations and broadcasting networks (Duffhues, 1991). Christian Democrats often play an important role in the administration and management of these organisations. Even so, the network has lost some of its cohesion.

Some religious organisations try to keep the Christian Democrats at a distance. This applies particularly to the churches. Relations between the CDA and the major Dutch churches were strained in the early 1980s, when the Peace Council of the churches led a massive campaign against the modernisation of nuclear weapons, while the CDA approved of modernisation (albeit with some hesitation). There seems to be a growing mutual awareness, however, that the gap between party and church(es) may have become too wide. Thus, attempts have recently been made to improve the relationship (CDA, 1991, p. 79–80).

Moreover, a membership survey held in 1986 indicated that 98 per cent of CDA members belonged to Christian churches (51 per cent Catholic, 47 per cent Dutch Reformed or Reformed). Furthermore, no less than 92 per cent of the CDA party members attended church at least once a month, 78 per cent at least once a week (Zielonka-Goei and Hillebrand, 1988, pp. 127–9).

Membership of the party has declined since 1981, but not as much as that of other major Dutch parties (see Table 3.2). Members still play an important role in the selection of candidates and in the financing of the party – about 80 per cent of the central party funds are contributed by the members (Koole, 1992, p. 191). Though the CDA has retained the organisation structure of a mass party, it can be better described as a 'modern cadre party' run by professional politicians, according to Koole (1992, pp. 406–12). The leaders remain accountable to the members (at meetings of the party council) but exercise considerable influence in practice. In a similar vein, the parliamentary party is subordinate to the extra-parliamentary party in theory, but almost independent in practice. Conflicts between the two are rare, however; the party chairman and parliamentary party leader consult each other frequently (Koole, 1992, p. 259). They also meet regularly with the prime minister – since 1977 always a Christian Democrat – who is in fact the political leader of the party, even if he does not hold any formal position within it.

The electorate

Belgium

Unfortunately, sample surveys have only taken root very recently in Belgium (Mughan, 1985, p. 328). What we do know, however, is that in 1970 92.7 per cent of the CVP voters identified themselves as 'practising Catholics' (Fitzmaurice, 1988, p. 150). De Winter more recently reported that 44 per cent of the CVP voters and 46 per cent of the PSC voters attend church services weekly, as against 21.3 per cent of the Belgian population as a whole. According to him, 16 per cent of the CVP voters and 12 per cent of the PSC voters do not attend church services at all, against 39 per cent of the overall population (1992, p. 50). Despite having no data available about the religion and church practice of their party members, it seems appropriate to conclude that the CVP and the PSC, like their predecessors, are still predominantly parties of church-attending Catholics.

This impression is confirmed by data analysed by Broughton according to which the Christian Democratic parties in 1977 attracted relatively few voters who did not attend church frequently (see Table 3.3) or who, in 1983, called themselves 'not a religious person' or 'a convinced atheist' (7.0 and 1.3 per cent respectively) (1988, p. 211).

Yet the same data also indicate that in 1977 the CVP/PSC was supported by hardly more than a quarter of the Catholic population, a significantly smaller percentage than that of the Dutch CDA (see Table 3.4). Similarly, no more than 40.3 per cent of the people who went to church several times

Table 3.2 Membership and electorate of the CDA

Year	Membership	Electorate	Membership ratio (%)
1977	150,712*	2,652,278	5.8
1981	152,885	2,677,259	5.7
1982	147,896	2,420,441	6.3
1986	128,588	3,172,918	4.1
1989	125,033	3,140,502	4.0

Note: *Direct membership of CDA combined with membership of the constituent parties ARP, CHU and KVP

Sources: Documentation Centre Dutch Political Parties

Table 3.3 Christian Democratic preference by church attendance in Belgium and The Netherlands (1977)

	CVP/PSC	CDA
Several times a week	40.3	74.7
Once a week	36.3	67.0
A few times a year or less	22.5	28.1
Never	12.2	16.1

Note: To read this table: 40.3% of all Belgian respondents who went to church several times a week would vote for CVP or PSC in 1977.

Source: Broughton, 1988, p. 200

Table 3.4 Christian Democratic preference by religious denomination in Belgium and The Netherlands (1977)

	CVP/PSC	CDA
Catholic	28.6	48.6
Protestant	12.5*	36.1
Other	12.5*	14.6*
Non Religious	5.4	3.9

Note: *Fewer than ten persons in this category
To read this table: 28.6 per cent of the Catholics in the Belgian sample would vote for CVP/PSC in 1977.

Source: Broughton, 1988, p. 198

a week voted CVP/PSC that year (Table 3.3). In 1983, finally, only 23.6 per cent of the people describing themselves as being religious voted CVP/PSC (Broughton, 1988, p. 211). Part of the explanation for this lies in the breakthrough of the 'community parties', of which especially the Flemish Volksunie (VU; People's Union) attracts a lot of practising Catholics (Fitzmaurice, 1988, p. 177). Even the Socialist Party (SP) and the Liberal Party (Partij voor Vrijheid en Vooruitgang) have become more open to Catholics than they used to be, while for example at the European elections of 1989 the Ecologists also turned out to be a major electoral threat. The effects of the recent transformation of the Liberal Party into the Citizens' Party (Partij van de Burger) are not yet clear, although opinion polls suggest a considerable impact on voting behaviour.

Despite the general secularisation of society after Vatican II (Dobbelaere, 1981), most of the Catholic social organisations in Belgium seem to have lost little of their considerable strength in terms of membership and viability (Dewachter, 1987; Huyse, 1987). Thus, in comparison to the Catholic pillar in general, the CVP performs badly and can without a doubt be considered the weakest stone in the Catholic pillar. In the long run, at least some Catholic social organisations might therefore adopt a system of plural political representation, as in the case of the PSC (de Winter, 1992, pp. 51–3).

Christian Democratic party supporters in Belgium differ little from the average Belgian party supporter. They are slightly older, however, and more often female; moreover, they identify less with the working class and slightly more with the middle classes (see Table 3.5). In addition, Broughton reports that there are somewhat more materialists and fewer post-materialists among CVP-PSC supporters than among party supporters in Belgium as a whole (1992). Compared to their electorates white-collar workers and cadres are manifestly over-represented in both the CVP and the PSC membership, while blue-collar workers are under-represented (Dewachter, 1987, p. 316).

The Belgian electoral system of proportional representation, with no formal threshold, benefits not only a relatively large party like the CVP, but also the much smaller PSC (see Table 3.6). A disadvantage of the system for the Christian Democrats, however, is that new (rival) parties can easily obtain representation in parliament.

The Netherlands

All available election data point in the same direction as in Belgium: the CDA appeals predominantly to religious people and, more specifically, to those who attend church regularly. Broughton, for example, found that in 1977 the party was supported by almost half of the Catholic population and more than a third of the Protestant population. Three quarters of the people who went to church several times a week voted for the CDA (see Table 3.3). Similarly, in 1983 38 per cent of the people describing themselves as being 'a religious person' voted CDA (Broughton, 1988, p. 211).

Table 3.5 Background variables of Christian Democratic
party supporters in Belgium (1989)

	CVP/PSC (%)	All party supporters (%)
Age		
< 24	15	19
25–39	26	28
40–54	24	23
55+	36	30
Total	101	100
Gender		
Male	40	48
Female	60	52
Total	100	100
Subjective social class		
Working	28	36
Lower middle	15	15
Middle	40	35
Upper middle	12	11
Upper	4	3
Total	99	100
Religion		
Catholic	95	95
Protestant	3	2
Orthodox/Free	0	0
Others	2	4
Total	100	101

Source: Broughton, 1992

Although in 1986 the CDA still appealed to the religious electorate significantly more than other parties, it attracted a significant number of non-
religious voters for the first time. In 1989 14 per cent of the voters with no
religion voted CDA, while almost 60 per cent of Catholic voters, and a
slightly smaller share of Protestant voters, preferred the Christian
Democrats to other parties (CBS, 1990, p. 22). Finally, according to a poll
held in 1991, 32 per cent of the CDA voters go to church once a week, 48
per cent less often and 19 per cent never, against 15, 32 and 53 per cent
respectively for the entire sample (*Nieuwsblad van het Noorden*, 1991).
    Apart from their religion and church attendance, CDA voters differ
little from the average Dutch voter. They are slightly older, however, and
more often female; moreover, they are more often married and less often

Table 3.6 Christian Democratic representation in parliament (Belgium)

Year	Seats in Parliament			Vote %		
	CVP	PSC	CVP+PSC	CVP	PSC	CVP+PSC
1968	50 (23.6%)	19 (9%)	69 (32.5%)	22.3	9.4	31.7
1971	46 (21.7%)	21 (9.9%)	67 (31.6%)	21.9	9	30.9
1974	50 (23.6%)	22 (10.4%)	72 (34%)	23.3	9.1	32.4
1977	56 (26.4%)	24 (11.3%)	80 (37.7%)	26.2	9.8	36
1978	57 (26.9%)	25 (11.8%)	82 (38.7%)	26.1	10.1	36.2
1981	43 (20.3%)	18 (8.5%)	61 (28.8%)	19.7	6.7	26.4
1985	49 (23.1%)	20 (9.4%)	69 (32.5%)	21.3	8	29.3
1987	43 (20.3%)	19 (9%)	62 (29.2%)	19.5	8.0	27.5
1991	39 (18.4%)	18 (8.5%)	57 (26.9%)	16.8	7.7	24.5

Source: Deschouwer, 1992, p. 127. Percentages, seats in parliament CVP and PSC, and totals CVP and PSC calculated by present authors.

divorced than the average voter (see Table 3.7; CBS, 1990, p. 21). As Broughton's (1992) analysis of Eurobarometer data indicates, the Christian Democratic voters identify less with the working class and slightly more with the middle classes. Furthermore, there are more materialists and fewer post-materialists in the CDA electorate than in the Dutch electorate at large.

The electoral system of almost pure proportional representation benefits a large party only slightly (see Table 3.8). Though the Christian Democrats would probably benefit more from a British-style first-past-the-post system, they have never advocated such a system in the Netherlands.

Ideology and policy

Belgium

How can the CVP be characterised ideologically? In its famous *Kerstprogramma* (Christmas Programme) of 1945, the newly formed CVP declared that it was a Christian party, because it wanted to build upon the human values that represented the foundations of Western culture and civilisation. Historically, these values were brought forth by Christianity; today, however, they might well be regarded as the common inheritance of believers and non-believers alike (Van den Wijngaert, 1976, pp. 92–3).

According to its most recent ideological document, entitled *Geloof, hoop en toekomst* (1986), the CVP wants to maintain its explicitly though not exclusively Christian character (section 4). Apart from the rather general notion of 'social-personalism' (previously 'personalism'), the party's basic concepts are: solidarity, responsibility and stewardship

Table 3.7 Composition of the CDA electorate (1989)

	CDA (%)	Total electorate (%)
Age		
18–24	7	7
25–34	22	· 26
35–44	20	25
45–54	16	14
55–64	16	12
65+	20	15
Total	101	99
N=1370		
Gender		
Male	48	52
Female	52	48
Total	100	100
N=1370		
Education level		
Elementary	18	19
Lower secondary	28	25
Higher secondary	33	34
College/university	21	22
Total	100	100
N=1370		
Religion		
Catholic	47	28
Dutch Reformed	18	15
Reformed	15	9
Other	3	6
None	17	42
Total	100	100
N=1369		

Source: CBS, 1990, p. 21–2, data recalculated.

(section 3). Subsequently, from these four principles a number of policy orientations and political values are deduced.

With regard to the economy, the CVP clearly accepts the capitalist and industrial market economy as a means of generating prosperity. Yet, it does not idealise capitalism, but stresses instead the need for a 'guided market economy' (*georiënteerde markteconomie*), which should be acceptable both from a social and an ecological point of view. The party pays

Table 3.8 Christian Democratic representation in cabinet and parliament (The Netherlands)

Period	Coalition	CDA seats in cabinet	CDA seats in parliament	CDA vote (%)
1977–81	CDA+VVD	10 (67%)	49 (33%)	31.9%
1981–82	CDA+PvdA+D66	6 (40%)	48 (32%)	30.8%
1982	CDA+D66	9 (60%)	48 (32%)	30.8%
1982–86	CDA+VVD	8 (57%)	45 (30%)	29.3%
1986–89	CDA+VVD	9 (64%)	54 (36%)	34.6%
1989	CDA+PvdA	7 (50%)	54 (36%)	35.3%

Source: *Parlement en kiezer* (Leiden: Martinus Nijhoff, 1991, pp. 10–55).

special attention to small- and medium-sized industries. Workers should be able to participate in the decision-making in their firms (1986, section 15).

Similarly, the CVP only very reluctantly accepts a secularised and individualistic culture. According to the notion of social personalism, an individual can develop and achieve his or her full potential only through interaction with other human beings and through participation in social groups and associations such as families, churches and trade unions (1986, section 11). Therefore, the party supports all kinds of pillarised organisations in the sectors of education, public health, socio-cultural work and so on, demanding that the state (co-)finance these organisations (1991, pp. 12, 45 for example). The Christian Democrats in Flanders would like the parliamentary debate on abortion to be reopened and euthanasia to remain prohibited (1991, p. 33), while they still regard the family as the basic social unit (*houvast voor de samenleving*). Thus, despite strong opposition from both Socialists and Liberals the CVP sticks, for example, to the tax system it introduced in 1988 and which favours families (1991, p. 43).

Although at least one of the constituent parts of its predecessors at times still regarded liberal democracy as a threat to the Church's position in society (Gerard, 1985, pp. 245–9), the CVP by now seems to have accepted wholeheartedly modern representative mass democracy (1986, § 16). Also, the CVP unconditionally (*zonder enig voorbehoud*) upholds political, social and individual rights and freedoms (1986, § 7).

The last time the PSC dealt with its ideology during a national party congress was in 1983. Like the CVP three years later, it adopted 'social-personalism', instead of just 'personalism', as its guiding ideological concept (Dierickx, 1992). For some time in the past, the party was less federalist than its Flemish counterpart, but recently the unitarists in the PSC seem to have lost ground. Also, as in the case of the two liberal parties (Rudd, 1988, p. 204), there are ideological differences between the CVP and PSC with respect to the issue of abortion, the Walloon party being the slightly more liberal of the two (see, for example, Moors, 1990, p. 152).

We might conclude therefore that the Belgian Christian Democratic parties accept the major aspects of modernisation, but two or three aspects of it only with substantial qualifications.

The Netherlands

Before the CDA could be established, substantial debate took place between the ARP, CHU and KVP about its Christian character. In 1978 it was agreed that the CDA would accept the Biblical evidence of God's promises, acts, and commandments as being of decisive significance for mankind, society and government. At the same time, however, the CDA would address itself as a 'people's party' to the entire Dutch population, irrespective of religious belief or social status. Its political conviction – elaborated in a programme of basic principles – is considered the political answer to the appeal made by the Bible. This conviction, rather than the Bible itself, was to be the binding element that everyone in the CDA must uphold (CDA, 1978; CDA, 1992, pp. 16-17).

The basic principles of the newly formed CDA are almost the same as those of the CVP – not surprisingly, because of the contacts between the two Dutch-speaking parties: justice, differentiated responsibility, solidarity and stewardship. Like the CVP, the CDA claims to deduce a series of policy orientations and political values from these principles.

Like the Belgians, the Dutch Christian Democrats have come to accept a capitalist market economy, albeit with qualifications. Corporatist ideas, which inspired the Catholic Party until the 1960s, have been quietly abandoned since then. Yet the Programme of Principles as well as the first election manifesto of the CDA (1977) still contained critical comments on the materialist and competitive aspects of modern society (1977, pp. 8, 24, 28, 38; 1980, pp. 23–5, 31). Production should be oriented towards society and be 'socially meaningful' (*maatschappelijk zinvol*). Economic power should not be concentrated and should be shared also by workers (CDA, 1980, p. 8).

However, certain sections of the more recent ideological document *Public justice*, published by the party research centre, seem to echo the neo-conservative and liberal critique of the bureaucratic welfare state. The state should focus on its proper responsibilities like the maintenance of (international) law and order. It should confront citizens with their social responsibility and promote competition, not only in the economic sphere but also in the area of education and health (Klink et al., 1990, pp. 116–32). Yet, as Lucardie has argued (1988, pp. 87–8), at least for the time being there remain important differences between the neo-conservative liberalism of Thatcher or Reagan and the reformist or social conservatism of the CDA. For one thing, the CDA also stresses the responsibility of the state to promote social justice. Hence, it seems reluctant to reduce social security and welfare payments, the more so since it once again formed a coalition with the Social Democrats in 1989. Between 1982 and 1989 the Christian Democrats did reduce social expenditure (in coalition with the Dutch Liberal Party), but not dramatically. They also made a modest effort to privatise parts of the public sector such as the State Printing Office and the Post Office Bank.

The CDA accepts modern representative democracy in practice, but with a theoretical qualification: the state is the servant of God (*dienaresse*

Gods) rather than the servant of a sovereign people (1980, p. 5). More-over, the state should recognise the responsibility of social institutions and the specific rights and character of the Church.

The CDA accepts modern secularised culture only very reluctantly. In its latest (draft) Programme of Principles it refers – like the Belgian CVP and PSC – to the notion of social personalism and rejects individualism (CDA, 1992, p. 8). The CDA strongly supports Catholic and Protestant schools and other pillarised associations and institutions. Officially it still rejects abortion; but, unlike the CVP, the party carefully tries to prevent this re-emerging as a political issue. The CDA also opposes the legalisation of euthanasia, and of commercial television or radio. To be sure, on some other issues – like, for example, the recognition of sexual relationships other than the traditional heterosexual marriage – the CDA has moved to a more liberal position (CDA, 1989). With respect to these moral and cultural issues the CDA is often criticised as being too secular and liberal by the three small Christian (Calvinist) parties in the Dutch Lower House; but the latter have not been able so far to benefit from this electorally. (These parties, which together collected only 4.1 per cent of the popular vote in 1989, will not be dealt with here; they are purely confessional parties which reject Christian Democracy [see Lucardie, 1988, pp. 91–2]).

In conclusion, it seems clear that although the CDA accepts the major aspects of modernity, it only does so with substantial qualifications.

Government record

Belgium

During most of the post-war period the Christian Democratic party has been the strongest political formation in Belgium, with its vote share varying between 48 per cent in 1950 and 24.5 per cent in 1991. While in Flanders the CVP has always been the dominant party, the PSC is only the second or even third party in Wallonia (after the Socialists and the Liberals). Apart from the years 1945–7 and 1954–8, the CVP has always been in the government; moreover, nearly all post-war prime ministers in Belgium – like Gaston Eyskens, Theo Lefèvre, Pierre Harmel, Paul van den Boeynants, Leo Tindemans and Wilfried Martens – have been (Flemish) Christian Democrats. Thus, the party has to a large extent been able to dominate both Flemish and national political life, which has at times given rise to the criticism of a 'CVP-state' (Coenjaarts et al., 1979). The impact of the Christian Democratic parties on government policies is further strengthened by the more general phenomena of 'political patro-nage' and 'clientelism' in Belgian politics. On the other hand, it has been remarked that as a result of the multiparty system with coalition cabinets and the international dependence of the economy, Belgian policy-making is to a considerable extent a reactive and incremental process, while the policy output of the Belgian system does not only, or even predominantly, depend on cabinet participation (Dewachter, 1987, pp. 347–53). An additional problem for the PSC is, moreover, that on the one hand it depends heavily on the pivotal power of the CVP for its own participation in government, while on the other hand the coalition preferences of the two parties often conflict. Too close a co-operation with its Flemish counterpart is increasingly disapproved of by its own (Francophone) electorate.

Table 3.9 Party composition of cabinets (Belgium)

Period	Party of prime minister	Other parties
1968–72	CVP	PSC+PSB/BSP
1972–73	CVP	PSC+PSB/BSP
1973–74	PSB/BSP	PRL+CVP+PSC+PVV
1974–74	CVP	PVV+PSC+PRL
1974–77	CVP	PSC+PVV+PRL+RW
1977–77	CVP	PSC+PVV+PRL
1977–78	CVP	PSC+PSB/BSP+VU+FDF
1978–79	PSC	CVP+PSB/BSP+VU+FDF
1979–80	CVP	PSC+BSP+PSB+FDF
1980–80	CVP	PSC+BSP+PSB
1980–80	CVP	PSC+BSP+PSB+PVV+PRL
1980–81	CVP	PSC+BSP+PSB
1981–88	CVP	PSC+PVV+PRL
1988–91	CVP	PSC+BSP+PSB+VU
1991–92	CVP	PSC+BSP+PSB
1992	CVP	PSC+BSP+PSB

BSP: *Belgische Socialistische Partij*
FDF: *Front Démocratique des Francophones Bruxellois*
PRL: *Parti Réformateur Libéral* (until 1976, PLP: *Parti de la Liberté et du Progrès*; 1976–79; PRLW: *Parti des Réformes et de la Liberté de Wallonie*)
PSB: *Parti Socialiste Belge*
PVV: *Partij voor Vrijheid en Vooruitgang*
RW: *Rassemblement Wallon*
VU: *Volksunie*

Source: Deschouwer, 1992, pp. 128, 126.

Certain ministries are virtually 'occupied' by factions within the CVP-PSC. Examples include the labour and employment, family and public health departments (ACW/MOC), agriculture (BB), and, albeit to a lesser extent the middle classes department (NCMV/CEPIC). In particular the ministry of finance is frequently headed by a *sans famille* Christian Democrat (de Winter, 1992, p. 44).

The Netherlands

The CDA has enjoyed governmental power ever since its creation. One of its constituent parties, the KVP, has been in government as a pivotal coalition party almost without intermission since 1917 (Koole and ten Napel, 1991). Dutch prime ministers have been affiliated with a Christian party from 1918 to 1940, from 1946 to 1948, 1959 to 1973 and from 1977 to the present. Apart from the prime minister's office, the Christian Democrats tend to run the department of agriculture; often they also hold the portfolios of education, culture and foreign affairs. The Christian Democrats have usually chosen as coalition partner either the Labour Party (PvdA, Social Democrats) or the (Conservative) Liberal party (VVD: Volkspartij voor Vrijheid en Democratie); but more often the latter than the former (see Table 3.8). In socio-economic affairs they try to occupy a position in the centre, between Labour and the Liberals. In this area they have been quite effective in moderating conflicts between Capital and Labour and in reconciling a capitalist economy with a strong welfare state. In cultural matters, they have been less successful in their opposition to secularisation and liberalisation, favoured by Labour and Liberals alike.

Conclusion

If Christian Democratic parties evolve from 'closed', anti-modern confessional parties towards 'open', modern liberal-conservative parties, as Horner asserted (1981), the CDA, PSC and CVP may lag behind some other European parties on this road. Nevertheless they are moving in the same direction.

From our analysis of party platforms and declarations of principles presented above we can conclude that the three parties have embraced liberal capitalist economic principles, giving up corporatism as well as Christian socialism, even if they remain critical of capitalist influence in the area of culture and ethics. They try to reconcile Christian principles with secularisation in a pluralist society, advocating personal freedom but fighting abortion and euthanasia. Personalism is still presented as an alternative to both individualism and collectivism. The sovereignty of the people is not accepted explicitly by the CDA; yet it accepts parliamentary democracy and does not contribute much to the power and influence of the churches.

The organisational networks of the three Christian Democratic parties declined in the 1960s and 1970s, especially in the Netherlands, but they still survive. Members of the parties are still predominantly practising Christians, who attend church regularly (once a week or so). Most voters belong to the same category, but a growing proportion of the Christian Democratic electorate does not practise any more and may even have left the church altogether.

The Dutch Christian Democratic party has expanded its non-religious electorate in recent years. Yet it has to compete with modern Liberal mass parties – not only the Conservative Liberal VVD but also the leftwing Liberal Democrats 66 – for the secular voters left and right of the centre in the political spectrum. Its Belgian sister parties face an even more arduous task: not only to win secular voters from the large Liberal party, but to maintain their hold on Catholic voters tempted by Nationalism (both the moderate Volksunie and the extremist Vlaams Blok in Flanders, the Front National in Wallonia), and even by the (originally also Catholic) Greens. In both countries, as a result Christian Democratic power may begin to wane towards the end of the twentieth century.

References

Anon, 1991, *Parlement en kiezer*, Martinus Nijhoff, Leiden.

Becker, Winfried, 1991, Zur Geschichte und Konzeption der Christlichen Demokratie, in Günter Baadte and Anton Rauscher (eds.) *Christen und Demokratie*, Graz, Styria, pp. 11–39.

Billiet, Jaak, 1987, Les relations complexes entre le CVP et l'Eglise, *La Revue Nouvelle*, 43: pp. 299–307.

Broughton, David, 1988, The Social Bases of Western European Conservative Parties, in Brian Girvin (ed.) *The Transformation of Contemporary Conservatism*. Sage, London, pp. 193–224.

Broughton, David, 1992, The Christian Democratic Voter: A Four Country Comparison, paper presented at the ECPR Joint Sessions of Workshops, University of Limerick, Republic of Ireland, 30 March–4 April 1992.

CBS, 1990, *Nationaal kiezersonderzoek 1989. Deel 1. Stemgedrag en politieke aspekten*, SDU, The Hague.

CDA, 1977, *Niet bij brood alleen*, CDA. The Hague.

CDA, 1978, *Rapport grondslag en politiek handelen*, CDA, The Hague.

CDA, 1980, *Program van Uitgangspunten*, CDA, The Hague.

CDA, 1989, *'Verantwoord voortbouwen'. Program van aktie '89–'93*, CDA, The Hague.

CDA, 1991, *Levensbeschouwelijke identiteit en politiek. Verslag van de conferentie van 22 en 23 februari 1991 te Noordwijkerhout*, CDA, The Hague.

CDA, 1992, *Ontwerp-Program van Uitgangspunten*, CDA, The Hague.

Coenjaarts, Henry, de Haes, Leo and Geens, Hilde, (1979) *De CVP-staat*, EPO, Berchem.

CVP, 1986, *Geloof, hoop en toekomst*, CVP, Brussel.

CVP, 1991, *Goed leven in Vlaanderen ook morgen. Programma van de Vlaamse christen-democraten voor de wetgevende verkiezingen*, CVP, Brussel.

Daalder, Hans, 1987, The Dutch Party System: From Segmentation to Polarization – And Then?, in Hans Daalder (ed.), *Party Systems in Denmark, Austria, Switzerland, the Netherlands and Belgium*, Pinter, London, pp. 193–284.

De Groof, Jan, 1977, Over de wording van de CVP-PSC. Enkele krachtlijnen, gegevens en bedenkingen bij de wording van de Christelijke Volkspartij, *Res Publica*, 19: 83–98.

Deschouwer, Kris, 1992, Belgium, in Richard S. Katz and Peter Mair (eds.), *Party Organizations. A Data Handbook on Party Organizations in Western Democracies, 1960–90*, Sage, London, pp. 121–98.

Deschouwer, Kris and Ruud Koole, 1992, De ontwikkeling van partij-organisaties in België en Nederland, 1960–1990, *Sociologische Gids*, 39: 324–45.

Dewachter, Wilfried, 1987, Changes in a Particratie: the Belgian Party System from 1944 to 1986, in Hans Daalder (ed.), *Party Systems in Denmark, Austria, Switzerland, the Netherlands and Belgium*, Pinter, London, pp. 285–363.

Dewachter, Wilfried et al., 1988, Morfologie van de Belgische politieke partijen 1970–1985, *Res Publica*, 30: 483–698.

De Winter, Lieven, 1992, Christian Democratic Parties in Belgium, in Mario Caciagli et al., *Christian Democracy in Europe*, Barcelona, Institut de Ciènces Politiques i Socials.

Dierickx, Guido, 1992, Christian Democracy and its Ideological Rivals. An empirical comparison in the Low Countries, Paper prepared for the ECPR workshop on Christian Democracy, University of Limerick.

Dobbelaere, K., 1981, Secularisatieprocesen in Vlaanderen, *Tijdschrift voor Sociologie*, 1: 5–20.

Duffhues, T., 1991, Confessionele partijen en maatschappelijke organisaties. Aspecten van een duurzame relatie, in Paul Luykx and Hans Righart (eds.), *Van de pastorie naar het torentje. Een eeuw confessionele politiek*, SDU, The Hague, pp. 124–46.

Fitzmaurice, John, 1988, *The Politics of Belgium. Crisis and Compromise in a Plural Society* (2nd edn.), Hurst and Company, London.

Fraeys, William, 1988, Les élections législatives du 13 décembre 1987. Analyse des résultats, *Res Publica*, 30: 3–24.

Gerard, Emmanuel, 1985, *De katholieke partij in crisis. Partijpolitiek leven in België (1918–1940)*, Kritak, Leuven.

Horner, Franz, 1981, *Konservative und christdemokratische Parteien in Europa*, Herold, Vienna.

Huyse, Luc, 1987, *De verzuiling voorbij*, Kritak, Leuven.

Irving, R. E. M., 1979, *The Christian Democratic Parties of Western Europe*, Allen and Unwin, London.

Klink, A. et al., 1990, *Publieke gerechtigheid. Een christen-democratische visie op de rol van de overheid in de samenleving*, Bohn, Stafleu, Van Loghum, Houten.

Koole, R. A., 1992, *De opkomst van de moderne kaderpartij: veranderende partijorganisatie in Nederland 1960–1990*, Het Spectrum, Utrecht.

Koole, R. A. and H.-M. T. D. ten Napel, 1991, De riante positie in het vermaledijde 'midden'. Confessionele machtsvorming op nationaal niveau, in Paul Luykx and Hans Righart (eds.) *Van de pastorie naar het torentje. Een eeuw confessionele politiek*, SDU, The Hague, pp. 72–92.

Kossmann, E. H., 1978, *The Low Countries (1780–1940)*, Clarendon Press, Oxford.

Lijphart, Arend, 1975, *The Politics of Accomodation. Pluralism and Democracy in the Netherlands* (2nd edn.), University of California Press, Berkeley (CA).

Lönne, Karl-Egon, 1986, *Politischer Katholizismus im 19. und 20. Jahrhundert*, Suhrkamp, Frankfurt am Main.

Lucardie, Paul, 1988, Conservatism in the Netherlands: Fragments and Fringe Groups, in Brian Girvin (ed.) *The Transformation of Contemporary Conservatism*, Sage, London, pp. 78–97.

Luykx, Paul, 1991, Van de dorpspastorie naar het torentje. Kerken en de macht der confessionele partijen, in Paul Luykx and Hans Righart (eds.) *Van de pastorie naar het torentje. Een eeuw confessionele politiek*, SDU, The Hague, pp. 35–71.

Mayeur, Jean-Marie, 1986, Les partis politiques d'inspiration chrétienne en Europe entre les deux guerres mondiales, in Hugues Portelli and Thomas Jansen (eds.) *La démocratie chrétienne, force internationale*, Institut de Politique Internationale et Européenne, Paris, pp. 25–30.

Moors, Johan, 1990, De partijpolitieke situatie in België, *Christen Democratische Verkenningen*, 10: 150–53.

Mughan, Anthony, 1985, Belgium, in Ivor Crewe and David Denver (eds.) *Electoral Change in Western Democracies. Patterns and Sources of Electoral Volatility*, Croom Helm, London, pp. 319–41.

Nieuwsblad van het Noorden, 1991, 30 November.

Rudd, Christopher, 1988, The Belgian Liberal Parties: Economic Radicals and Social Conservatives, in Emil J. Kirchner (ed.) *Liberal Parties in Western Europe*, Cambridge University Press, Cambridge, pp. 178–212.

Smits, Jozef, 1982, De standenvertegenwoordiging in de Christelijke Volkspartij en de Parti Social Chrétien, *Res Publica*, 24: 73–127.

Ten Napel, H.-M. T. D., 1992, *'Een eigen weg'. De totstandkoming van het CDA (1952–1980)*, Kok Agora, Kampen.

Van den Wijngaert, M., 1976, *Ontstaan en stichting van de CVP/PSC. De lange weg naar het Kerstprogramma*, Nederlandse Boekhandel, Antwerpen.

Vandeputte, Robert, 1991, *De Christelijke Volkspartij 1944–1988. Wezen en ontwikkelingen*, CEPESS, Brussel.

Van Holsteyn, J. J. M. and G. A. Irwin, 1988, CDA, naar voren! Over de veranderende verkiezingsstrategie van het CDA, in *Jaarboek 1987 DNPP*, Documentatiecentrum Nederlandse Politieke Partijen, Groningen, pp. 66–98.

Verkuil, Dik, 1992, *Een positieve grondhouding. De geschiedenis van het CDA*, SDU, The Hague.

Verminck, M., 1991, Morfologie van de Vlaamse politieke partijen in 1989 en 1990, *Res Publica*, 33: 523–584.

Vos, Mieck, 1992, Morphologie des partis politiques francophones en 1990 et 1991, *Res Publica*, 34: 453–490.

Whyte, John, 1981, *Catholics in Western Democracies*, Gill and MacMillan, Dublin.

Zielonka-Goei, M. L. and R. Hillebrand, 1988, De achterban van parlementariërs. Kiezers en partijleden, in *Jaarboek 1987 DNPP*, Documentatiecentrum Nederlandse Politieke Partijen, Groningen, pp. 116–37.

4

DEMOCRAZIA CRISTIANA: PARTY OF GOVERNMENT

Mark Donovan

The DC, as the Italian Christian Democratic Party is usually known, has its immediate origins in the disintegration of the twenty-year Fascist regime in 1943. For the next fifty years the Christian Democrats dominated Italian government, mostly in coalition with other parties. From December 1945 until 1981 every prime minister was a Christian Democrat. Then the party's strangle hold was broken: first by the Republican, Giovanni Spadolini, and then by the Socialist, Bettino Craxi. And yet, throughout the 1980s, the DC alone still provided cabinets with half their ministers, including the premier on six occasions, while the remaining portfolios were shared between four other parties. At the end of the 1980s the DC's predominance had been challenged, but not undone.

The crisis of the party system in the early 1990s, however, raised questions about the very survival of the DC, indeed, of all of Italy's traditional parties. The interaction of three highly disruptive forces – the referendum-based attack on the existing party-cum-political system; the electoral advance of the Northern League; and the snowballing corruption scandals (known collectively as *tangentopoli*, roughly 'rake-off city') – threatened to reduce the DC to a party essentially of the south, and two leading figures left the DC to challenge it externally. By the spring of 1993 opinion polls were showing support for the party to have collapsed to about 20 per cent, similar to that for the (ex-Communist) Party of the Democratic Left, and it seemed inevitable that the DC would formally cease to exist. The extent to which its heir, or heirs, would inherit the Christian Democratic tradition was uncertain.

The DC's crisis was triggered by the collapse of communism and the disappearance of its principal rival for power, the Italian Communist Party. But the roots of the crisis were far deeper, reflecting the fact that the party's quasi-permanent occupation of power had never been a happy one. If in the 1950s the party was accused of clerico-conservatism, of building a confessional state, and even of presiding over a new totalitarianism (Jemolo, 1960; Spotts and Wieser, 1986, p. 245), in the 1960s it was realised that these accusations were exaggerated, not least because the ideological diversity within the party was greater than that found in most other West European party systems. The DC was not the long arm of the Vatican (Sassoon, 1986, pp. 143–6). But equally it was not capable of coherent government, or even of governing at all; it merely survived (Di Palma, 1977). Moreover, by the 1970s it was widely seen as reeking with corruption, so much so that one influential newspaper editor urged voters to support it casting their vote with one hand and holding their nose with the other! The justification for this ambivalent advice was that the DC remained the country's anti-Communist bulwark. If the anti-Communist vote split, ending the DC's non-socialist 'catch-all' function, the Italian Communist Party (PCI), the West's largest, and the second strongest party in Italy, might become Italy's leading political force. Regardless of the PCI's declared democratic intentions, such a development was likely to precipitate a crisis of the entire political system.

The collapse of Soviet and Italian communism in the late 1980s and early 1990s thus removed one of the main reasons for the DC's post-war success. Its leaders reacted by reaching back into history. Denying that the DC's origins lay in the founding of the Republic (by then widely described as a 'First Republic' with the implied hope that it was due to give way to a 'Second Republic') the party's factions increasingly adopted a common line: that the DC's origins really lay in the Italian Popular Party (PPI), founded in 1919. In this way the origins of the DC pre-dated the foundation of the PCI by two years. By this leap of historical imagination, the DC sought to escape both identification with the despised post-war 'regime' and reduction to mere anti-communism.

The PPI itself had survived only until 1926 when it had fallen victim to Fascism and the Vatican's rapprochement with it (Molony, 1977), leading to the 1929 Church–state Concordat. Nevertheless, in combining liberalism and Catholicism the PPI's founder, Don Sturzo, laid the basis for the creation of a distinct Catholic political identity. When Fascism disintegrated, 'political Catholicism' underpinned the DC's claim to represent a 'third way'. From the 1940s until the 1980s, though with ever less plausibility, this third way lay between Fascism and Communism. By the early 1990s the essential contrast (with liberalism and socialism) had to be restated, and the superiority of 'Popularism' asserted (Fontana, 1993).

Governing during a protracted democratic consolidation

The PPI was born of a culture long hostile to the lay state and uncertain whether compromise with other political forces was tolerable. The DC emerged from the Fascist period determined to govern Italy and well aware that non-co-operation between moderate socialists and Catholics had let 'barbarism' usurp parliamentary government from 1922. The new spirit of accommodation resulted in the formation of a grand anti-Fascist coalition, known as the Committee for National Liberation (CLN), which by 1944 had won international recognition as Italy's new governing class. Uniting a wide range of political traditions, the CLN established a practice of broad coalition government. This elite-level development preceded the holding of parliamentary elections. The first parliament was not elected until 1948, by which time several cabinets had come and gone. The CLN ended in 1947, with the onset of the Cold War, because the imminent participation of the Italian people in electing a parliament and government forced the elites into confrontation. Well into the 1970s, the two major subcultures in Italy, the Catholic and the Socio-Communist, identified each other as would-be bearers of totalitarianism with whom co-operation was inconceivable (Farneti, 1980; Di Palma, 1982).

The first prime minister to govern all of Italy, independently of the Allied Military Government, was Alcide De Gasperi, the DC's key founding figure. De Gasperi dominated the party until 1954 when he died, having led eight successive governments. His combination of anti-communist politics and reformist policies encouraged the development of a three-bloc party system in which the DC dominated the centre bloc, with which government was identified, while forcing both the Socio-Communist left and the Monarchist and neo-Fascist right into permanent opposition. Thus was established a party-cum-political system via which was managed the difficult, and protracted, process of democratic consolidation in post-Fascist Italy. The governmental or oppositional stances assumed by the parties became quasi-permanent roles – and the governing party *par excellence* was the DC.

After De Gasperi's death the DC was briefly dominated by Amintore Fanfani. Fanfani was associated with the Catholic left, and both business interests and the Vatican regarded him as socialistically inclined. The left, however, saw him as a dangerous autocratic foe. He was actually more interested in consolidating the power of the DC than that of the Church. Certainly the exclusionary nature of the DC's centrist domination of government, combined with Fanfani's personality, rendered credible both left and liberal right-wing interpretations of Fanfani as a potentially authoritarian figure.

From 1959, however, the oligarchic nature of the DC became clear. The existence of different ideological strands within the party, and more importantly the party's dendritic rootedness in civil society, prevented any individual dominating the party. Having displaced Fanfani, the so-called *Dorotei* cluster of faction leaders took charge of the party and ran it, and the Italian state, for the next twenty to thirty years.

The party and the state became increasingly intertwined as government intervention in the economy, in all its aspects, and especially regarding 'the problem of the South', led to the proliferation of special agencies dominated by Christian Democrats or by interest groups having tight relations with the party. From the 1960s the very basis of government moved away from parliament and cabinet into the world of 'sub-government' (*sottogoverno*), that is to the 'quasi-governmental' networks linking the DC with various public bodies and interest groups. The development of 'post-parliamentary democracy' was a post-war European trend (Heisler, 1974; Richardson and Jordan, 1979). However, in Italy this diffusion of power also reflected the DC's concern to avoid confronting the Socialists and

Communists in parliament. Many Catholics, moreover, still believed that
government by a 'third (Catholic) way' was both a duty to be implemented,
and a blessing for the Italian people.

Most illusions that the 'DC-state' was not about 'power for power's sake'
were dispelled, first by the fact that even the Catholic subculture took a
critical stance regarding the Christian Democrats in the 1960s, then by the
financial scandals of the 1970s which coincided with the end of the public
sector's innovative and entrepreneurial protagonism. In the 1970s the DC
thus faced a pressing legitimacy crisis. It was saved by the gravity of
the challenges facing the political system: apparent economic collapse,
Europe's most violent experience of non-regional terrorism, and the fact
that the force likely to succeed it was still Communist. The PCI, indeed,
reached its greatest strength in 1976, only a few points behind the DC (34.4
per cent compared to 38.7 per cent). The result was an emergency DC
minority government backed in parliament by the so-called 'constitutional
arc' – in effect the parties of the CLN. This partially legitimised the
Communists; but fortunately for the DC, the party which suffered from
this second demonstration of elite preparedness to collaborate in the face
of grassroots radicalism was the PCI itself.

The PCI was torn between its revolutionary identity and the *de facto*
moderation of its dominant leadership group. The Radicals, a new party,
condemned the Communist Party for combining empty revolutionism with
conservative practice. A major component of the Radicals' critique was the
resurrection of the term *partitocrazia* ('partyocracy' – party rule). This
term was first used by liberal critics of the nascent post-war democracy
(Maranini, 1950, 1963). The crucial point of the Radicals' use of the term
was that as criticism shifted from the 'DC-state' (the villain of the 1970s)
back to the *partitocrazia*, it shifted from the DC alone to the entire party
system. All the traditional parties, including the PCI to some extent, were
seen as stifling civil society; and increasingly, Italians rejected those parties
(Morlino, 1984).

Disenchantment with the DC in the 1960s and 1970s did not result in
significant vote losses because there was still little alternative to it: the
Communist spectre lingered on. But in the 1980s the DC vote weakened,
and in 1992 it fell to just under 30 per cent, prompting fear that the DC
could be facing the vicious circle of decline that had afflicted the PCI from
1979. But an even greater danger existed.

That party-system and governmental change in the 1970s and 1980s had
not been decisive was deeply unsatisfactory to many Italians. Electoral
competition seemed to be a farce, with the DC apparently doomed to
govern and no credible alternative in sight. In response to the inability of
the party system to produce significant governmental turnover or otherwise
enhance its authority, leading politicians resorted to direct democracy.
Unusually, the Italian constitution allows referenda to be initiated by
popular request. From 1989 they were used to force the parties to change
and innovate, so that the early 1990s saw continuous mobilisation of an
explicitly *anti-partitocrazia* nature via the repeated multiple deployment of
the referendum instrument. This reinforced the delegitimisation of the

traditional parties, especially in northern Italy, and contributed to the success of a new political phenomenon, the regional Leagues. In 1992 the Northern League not only became the fourth largest party in parliament, threatening to replace the left as the DC's main challenger, but it also broke into the DC's electoral strongholds in northern Italy, radically undermining the so-called white (Catholic) subculture in those areas. The DC thus faced the prospect that its Catholic identity would disappear along with its anti-Communist one. At the same time, the message was clear that a centrist party dominating government in an exclusive way was no longer needed. The protracted transition to democracy was over. A new way of structuring politics was called for.

Organisation

The DC is not a clerical institution. It is an independent organisation. However, its position *vis-à-vis* what is known as the 'Catholic world', and its interpenetration with both civil society and the state, have been so intimate that all three can be considered in some way as part of the structure of Italian Christian Democracy. In addition, of course, civil society and the Catholic world, or 'subculture', themselves overlap extensively, giving rise to the term 'religious society'.

The partial fusion of party, state and civil society

The trade union confederation CISL can be taken as an example of the complex interrelations between the DC, the state and civil (especially religious) society. Deeply rooted in the Catholic world via the pre-Fascist 'white' trade unions and its relationship with the Association of Catholic Workers (ACLI), the CISL nevertheless deliberately avoided joining the International Catholic Federation of Trade Unions. Its interest lay in autonomy via allegiance with the DC, as opposed to subordination to the Vatican. Nevertheless, when, from the late 1960s, the CISL flirted with the Socialists, its Catholic roots prevented a radical change in direction and subsequently, in the late 1980s, it took on again a Christian Democratic identity.

More generally, the term 'Christian Democracy' is itself ambiguous, referring both to the tradition of democratic modernisation within Italian Catholicism (Webster, 1961; Zoppi, 1991) and to the party specifically. Thus, while no specific post-war Christian Democratic movement can be identified, the interdependent, often conflictual, relationship between the DC, the Vatican and the various components of the Catholic world has been such that political Catholicism has been more than just the party alone.

In 1942–3 a skeleton party organisation was quickly established throughout the national territory. This, backed by De Gasperi's close contacts with the Vatican and some strategic manoeuvring, established the principle of the political unity of Catholics and pre-empted the possibility that a plural political Catholicism would develop. The new party was dependent upon the Church for the mobilisation of its electorate and it also drew many of its leading cadres from organisations such as Catholic Action.

Not wishing to repeat the fate of the PPI, however, the DC put much effort into seeking its long-term independence from the Vatican by ensuring that the organisation of millions of peasant farmers and workers in *Coldiretti* and the CISL was not simply dominated by the Church. These autonomous Catholic associations, combining distinct cultural identity with economic self-interest, laid the bases for the intertwining of party, state and civil society. This interweaving burgeoned with the development of the 'DC-state', and the term *parentela* was devised to describe it (LaPalombara, 1964). The term was contrasted to *clientela*, i.e. the (non-party-based) 'corporatist' link between an interest group and a state institution typical of 'post-parliamentary' government. In many cases the *parentela* linkage degenerated into mere mutual self-interest, centred on the exchange of commercial benefit for political support. In the scandals of the early 1990s some of these links and organisations were revealed as little more than politico-financial swindles. As demands that the parties withdraw from the state, and that interest-group activity be properly regulated, became irrefutable, the DC was forced to rethink its entire mode of operation.

A particular aspect of the new situation, again affecting all the parties, was the need to develop a new method of party funding. A system of public funding for the parties had been hurriedly introduced in the 1970s in response to the corruption scandals involving party slush funds provided by IRI, the public sector industrial conglomerate. By early 1993 the year-old *Tangentopoli* investigation involved no less than a quarter of parliament's deputies and senators. A new system based on tax payers voluntarily allocating a tax-deductible proportion of their income seemed likely to result (*Corriere della Sera*, 4 February 1993, p. 6).

Towards 'normalisation' of party organisation

An early indicator of the normalisation of state–interest group relationships was provided by the revision of the 1929 Concordat in the mid-1980s. Effected under a Socialist-led government and requiring extensive subsequent negotiation to thrash out the detailed legislation, a more 'normal' corporatist relationship became apparent, with the Church losing a number of its privileges and having to act as an interest group working with government departments and agents. Even for the Church, the DC was no longer necessary to the governmental process. Indeed, the DC's prior monopoly of government leadership had rendered reform in this important area impossible; the whole complex of issues was too sensitive for the DC either to handle, or be seen to handle.

In other ways too the DC's dominant governing role had become unhelpful to the Church and of ambiguous benefit to the party. Financial corruption, arising from the party's notorious 'occupation of the state', we have seen, undermined the party's legitimacy. In addition to the numerous social and economic ministries and agencies dominated by the DC, both the Interior Ministry and the Education Ministry were virtually monopolised by the DC. This had involved the party in, respectively, the misuse of the intelligence and security services and responsibility for guaranteeing a dominant position for Catholicism in state education. The development of national radio, and subsequently television, had initially also been kept firmly in the hands of trusted Catholics and Christian Democrats. From the 1970s, however, control of public radio and television was divided up among the three larger parties (DC, PCI and PSI).

A further major factor in maintaining DC influence at the grass roots level has been the nature of Italy's financial system which is dominated by bank lending and a proliferation of credit institutions, rather than by the stock exchange. Two factors enhanced the political significance of Italy's credit system. On the one hand it has always been highly fragmented, giving not only individual branches but the whole profusion of independent regional and town-based offices immense influence at the deepest level of Italian society. On the other hand, the whole fragmented system was tightly overseen by a treasury-based government committee, allowing the DC to ensure the loyalty of directors. This control was specifically, and massively, repudiated by one of the eight referendums of April 1993, and was in any case becoming impossible to reconcile with the growing 'Europeanisation' of banking activities.

Party organisation and factionalism

The formal structure of the party, then, has to be understood in the context of its extensive and profound penetration of Italian society and of the distended Italian state. Even the formal organisation was bound to be transformed by the disintegration of the old politics in the early 1990s. In that system (Leonardi and Wertman, 1989, pp. 90–158), local party organisations were de facto divided between the mass membership, essentially inactive, and the core which represented local interests and structures of power. Often the local organisation was the link between those who controlled bureaucratic and economic power and those who organised a clientelistic vote for the party.

As a consequence of the party's locally entrenched nature and its operation in and via various public sector bodies, the potential for division inherent in the party's ideological flexibility was maximised. Thus, the existence of various tendencies in the 1940s gave way to the development of highly organised and distinctive factions in the 1950s. From 1964 the factions' fundamental role in party life was officially sanctioned in that the allocation of seats in various party organs was determined by the proportion of the vote obtained in the national Party Congress.

The national Party Congress represents the pinnacle of a hierarchy of sections, and municipal, provincial and (since 1970) regional tiers of organisation. At the subnational level, the provincial level is the most important, except where its functions are assumed by large city municipalities. It is this level which selects most parliamentary deputies and senators, and it is also the pivot between the party's national leaders and the grassroots. It is thus the target which the ambitious aim for in a system heavily based on co-optation along factional lines.

Congresses are supposed to be held every two years, but crises have frequently resulted in delay. Some thousand delegates participate in these Congresses which debate general policy and have the right to change the party statutes. They are simultaneously highly orchestrated yet intensely competitive affairs, important because they seal, for a time, the balance of forces in the National Council which they elect. This latter, comprising some 220 members, in turn elects the National Executive Committee, a smaller body of some forty members, which is where the faction leaders exercise their power. It is this machinery, rather than the parliamentary party, which is the core of the DC. The consequent tension is revealed by the way disgruntled back-benchers refer to themselves as 'peons'.

Failed attempts at reform

From 1976 the party leader, or Political Secretary, has been elected directly by Congress, partly in an attempt to outflank the faction leaders and thus rejuvenate the party. For the 1980 Congress the old system of indirect election by the National Council was briefly reasserted, but from 1982–9 Ciriaco De Mita was thrice elected directly on a platform of reform. None the less, the party remained essentially oligarchic, both because the Congress itself remained largely the creature of the factions and because De Mita was himself one of the party's southern *notabili*. He was more successful in reforming the party's position in the para-state than in reforming the party itself. Attempts to make the regional tier more important bore little fruit, while central intervention in local party affairs often turned into inconclusive wars of attrition. The return of Arnaldo Forlani to the secretaryship in 1989, backed by the septuagenarian Giulio Andreotti, who again took over as prime minister, demonstrated the continuing grip of the old faction bosses. One consequence of the return of Forlani was the subsequent resignation of Leoluca Orlando, the leader of the DC-left in Palermo, Sicily's capital. The left-wing party he subsequently formed, known as The Network (*la Rete*), gained eight deputies in the 1992 election.

The electoral disaster of 1992 forced Forlani to resign. The new Secretary, Martino Martinazzoli, was neither elected (since no Congress had taken place) nor was he a factional boss. Like Zaccagnini, appointed in 1975 and confirmed by the new election procedure in 1976, Martinazzoli was a co-opted 'clean' face. He had the additional advantage of representing the northern DC, thus improving his party's chances in the confrontation with the Northern League, while cloaking the DC's growing identification with the (corrupt) south.

De Mita's failure to reform the party was confirmed by the emergency nature of Martinazzoli's appointment and by the fact that his principal challenger was formally no more than a back-bencher, Mario Segni, identified with a conservative wing of the party. Segni's power lay in the referendum mobilisation, for he was President of the key Committee for Electoral Reform (COREL) which spanned the spectrum of Italian parties.

In the immediate run-up to the April 1993 referenda, Segni resigned from the party, though his Catholicism and devotion to Christian Democracy in its more abstract sense remained clear. The organisational reforms which the DC was in the process of implementing, such as the reduction of the National Executive Committee to just fifteen voting members, were too little too late. Not least in a context in which Andreotti, the DC's (and the Republic's) most distinguished politician, was being accused of plotting murder with the mafia; while the leadership of the DC's Naples stronghold was under suspicion of long-term collusion with the Camorra (the Neapolitan mafia). As far as Segni was concerned, years of rhetoric about rebuilding and refounding the DC, and the absence of progress in this direction, underlined the impossibility of reforming it. Only the destruction of the party machine could bring real change, and the single ballot, first-past-the-post electoral system embraced by referendum voters seemed the ideal means for achieving this. Martinazzoli appeared to agree (Panebianco, 1993).

The Christian Democratic electorate

How much of the DC's electoral support has actually identified with the party, thus forming a truly Christian Democratic electorate, and how much of it has been 'lent'? In other words, to what extent has an anti-Socialist/ anti-Communist vote backed it out of necessity, in the absence of a strong lay alternative? And how much has the Catholic vote itself been constrained by the same anti-Communist imperative to back a party felt to be too conservative, too corrupt, or only luke warm and ambiguous in its support for Catholic aims? These questions have much exercised the DC elite since the late 1960s, and many commentators have argued that the party is becoming, or should become, a catch-all centre-right conservative party, with its Catholic base essentially subordinated or even marginalised (Furlong, 1984; Caciagli, 1985).

Anti-Communism, religion and regional tradition

In 1948 the DC amassed 48.5 per cent of the vote, reflecting the 'aligning' nature of that election between the Socio-Communist Popular Front and the DC (Allum and Mannheimer, 1985). A permanent two-bloc alignment did not endure, however, for in 1953 the extreme right gained nearly 13 per cent of the vote; and with the Liberals also being on the DC's right flank, the DC was able to claim a centre position (Farneti, 1985). The DC's subsequent 'centrism', based on its command of some 40 per cent of the vote (1953–79), enabled it to retain its left factions and to have a degree of credibility with moderately reformist currents in the Catholic world. This became particularly important in the general politico-cultural shift to the left of the 1960s and 1970s, a shift which embraced the Catholic subculture, the so-called 'contestation'. Thus, while the Catholic left condemned the DC for its conservatism the party did not, as we have seen with reference to the CISL, lose its links either with the working class or with its populist base.

Class, in fact, has never been a particularly good indicator of voting behaviour in post-war Italy. Institutionalised political traditions and cultural factors have been supremely important (Galli and Prandi, 1970; Barnes, 1977), so that religion and region have been strikingly important in dividing much of central and northern Italy between the Red Belt (Emilia-Romagna, Tuscany, Umbria, the Marches) on the one hand, and the northern and north-eastern strongholds of the White subculture on the other. The encompassing nature of DC allegiance in these strongholds has ensured that the DC has always been able to claim to be an inter-class people's or 'popular' party. Yet the party's electorate has never mirrored Italian society. The regional strongholds, based on intense religious associationalism, are themselves special features of voting behaviour, and the DC's electorate has been disproportionately drawn from rural areas and small towns, older voters and women. This last category has been particularly significant, providing up to two-thirds of the party's vote in the 1950s, and falling below 60 per cent only in the 1980s (Leonardi and Wertman, 1989, p. 166).

By the 1970s, Catholic voting for the DC was far from being a simple matter of subcultural identity or a mere ritual. Italy had never, in any case, been witness to the so-called 'pillarisation' phenomenon of the Netherlands in which distinct subcultures marshalled voters into well-defined political blocs (Allum and Mannheimer, 1985). Nevertheless, the mobilisations of the 1960s and 1970s resulted in active Catholics ceasing to regard their vote as predetermined by their faith. They even showed themselves to be prepared to vote across the divide that separated the centre and right from the left. This cross-bloc volatility was aided by the passage of the Socialists (PSI) into the government in the early 1960s, a development which coincided with the second Vatican Council. Although this Council, launched by John XXIII, was of global significance, its local impact was to sanction and accelerate the changes taking place within Italian Catholicism, reinforcing the fusion of Catholic and Socialist reformism represented by the new government. The prominence of leading Catholics on Communist Party electoral lists from 1976 encouraged some former DC voters to go so far as to vote Communist, at one time sufficient grounds for automatic excommunication.

Parallel with these changes, the proportion of the DC vote made up of practising Catholics declined, leading to speculation that the DC was being 'laicised'. This trend appeared to come to an end in the 1980s as

Catholicism reconsolidated, and the DC electorate was left split, roughly half and half, between practising Catholics and a component widely defined as 'secular' (Sani, 1991). Other research has indicated that this latter component was markedly Catholic despite being weak in its devotional practice (Garelli, 1991, pp. 100–101). Such findings lent weight to speculation that Italy's dominant future political cleavage would be a lay–clerical one. The likelihood of this was increased by the historic weakness of social democracy in Italy (Padgett and Paterson, 1992) and the alleged collapse of socialism as a defining feature of the left (Vertone, 1993). Yet by the summer of 1993 even the Conference of Italian Bishops was forced to concede that the principle of Catholic political unity was disintegrating under the stress of polarisation between the Northern League and a variegated left which included Orlando's increasingly successful party The Network (*Corriere della Sera*, 11–14 May and 8 June 1993).

The regime vote

The possible development of a lay–clerical cleavage as the dominant determinant of voting behaviour, in any case, assumes that the DC, or its heir, will remain one of the country's dominant political forces, and this may depend on its ability to stay in government. While the religious element remains fundamentally important in shaping voting behaviour, even among the young (Franklin et al., 1992), voting for the DC was never rooted solely in Catholicism, or even anti-Communism. A third major component was what can be called the regime vote, concentrated in southern Italy. This vote is associated with the practice of clientelism, that is the exchange of votes for favours, ranging from the finding of jobs and the award of pensions, to the granting of licenses, the waiving of rules and regulations, etc. As a type of vote, it was loyal to the Liberal notables of the pre-Fascist regime so long as they were in control, but it quickly passed to the new Fascist elites in the early twenties, and it shifted again to the DC in the 1950s. Another such massive shift, resulting from the DC's being forced into the opposition, would wreck the DC. This judgement is supported by the Northern League's destruction of DC dominance in the so-called White regions of northern Italy (Donovan, 1992).

Centrism as policy and practice

The land reforms of the 1948–53 government, together with the establishment of the Fund for the South in 1950, which provided for massive state investments in southern Italy, were critical in provoking the enlargement of the electoral fringe to the right of the DC in the 1953 election. Thanks to the survival of the highly proportional system of electoral representation (Seton-Watson, 1983) the existence of a three-bloc party system was confirmed, and this endured into the 1970s. A blueprint for this development had been presented by the 1946 election to the (non-parliamentary)

Constituent Assembly when the DC had taken only 35 per cent of the vote, rather than nearly half as in 1948. It was in this situation that De Gasperi described the DC as a 'centre party leaning left'. In so far as the three-bloc system was asymmetrical (with the left over twice the size of the right at the outset), the DC was a centre party which had to compete with the growing challenge from the left even while seeking to absorb the electorate from the right in order to ward off the left's threat of becoming the country's largest political bloc. This situation, made possible by, and expressed via, the party's variegated ideological mix and popular electoral base, rendered the party's policy stances highly ambiguous. It also necessitated the use of highly abstract and ambiguous language for which Italian political speech is particularly notorious (Furlong, 1984, p. 116).

Conservative modernisation

In retrospect, the defining practice of the DC (ideology would imply a degree of homogeneity which was absent) can usefully be described as conservative modernisation. The same term has been applied to Fascism (Moore, 1967), but here the additional adjective 'democratic' is understood, and distinguishes the two sharply. Within a democratic context, the DC was never genuinely progressive enough to be regarded as a centre-left party, despite the professed desire of several of its leaders to be regarded thus. The DC was, nevertheless, far from being a reactionary party, least of all in the context of Italy's own past. It was essentially pluralist, despite its rather vanguardist view of itself and a certain tendency to assume the party's near mystical union with the Italian people; and its forceful proponents of economic liberalism were countered by the party's Catholic social inheritance. The DC thus moved beyond a narrowly liberal understanding of democracy while imbuing the implantation of democracy in Italy with paternalism and some strongly conservative, even reactionary traits, for example with regard to the role of women in society. Not that other Italian parties were free from such limitations. This combination of pluralistic, conservative Catholicism directed to a modernising strategy can be seen in the broad outlines of post-war economic and social policy.

The Italian economy is sharply divided between a mass of small and medium-sized firms, often family-based, and a small group of very large firms split between the public and private sectors, the latter again often family-based, as per FIAT (Agnelli), Pirelli, Olivetti, etc. The *dirigiste* aspect of Catholic corporatism was perfectly at home with the idea of managing, or working with, the large-scale public and private concerns. Thus it was established early on that IRI would be maintained and that within IRI a steel production branch would be established (FINSIDER in 1947) to provide the inputs for FIAT, thus laying the basis for the automobile sector which was, in turn, the key to the development of a mass-production, mass-employment, mass-consumption economy. The creation of the public energy agency ENI in 1953, with De Gasperi's blessing, similarly helped growth-orientated business sectors by launching a frontal attack on the stagnant private electricity monopoly based in Lombardy, the heart of Italian capitalism. The vigorous state entrepreneurialism of ENI in the 1950s and 1960s was not, then, socialist, but fed off strong anti-capitalist feelings within Catholicism.

At the other extreme, a series of legislative acts aimed at the small and medium-sized business, particularly the world of artisan production, accorded not only with the reality of Italian socio-economic structure, but also with Catholic economic doctrine (Weiss, 1988). The latter aimed at creating a property-owning democracy not via socialisation/ nationalisation, nor by share ownership, but on the basis of petty commodity production and direct ownership of the means of production. In the long run this sector was to prove very helpful to Italy in surmounting the financial and industrial crises of the 1970s.

In so far as Italy's modernisation was based on promoting the growth of its industrial-bourgeois heartland in the north-west, fed by the migration of 'surplus' labour from the south, massive social upheaval was inevitable. No overarching plan was ever developed to cope with the huge social and economic transformations which took place, and this became a constant complaint of the left. Rather, an *ad hoc* response developed, resulting in the early and rapid growth of social expenditure in Italy. Responding to political pressures, rather than need or rationally planned analyses of requirements, such expenditure assumed a particularistic format mediated by both government and opposition parties (Ferrera, 1986; Ascoli, 1987).

If the broad thrust of economic policy showed a degree of long-term thinking, at least in the 1940s and 1950s, social policy was always the epitome of 'muddling through'. Foreign policy too reflected the domination of consensus-seeking politics and domestic policies over any attempt to rationalise or enhance the policy process: once the twin pillars of NATO and EC membership had been established, foreign policy atrophied.

Governing record: a self-serving democratic consolidation

Democrazia Cristiana has been the predominant governing party in Italy. This record of success stems essentially from its ability to dominate the coalition-making process, an ability in turn derived from its domination of the centre bloc in a party system based on a three-bloc structure. By preventing left–right polarisation and confrontation, the DC's promotion of tripolarism served both its own interest in securing a quasi-permanent governmental role and the consolidation of government based on consent. This coincidence was clearly ambiguous and ultimately it proved difficult to reproduce. Centre domination of government fostered centripetal competition, even by the Communist Party, while large parts of the DC's electorate came to be disgusted with the self-serving aspect of its domination of the centre.

In fostering the consolidation of this system the DC took three key coalition decisions. The first was the maintenance of the CLN, via the

privileging of the link with the PCI. This enabled the Constituent
Assembly to ratify the new Republican constitution in December 1947.
This behaviour was attacked by both the Vatican on the right and the
Actionist and Socialist parties on the left. The second major coalition
decision was the formation of the centrist coalition in 1947–8. This linked
three small lay parties to the government, denying the Catholic right its
wish to see a one-party confessional government, and allowed the transition from the centrism of the post-war grand coalition to a centrism based
on the three-bloc system. The third key decision was to link up with the
Socialist PSI in the early 1960s, pushing the Liberals out and again avoiding
a left–right polarisation. The preferential link with the Socialists was
retained for the next thirty years.

The consequence of these consensus-seeking decisions was weak government, but government responsive to the electorate (Pasquino, 1987; Ware
1987, p. 213), even though the electorate (like many onlookers) was never
convinced of this. Perhaps it is more accurate to say that the system was
responsive primarily to the various centre parties and their supporters,
then in second place, to the formally excluded left and right elites, and only
lastly to the latters' electorates. Nevertheless, even the Communist Party
was co-opted into governing Italy, albeit from outside the cabinet (Tarrow,
1977).

It has already been seen that the DC has dominated the prime minister-
ship, interior ministry and public instruction throughout the post-war
period. In addition the agricultural and the post and telecommunications
ministries have also been in the hands of DC ministers in over 80 per cent
of all governments, while the treasury and ministry of foreign affairs have
also been portfolios much sought after (Leonardi and Wertman, 1989,
p. 229). In general, it can be said that the DC has sought to occupy both
strategic state offices and strategic economic ones, and that in so doing it
has, despite the frequency of cabinet turnover, provided the country with a
highly stable governing core (Dogan, 1989), perhaps even a partially extra-
cabinet core executive.

While policy output has been largely secondary to the inter-party
and even intra-party game around which democratic consolidation took
place, an overall thrust in the direction of modernisation, understood as
enhanced competitiveness in the dominant global economic order, has not
been absent. It must be conceded that policy-making in Christian
Democratic-dominated Italy has been essentially of a distributive rather
than a regulatory nature. This is a concession in that it signals the particularistic, and often clientelistic, indeed corrupt, nature of policy-making in
Italy. It is a fact, too, that the political elites have been unable to control
the budgetary process for twenty years. However, the fragmentation and
particularistic nature of policy output, and the lack of cohesion resulting in
weak, or even nonexistent governmental control, is a cause as well as an
effect of the DC's formal domination of the policy process – a domination
which, all things considered, has actually been very weak. In fact, the so-
called DC regime has to be seen as one of 'weak hegemony' (Tarrow,
1990). For many Catholics it has been no hegemony at all. The DC may

have won many battles, but the war to build a Christian Democracy in Italy has been lost.

Acknowledgement

I should like to thank Gino Bedani, Hugh Compston and John Dickie for their very useful comments (not all of which I have been able to respond to) on a first draft of this chapter.

References

Allum, P. and Mannheimer, R., 1985, Italy, in Crewe I. and Denver, D. (eds), *Electoral Change in Western Democracies*, Croom Helm, London, pp. 287–318.
Ascoli, U., 1987, The Italian Welfare State: Between Incrementalism and Rationalism, in Friedmann R., Gilbert, N. and Sherer. M. (eds), *Modern Welfare States. A Comparative View of Trends and Prospects*, New York University Press, New York, pp. 110–50.
Barnes, S. H., 1977, *Representation in Italy, Institutionalised Tradition and Electoral Choice*, University of Chicago Press, Chicago and London.
Caciagli, M. 1985, Il resistibile declino della Democrazia cristiana, in Pasquino, G. (ed.), *Il sistema politico italiano*, Laterza, Bari, pp. 101–27.
Clark, M., 1984, *Modern Italy, 1871–1982*, Longman, London and New York.
Di Palma, G., 1977, *Surviving Without Governing*, University of California Press, Berkeley.
Di Palma, G., 1982, Italy: Is there a Legacy and is it Fascist?, in Herz, J. (ed.), *From Dictatorship to Democracy: Coping with the Legacies of Authoritarianism and Totalitarianism*, Greenwood Press, Westport, pp. 107–34.
Dogan, M. 1989, Italy, in Dogan, M (ed.), *Pathways to Power. Selecting Rulers in Pluralist Democracies*, Westview Press, London, pp. 99–139.
Donovan, M., 1992, A Party System in Transformation; The April 1992 Election, *West European Politics*, 15 (4): 170–177.
Farneti, P., 1980, Italy: The Response to Overload, in R. Rose (ed.), *Challenge to Governance: Studies in Overloaded Politics*, Sage, Beverley Hills, pp. 199–214.
Farneti, P. 1985, *The Italian Party System*, Pinter, London.
Ferrera, M., 1986, Italy, in Flora P. (ed.) *Growth to Limits. The Western European Welfare States Since World War II*, vol. 2, *Germany, United Kingdom, Ireland Italy*, de Gruyter, Berlin, pp. 385–499.
Fontana, S., 1993, *Il decalogo del popolarismo*, Cinque Lune, Roma.
Franklin, M., Mackie, T. and Valen, H., 1992, *Electoral Change: responses to evolving social and attitudinal structures in Western European countries*, Cambridge University Press, Cambridge.
Furlong, P. 1984, Italy, in Ridley, F. (ed.), *Policies and Politics in Western Europe*, Croom Helm, London, pp. 115–53.
Galli, G. and Prandi A., 1970, *Patterns of Political Participation in Italy*, Yale University Press, New Haven.
Garelli, F., 1991, *Religione e Chiesa in Italia*, Il Mulino, Bologna.
Heisler, M. 1974, *Politics in Europe*, McKay, New York.
Jemolo, A. C. 1960, *Church and State in Italy*, Blackwell, Oxford.

LaPalombara, J. 1964, *Interest Groups in Italian Politics*, Princeton University Press, Princeton.

Leonardi, R. and Wertheim, D., 1989, *Italian Christian Democracy*, Macmillan. London.

Mackie, T, Mannheimer, R. and Sani, G., 1992, Italy, in Franklin, Mackie, T., Valen, H. et al. *Electoral change: Responses to evolving social and attitudinal structures in western countries*, Cambridge University Press, Cambridge, pp. 238–54.

Maranini, G., 1950, *Governo parlamentare e partitocrazia*, Editrice universitaria, Firenze.

Maranini, G. 1963, *Il tiranno senza volto*, Bompiani, Milano.

Molony, J. N., 1977, *The Emergence of Political Catholicism in Italy*, Croom Helm, London.

Moore, B., Jnr, 1967, *Social Origins of Dictatorship and Democracy*, Allen Lane, London.

Morlino, L. 1984, The Changing Relationship Between Parties and Society in Italy, *West European Politics*, 7 (4): 46–66.

Padgett, S. and Paterson, W., 1992, *A History of Social Democracy in Post-war Europe*, Longman, London and New York.

Panebianco, A., 1993 Per un turno in più, *Corriere della Sera*, 8 May 1993, pp. 1, 3.

Pasquino, G., 1987, Party Government in Italy: Achievements and Prospects, in Katz R. (ed.), *Party Governments: European and American Experiences*, de Gruyter, Berlin, pp. 202–42.

Richardson, J. J. and Jordan, A. G., 1979, *Governing Under Pressure: The Policy Process in a Post-Parliamentary Democracy*, Basil Blackwell, Oxford.

Sani, G., 1991, Church Attendance and the Vote for the DC: Evidence from the 1980s, *Italian Politics and Society*, Fall: 13–18.

Sassoon, D., 1986, *Contemporary Italy: Politics, economy and society since 1945*, Longmans, Harlow.

Seton-Watson, S. 1983, Italy, in Bogdanor, V. and Butler, D. *Democracy and Elections. Electoral Systems and Their Political Consequences*, Cambridge University Press, Cambridge, pp. 110–21.

Spotts, F. and Wieser, T., 1986, *Italy, A Difficult Democracy: A Survey of Italian Politics*, Cambridge University Press, Cambridge.

Tarrow, S. 1977, *Between Center and Periphery*, Yale University Press, New Haven

Tarrow, S. 1990, Maintaining Hegemony in Italy: The softer they rise, the slower they fall!, in Pempel, T. J. (ed.) *Uncommon Democracies. The One-Party Dominant regimes*, Cornell University Press, Ithaca and London, pp. 306–32.

Vertone, S., 1993, Il sol senza avenir, *Corriere della Sera*, 1 February, p. 15.

Ware, A., 1987, *Citizens, Parties and the State. A Reappraisal*, Polity, Cambridge.

Webster, R., 1961, *Christian Democracy in Italy, 1860–1960*, Hollis and Carter, London.

Weiss, L. 1988, *Creating Capitalism. The State and Small Business since 1945*, Basil Blackwell, Oxford.

Zoppi, S., 1991, *Dalla Rerum novarum all democrazia cristiana di Murri*, Il Mulino, Bologna.

5

CHRISTIAN DEMOCRACY IN AUSTRIA: THE AUSTRIAN PEOPLE'S PARTY

Wolfgang C. Müller and Barbara Steininger

Origins and development of the Austrian People's Party

The Austrian People's Party (Österreichische Volkspartei, ÖVP) was founded in April 1945 after the liberation of Vienna from Nazi occupation. Initially it claimed to be a completely new party, rather than the successor of the Christian Socials. The Christian Socials had been the dominant force of the interwar years but had set up an authoritarian (Austro-Fascist) regime in 1934 and therefore did not constitute an appropriate point of reference in 1945. Nevertheless, the new party was characterised by several continuities with the Christian Socials. First, it recruited its leaders from the ranks of the predecessor party or the 1934–8 regime. Second, the ÖVP organised and appealed to the same constituency as the Christian Socials, in particular farmers, the petty bourgeoisie, civil servants and white-collar workers. Third, the ÖVP accepted large parts of the ideological heritage of the Christian Socials. Fourth, the ÖVP had maintained a special relationship with the Catholic Church, although this was less important and less manifest than in the interwar period. Over the course of time, the ÖVP increasingly accepted its position as successor to the Christian Socials.

Despite these continuities the ÖVP does have some distinct qualities. By not returning to the confessional label, the ÖVP appeals to a broader constituency than the Christian Socials, in particular to anti-clerical German-Nationals who had been previously represented by the Greater German People's Party (Großdeutsche Volkspartei) and the Agrarian League (Landbund) in the interwar period. The party's concept of itself is that of a non-socialist catch-all party (*bürgerliche Sammlungspartei*) containing different ideological tendencies: Catholic social doctrine, conservatism and liberalism. Certain personalities and a high degree of pragmatism, which allowed the simultaneous existence of partly contradictory claims, served to bridge these tendencies.

In applying the concept of the non-socialist catch-all party, the ÖVP was remarkably successful in the first two post-war decades. During this time the ÖVP was the strongest party in parliament; it led the grand coalition government and formed the first single-party government (1966–70). Since then, however, the fortunes of the ÖVP have declined considerably. This chapter will concentrate on recent developments, particularly since the 1980s.[1]

Organisation

The ÖVP is an indirect party (Duverger, 1954) with the Farmers' League, the Business League and the Workers' and Employees' League as its constituent units. These organisations (or their respective predecessor organisations) had already existed in the pre-war period and had survived the Nazi period as personal networks. Thus the leagues constituted an excellent basis for building up a party organisation in 1945 and their leaders were careful to maintain this key position. According to a contract between the central party and these three leagues it would be the task of the latter to recruit and organise the members from December 1945. The party at each level was only allowed to keep a list of the leagues' functionaries at that level. Several attempts were made during the course of time to roll back the power of the leagues (Müller and Steininger, 1992; Leitner and Pleschberger, 1992). In the 1970s, the party's women, youth and pensioners' organisations were formally given the same status as the leagues, with all six officially called constituent organisations (*Teilorganisationen*). Since 1980, members *de jure* first become members of the party and then may decide to enrole in a league or in one of the three other constituent organisations. *De facto*, however, the ÖVP is still an indirect party with the bulk of the members still being recruited and organised by the three leagues. Although the other constituent organisations now have considerable membership and the smallest league, the Business League, is outnumbered by the pensioners' organisation, the leagues are still extremely powerful intra-party players and virtually no observer would consider the pensioner organisation to be more powerful than the Business League within the party.

Because of the ÖVP's complex organisational structure and the fact that membership figures are an important intra-party resource, official party statistics are highly inflated. According to a realistic adjustment the ÖVP (in the early 1990s) has about 500,000 full members[2] (Müller 1992, pp. 46–8; see also Busek 1992, p. 364), making it still one of the largest European party organisations (Katz and Mair, 1992). In 1990, the Workers' and Employees' League constituted the strongest league, with about forty-eight per cent of the full members. The Farmers' League organises about 38 per cent of the full party members and the Business League thirteen per cent. Most of the members of the remaining consituent organisations (women, pensioners, youth) are also members of one of the leagues and thus increase the size of the membership but not the number of members. For this reason, it is not possible to break down party membership for all six constituent organisations. Direct membership of the ÖVP is possible, but has remained irrelevant with a mere 4,449 direct members in 1990.

The power of the leagues in part lies in their domination of the corporatist interest group organisations, the chambers. The Business and the Farmers' Leagues dominate the Chamber of Business and the Chamber of Agriculture respectively. These positions furnish them with access to resources such as expertise, money and legitimacy. In contrast, the Workers' and Employees' League is in a minority position *vis-à-vis* the Socialist trade unionists in the Trade Union Congress (ÖGB) and the Chamber of Labour, the interest group organisations of the blue- and white-collar workers, thus it enjoys only very limited access to the resources of these interest groups.

The ÖVP is not only a highly factionalised but also a very federalised party. Although the division of the party into six constituent organisations is replicated at the *Land* (regional) level, the *Land* party organisations are important intra-party players. This is due to the fact that the ÖVP in *Land* elections is the strongest party in six of the nine *Länder*. Although most of the *Länder* have *Proporz* (coalition based on share of vote) governments and the ÖVP therefore shares executive power with other parties, occupancy of the position of governor (*Landeshauptmann*) provides the *Land* party and particularly the incumbent himself (who usually also holds the office of *Land* party chairman) with power and a public profile. Unlike the relations between the leagues, there is no permanent conflict of interest between the *Land* party organisations themselves and between them and the national party organisation. Nevertheless, whenever their narrow interests are at stake, *Land* party organisations usually give preference to them over the national party's interests. One example of this would be state subsidies to nationalised industries which are rejected by the national party but demanded by the *Land* party organisations of those *Länder* in which these industries are concentrated. Similarly, while the national party favours private competition in the electronic media, the strong *Land* party organisations defend the existing monopoly of the public radio and television corporation which allows governors privileged access. There have also been considerable differences between the *Land* party organisations about the party's style, for instance between *Land* party organisations employing a clientelistic style and those employing a more populist style.

Membership fees are paid to the *Land* organisations of the leagues, which should provide the central organisations of the leagues, the *Land* party organisations and the central party organisation directly or indirectly with a fixed share of the income from membership fees. While this system has worked well concerning the finance of the central organisations of the leagues, and reasonably well concerning the finance of the *Land* party organisations, finance for the central party organisation has not been readily forthcoming and has always been a matter of negotiation rather than the strict application of intra-party rules. Therefore the central party traditionally has been forced to rely on private donations to a large extent, in particular from economic interest groups. The introduction and gradual increase of public party finance at the *Land* and national levels since the

1970s has made life easier for the ÖVP, but has not solved the problem altogether (Müller 1991, pp. 233ff). Sickinger and Nick (1990, p. 131) have estimated that the ÖVP's total income, including the leagues and the *Land* party organisations, amounted to AS 850 millions in 1989. This still seems to be a conservative estimate and increases in public subsidies since then (Müller 1992, p. 117) may have pushed total party income over a billion AS per year.

According to the party statute, the party congress is the highest decision-making body of the party.[3] It is composed of delegates from the leagues and the other constituent organisations (according to membership figures) and the *Land* party organisations (according to electoral support at the most recent general election). In addition many party leaders and elected officials participate *ex officio*. The party congress elects the party leader, two deputy leaders and the treasurer, and may decide on fundamental questions such as a new party programme. However, the party congress is required by statute to take place only every four years and as a rule it is more a carefully planned media event than a forum of intra-party debate and substantial decision-making (Müller et al., 1992). These tasks are carried out by the party executive bodies, a presidium (*Parteipräsidium*) with nine places (occupied by eight people) and a party executive (*Partei-vorstand*) with thirty-four members. The party presidium is composed of the party chairman, his two deputies, the honorary chairman, the leader of the parliamentary party, the party's representative in the presidium of the parliament, and the federal chancellor or vice-chancellor (if he is from the ÖVP). Its task is to make day-to-day decisions. The main building blocks of the party executive are the party presidium, the heads of the six constituent organisations and those of the nine *Land* party organisations. Since the party executive comprises the most powerful intra-party players but still has a relatively workable size, it is the most important party body. Although the party leader has to work in a difficult environment in terms of party organisation, he has considerable leeway as long as he respects the interests of the leagues and *Land* party organisations, and is usually considered to be an electoral asset for the party.

Although the ÖVP's organisational structure must still be seen as out-dated and as disadvantageous for the party's competitiveness, its worst effects on performance may be a thing of the past. Since 1980, the central party has drawn up its own membership list, allowing direct communi-cation with the members. The centralised training system of party functio-naries, which has been built up since the early 1970s, has provided the ÖVP with functionaries who at least partly have a common training (Busek, 1992). The generous state subsidies to the central party and the party in parliament have reduced the national leadership's dependence on wealthy leagues and *Land* party organisations. More recently, the crisis of the chamber state (Gerlich, 1992) has also tended to undermine the power base of the leagues.

The ÖVP has no official organisational relations with the Catholic Church, which in 1945 reconfirmed its 1933 decision to withdraw from party politics. Accordingly, priests are not allowed to accept political office and even the official lay organisation, the Katholische Aktion, does not allow its functionaries to hold parliamentary seats at the national and *Land* levels or leading positions in political parties. At a more informal level, however, there are important links between the ÖVP and the Catholic Church. Many leading ÖVP politicians have held functions in the lay organisations of the Catholic Church before or after their political careers (Steger, 1985, p. 69). The Church provided organisational help for the setting up of the party in 1945 and supported the ÖVP in election campaigns until the 1960s. At this time the relationship between the Catholic Church and the ÖVP's main competitor, the Sozialistische Partei Österreichs (SPÖ), normalized, with the SPÖ accepting many of the Church's demands *vis-à-vis* the state. Consequently the Church reduced its involvement in party politics, and some observers introduced the concept of an equidistance between the Catholic Church and the two main political parties. Athough the Church itself never accepted this characterisation of its relations with the political parties, it was criticised by many ÖVP politicians. They claimed that the core of practising Catholics still have their home in the ÖVP, and that it was this party which based its policy on Christian principles. The Social Democrats, on the other hand, referred to equidistance as a principle which should guide the Church's political behaviour. In reality, however, the Church never practiced equidistance. This became clear in the 1970s when the SPÖ government's abortion and divorce reforms brought the party into open conflict with the Church, which explicitly announced that the ÖVP, in line with the Church on these issues, would provide better chances for Catholics to see their principles implemented in politics. However, both the Church and the SPÖ were careful not to escalate these conflicts into a new *Kulturkampf*. This, in turn, intensified criticism from the ÖVP that it was expected to do the Church's dirty work, while the Church itself maintained good relations with the government (Khol, 1984; Leitner, 1988).

The Vatican was also dissatisfied with the Austrian bishops, in particular because of their liberal policy on contraception and other moral issues. In 1987, Pope John Paul II appointed a number of bishops in Austria, who were committed to an extremely conservative course. Both because of the nature of these appointments and the positions of the new bishops, the Austrian Catholic Church itself has been split in recent years, the new appointments having alienated not only progressive groups but also the broad, active core of Austrian Catholics (Schneider, 1992, p. 556). Rumour has it that the conservative wing of the ÖVP had exerted considerable influence on Rome's evaluation of the Austrian Church and thus indirectly also on its appointments (Schulmeister, 1987; Horner and Zulehner, 1991; Schneider, 1992). The ÖVP is as divided as the Church; while its conservative wing is happy with the new bishops and their teaching on moral issues, the party's mainstream is not (see Schneider, 1992, p. 557). Thus the main divisions now can be found within the Church and the ÖVP rather than between these and the Social Democrats.

Beside the Church's official lay organisations, there is a network of independent Catholic organisations united in the Arbeitsgemeinschaft

Katholischer Verbände. They include the Catholic student fraternity (Cartellverband der katholischen österreichischen Studentenverbindungen, CV), to which many university graduates among the ÖVP leaders belong (Welan, 1985), and a variety of social organisations, including, for instance, the Catholic family association (Katholischer Familenverband) and the largest federation of sport clubs, the Turn- und Sportunion. Because of these Catholic organisations, the ÖVP did not build up as extensive a network of ancillary organisations as the Social Democrats, and some of the ÖVP's ancillary organisations were created only reluctantly. To a large extent the party chose to rely on the Catholic organisations as the Christian Socials had done in the pre-war period. Initially this was an advantage for the party *vis-à-vis* the Social Democrats who built up a network of ancillary organisations out of their own resources. In contrast, the Christian Social Party (CSP) and the ÖVP did not spend resources on this activity and the less party-political character of these organisations allowed them to appeal to a broader constituency than would have been possible for party organisations. However, their independence also allowed them to develop their own policy (Houska, 1985). Within the ÖVP they have often functioned as a lobby for conservative Catholic positions, to which they are at times more committed than to the party's electoral strategy. The Catholic organisations have also functioned as a base for criticism of the Catholic Church for its 'accommodative' behaviour and have allegedly played a role in the appointment of conservative bishops in recent years.

Electorate

The ÖVP was the strongest party in terms of both seats and (with the exception of 1953 and 1959) votes until 1970. Even after its replacement by the SPÖ as the leading party, the ÖVP remained one of the few West European parties which polled more than 40 per cent of the electorate. The year 1990 was a watershed in the party's electoral history. The ÖVP lost almost a quarter of its votes, polling a mere 32 per cent of the vote. According to its own definition, it is now no longer a big party but only a medium-sized one. The decline of the ÖVP is no less dramatic in relative terms. Before the 1990 election the ÖVP almost equalled the SPÖ in electoral terms; since then the SPÖ's lead is as much as a third of the ÖVP's vote. The 1986 and 1990 elections had an even greater impact on the ÖVP's relative strength *vis-à-vis* the Freiheitliche Partei Österreichs (FPÖ). The ÖVP's electoral support used to be seven times stronger than that of the FPÖ but since these elections it is only twice as strong (see Table 5.1).

Surveys carried out since the 1990 election reported a further decline of the ÖVP. Under the leadership of its new chairman, Erhard Busek, and particularly after the success of the ÖVP-sponsored candidate Thomas Klestil in the presidential election of 1992, however, the ÖVP has recovered in the polls. Nevertheless, even optimistic forecasts do not suggest that the ÖVP will be able to improve substantially at the next general

Table 5.1 Austrian elections, 1945–90

	Percentage of votes				Seats in parliament[1]			
	ÖVP	SPÖ	FPÖ[2]	Others[3]	ÖVP	SPÖ	FPÖ[2]	Others[4]
1945	49.79	44.59	–	5.6	85	76	–	4
1949	44.03	38.71	11.66	5.6	77	67	16	5
1953	41.25	42.10	10.94	5.7	74	73	14	4
1956	45.95	43.04	6.52	4.5	82	74	6	3
1959	44.19	44.78	7.70	3.3	79	78	8	–
1962	45.43	43.99	7.04	3.5	81	76	8	–
1966	48.34	42.56	5.35	3.7	85	74	6	–
1970	44.69	48.42	5.52	1.4	78	81	6	–
1971	43.11	50.03	5.45	1.4	80	93	10	–
1975	42.94	50.42	5.40	1.2	80	93	10	–
1979	41.90	51.02	6.06	1.0	77	95	11	–
1983	43.22	47.65	4.98	4.2	81	90	12	–
1986	41.29	43.12	9.73	5.9	77	80	18	8
1990	32.06	42.80	16.63	8.5	60	80	33	8

Notes:
1 1945–70: 165 seats; 1971–90: 183 seats.
2 Before 1956 VdU (Verband der Unabhängigen).
3 1945–62 mainly Communist Party (KPO); 1966 mainly DFP, a splinter group from the SPÖ; 1970–79 mainly Communist Party; 1983–90 mainly green parties.
4 1945–56: Communist Party; 1986 and 1990: Green Alternative

Source: Dachs et al. (eds), 1992.

election. The decline in the party's electoral fortunes is paralleled by the decline in ÖVP identifiers. While the ÖVP had a stock of 28 per cent identifiers in the second half of the 1970s and the first half of the 1980s, it has fallen to 17–19 per cent since its return to government in 1987 (Plasser and Ulram, 1992, p. 151).

According to Table 5.2 the ÖVP is a genuine people's party. It wins support from all population groups and does so almost in proportion to their respective strength. According to 1991 figures, only farmers, who constitute 4 per cent of the population but 11 per cent of the ÖVP supporters, were significantly over-represented. Only white- and blue-collar workers, who make up 23 per cent and 11 per cent of the population respectively, are underrepresented among the ÖVP supporters. Since the 1980s, white-collar employees (including low- and medium-ranking civil servants) have constituted the largest group of economically active ÖVP supporters and even the blue-collar workers outnumbered farmers. According to Table 5.2, the traditional core groups of the ÖVP, farmers and otherwise self-employed, fell from twenty-seven per cent in 1978 to a mere sixteen per cent in 1991. However, they still constitute the bulk of the party members and are strongly over-represented among the MPs and party functionaries. This in turn often makes it difficult for the party

Table 5.2 Social structure of ÖVP supporters (%)

Occupation	1978	1983	1985	1991
Self employed, professions	1	1	1	2
Shop keepers	6	4	5	3
Managers, higher civil servants	5	5	4	4
White-collar workers	16	22	21	19
Qualified workers	7	7	8	9
Blue-collar workers	10	7	9	7
Farmers	20	12	10	11
Housewives	13	15	16	15
Pensioners, students	21	26	26	30

Source: Representative surveys of the Dr Fessel & Gfk Institut.

leadership to put forward policy positions that appeal to the population at large. The high share of the pensioner and student group (the latter constitutes only a small minority of the group) reflects the problematic age structure of the party.

According to a 1990 survey, sixty-three per cent of Catholics (which did not differ from the population at large in this respect) identified the ÖVP as the party which would be most likely to represent Christian principles in its policies, while the SPÖ and the FPÖ were mentioned by a mere nine per cent and one per cent respectively (Zulehner et al., 1991). Indeed, in 1990, sixty-one per cent of the regular church-goers voted for the ÖVP, twenty-two per cent for the SPÖ, ten per cent for the FPÖ and two per cent for the Greens (Plasser et al., 1992, p. 34). Although the majority of practising Catholics have thus maintained their traditional loyalty to the ÖVP, the importance of religion as cement for the party has considerably declined, since Austria has been no exception to the international trend of secularisation. The share of nominal Catholics in the population dropped from eighty-nine per cent in 1951 to seventy-eight per cent in 1991. According to official statistics of the Catholic Church, the percentage of Catholics (above the age of seven years) who go to church on Sunday has dropped from forty per cent in 1950 to twenty-one per cent in 1990. While in the 1950s and 1960s almost sixty-seven per cent of the ÖVP supporters were regular church-goers, in the 1970s this dropped to fifty-five per cent, and fell further to forty-five per cent in the middle of the 1980s, a level which has remained stable since then (Stiefbold, 1975, p. 208; Ulram, 1990, p. 27; Zulehner et al., 1991). Thus active Catholics still constitute a core group of the ÖVP, but the majority of ÖVP supporters are not bound to the party by the cement of religion.

Major ideological and policy positions

The ÖVP has, since its foundation, defined itself ideologically as a non-socialist catch-all party. The party has always seen itself as being non-socialist rather than having a positive identity (Müller, 1988). The party's ideology is comprised of elements of Catholic social doctrine, conservatism and liberalism. Programmatically, Catholic social doctrine has been the most important element. Thus party programmes have contained the principles of subsidiarity, personalism and solidarism (*Subsidiarität, Personalismus, Solidarismus*). In the 1950s and 1960s the ÖVP characterised itself as the party of Western Christian culture. In the basic party programme, which dates from 1972, it describes itself as 'open to all Christians and all those who hold a humanistic view of mankind'. In practical politics, however, economic liberalism has been at least as important as Catholic social doctrine. An enormous degree of pragmatism has allowed the party to tolerate inconsistencies or even contradictions in its programmatic statements, and between them and actual policies.

The relative importance of the three ideological traditions has varied considerably in the post-war period. In the immediate post-war years, the ÖVP occupied a left of centre position, accepting a substantial amount of state intervention (Kriechbaumer, 1990). While in this phase of party history the French Mouvement Républicain Populaire (MRP) constituted a model for the ÖVP, in the 1950s it was the German Christlich Demokratische Union (CDU). The ÖVP converted to supply-side economics. In the 1960s, this was replaced by 'technocratic conservatism' and the belief that the government had the means for fine tuning the economy. In the 1970s, the ÖVP lukewarmly supported the 'Austro-Keynesian' economic policy of the Social Democrats, but not without claiming that it could execute such a policy with greater skill. However, when the country's macro-economic performance deteriorated and the costs of Austro-Keynesianism (public debt, taxation, structural sclerosis) became visible in the early 1980s, the ÖVP adopted a neo-liberal economic programme (Aiginger, 1985; Müller, 1988, 1991), including the privatisation of the huge public sector, reduction of the budget deficit, and the creation of more tax incentives for business. In the late 1980s, when environmental protection became the most important political goal for the population (Ulram, 1990), the ÖVP tried to incorporate it into its economic programme. The party therefore developed the vision of the so-called 'eco-social market economy', in which environmental protection would be achieved by market forces within a system of incentives set by the state rather than by regulative policy.

There are important differences between the constituent organisations on the question of social policy. The Business League, the members of which bear the brunt of the costs of social policies, are more reluctant than the other constituent organisations to expand or maintain social policies. The other constituent organisations are particularly interested in those social policies which affect their clientele, thus the women's organisation in recent years has been a driving force behind the increase of paid maternity leave and the reform of pension regulations for women. Similarly, the pensioner's organisation and the Farmers' League look after their clientele. The Workers' and Employees' League has traditionally been the driving force of the ÖVP's social policy, sharing the desire for an expansive policy with the Social Democrats. It differs from the SPÖ, however, not only by a special concern for their particular clientele, i.e. civil servants and white-collar employees, but also in that it applies the Catholic social doctrine principle of subsidiary 'horizontal' pluralism (Fogarty, 1957, p. 90). Accordingly, social policy should be selective, and welfare benefits given only to those who really need them rather than being generally available. Moreover direct state intervention ought in many cases to be replaced by help for the individual from smaller units, in particular the family. State policy should therefore enable these smaller units to fulfil their tasks rather than take them over itself. This approach to social policy fits together well with other traditional Catholic ideological considerations such as the promotion of the family. Social policy and tax policy should provide the required support for families to allow wives to take care of the children rather than to work, and welfare and tax benefits should increase progressively with the number of children.

In order to highlight the impact of Christian values on the ÖVP's ideology it is also necessary to look briefly at moral issues. Here the ÖVP has traditionally assumed the policy positions occupied by the Catholic Church. Thus it has fought against the softening of abortion and divorce laws, and has occupied a similar position on other moral issues (Müller, 1988). The ÖVP's stand on these issues was clearly not a catch-all position and did not help it in elections. In recent years the ÖVP has given more attention to the electoral consequences of policy positions on moral issues. Thus it has, for instance, rejected the idea of reintroducing criminal prosecution for abortion but rather argues for social policy measures in order to prevent it. However, the ÖVP has done no more than minimise the electoral damage. On new issues such as the legalisation of the abortion pill, which came up in the late 1980s, it usually assumes positions which are ideological rather than electorally viable under the pressure of the Catholic Church and its own conservative wing.

Government record

During the first two post-war decades the ÖVP was the dominant government party. After having participated in the national government from April until December 1945, it became the leading party first in an all-party coalition (until 1947) and then in the famous ÖVP–SPÖ grand coalition. In 1966, the ÖVP won an absolute majority of parliamentary seats and formed the first single-party government in Austria. In 1970, however, the SPÖ won a plurality of seats and formed a single-party minority government with the tacit support of the Freedom Party (FPÖ). For the first time since 1918 the major party of the non-socialist camp (the Christian Socials and the ÖVP respectively) was excluded from government. The ÖVP remained in opposition for sixteen years since the SPÖ managed to govern alone until 1983 (with majority status from 1971) and to lead a coalition with the FPÖ between 1983 and 1986. In 1987, the ÖVP returned to government as the junior partner of the SPÖ in a new grand coalition. It occupies portfolios which correspond closely to its traditional clientele, including agriculture, economics, defence and the family.

The ÖVP has been much more successful in winning and maintaining government office at the *Land* and local levels. The *Land* governments have been the party's real stronghold. In the 1970s, the ÖVP electoral defeats at the national level were not parallelled at the *Land* level. Since the late 1980s, however, the ÖVP has experienced an unprecedented series of relative defeats in *Land* elections. Although maintaining its position as the strongest party in six of the nine *Länder*, it is no longer possible to separate electoral fortunes at the national and *Land* levels. In local politics, the ÖVP dominates the small rural communities. In 1990, about 1,700 mayors, that is more than 80 per cent of all mayors, had been put up by the ÖVP.

What have been the ÖVP's main achievements since its return to government at the national level in 1987? Having been excluded from government for twenty years the ÖVP, unlike during the first two post-war decades, could not be satisfied with maintaining the status quo. Its pivotal position between its coalition partner, the SPÖ, and the oppositional FPÖ has provided the ÖVP with a good chance of succeeding with its policy proposals, although the necessity of compromise in a coalition government puts a limit on its influence.

A brief look at the economic policy of the grand coalition reveals that several major demands of the ÖVP have been integrated into the government programme, including privatisation, tax reform and the reduction of the budget deficit. The ÖVP's influence was twofold, direct and indirect. The mid-1980s saw a major economic policy reorientation of the SPÖ, which accepted in principle a large part of the ÖVP's proposals. This can be attributed to the increasing acceptance of the ÖVP's neo-liberal approach by voters and hence the ÖVP's indirect impact via political competition.[4] The direct influence of the ÖVP, exercised in the negotiation of the coalition programmes in 1986–7 and 1990, and in their implementation, has also been considerable. Although it can be argued that the breakthrough in terms of privatisation has been greater in government declarations than in practice, and that despite the successful cutting-back of the budget deficit its structural problems have not been solved, economic policy has undoubtedly seen a major reorientation since the ÖVP's return to government.

The ÖVP has been considerably less successful in making its genuinely Catholic demands part of the government's policy. Where it has succeeded, in particular in reducing the taxation of families, this was due to verdicts of the constitutional court rather than to the ÖVP's ability to put these matters on the government's agenda.

Conclusion

The ÖVP has by any standards been an important and powerful party over the whole post-war period. However, as we have seen, its fortunes have declined since 1970 and it has experienced particularly hard times in recent years. This can, to a large extent, be attributed to changes in the ÖVP's environment. Its traditional core groups in the population, the self-employed, the practising Catholics, and in particular the farmers, have declined numerically. Because of its outdated party structure, the ÖVP has not responded adequately to these environmental changes. Moreover, as a major and powerful party it is victim to the mood of the time which is definitely anti-party (Plasser et al., 1992). Finally, the ÖVP's diminished capacity to attract voters is also a result of the successful strategies of competing parties. The SPÖ became a catch-all party in the 1960s; more recently the FPÖ has begun to exploit the anti-party mood, and the Greens attract non-socialist conservationists.

Although rather gloomy scenarios for the ÖVP's further development have been put forward in recent years it seems (at the beginning of 1993) that its decline has come to a halt. The party has stabilised its position in the polls, open internal fighting has come to an end, and the coalition government is working relatively smoothly (and therefore does not attract negative headlines upon the parties involved). Moreover the FPÖ now concentrates its attacks on the SPÖ. The ÖVP is aiming to restore its image as a natural party of government. As it is the pivotal party, government formation without the ÖVP is indeed unlikely in the forseeable future. In 1992, the ÖVP decided to work out a new basic party programme in order to improve its appeal. It also hopes to profit from the personalisation of parliamentary elections as introduced by the 1992 electoral law. If the 1990s indeed return the ÖVP to relative success this will probably be less due to the party's successful adaptation to a changed political environment than to the structural changes which have hit other parties harder than the ÖVP.

Notes

1 For the history of the ÖVP see Reichhold (1975), Gottweis (1983), Pelinka (1983) and Müller (1988, 1991).
2 We leave aside so-called family members who pay a symbolic membership fee only (see Müller, 1992).
3 The composition and functions of the party bodies have been subject to frequent changes (see Müller, 1992 for an exhaustive analysis). The following paragraphs are based on the valid party statute as amended in 1991.
4 The SPÖ was already in a process of rethinking its economic policy, but without the pressure from the electoral market this process would have taken longer and might not have led to such a radical reorientation.

References

Aiginger, K., 1985, Die wirtschaftsprogrammatischen Vorstellungen der ÖVP 1945 bis 1985, in *Schwarz-bunter Vogel*, Junius, Vienna, pp. 95–124.

Busek, E., 1992, Die Österreichische Volkspartei, in W. Mantl (ed.), *Politik in Österreich*, Bohlau, Vienna, pp. 349–367.

Dachs, H. et al. (eds), 1992, *Handbuch des österreichischen politischen Systems* (2nd edn), Manz, Vienna.

Duverger, M., 1954, *Political Parties*, Methuen, London.

Fogarty, M. P., 1957, *Christian Democracy in Western Europe 1820–1953*, University of Notre Dame Press, Notre Dame, Ind.

Gerlich, P., 1992, A Farewell to Corporatism, in K. R. Luther and W. C. Müller (eds), *Politics in Austria: Still a Case of Consociationalism?*, Frank Cass, London, pp. 132–46.

Gottweis, H., 1983, Zur Entwicklung der ÖVP: Zwischen Interessenpolitik und Massenintegration, in P. Gerlich and W. C. Müller (eds), *Zwischen Koalition und Konkurrenz. Österreichs Parteien seit 1945*, Braumuller, Vienna, pp. 53–68.

Horner, F. and Zulehner, P. M., 1991, Kirchen und Politik, in H. Dachs et al. (eds), *Handbuch des politischen Systems Österreichs*, Manz, Vienna, pp. 441–56.

Houska, J. J., 1985, *Influencing Mass Political Behaviour*, Institute for International Studies, Berkeley.

Katz, R. S. and Mair, P. (eds), 1992, *Party Organisations*, Sage, London.

Khol, A., 1984, Katholikentag und Papstbesuch 1983: Eine kritische Würdigung, *Österreichisches Jahrbuch für Politik*, pp. 401–35.

Kriechbaumer, R., 1990, *Parteiprogramme im Widerstreit der Interessen*, Verlag für Geschichte und Politik, Vienna.

Leitner, F., 1988, *Kirche und Parteien in Österreich nach 1945*, Schöningh, Paderborn.

Leitner, L. and Pleschberger, W., 1992, Warum scheitern 'Parteireformen'? Eine Analyse am Beispiel der ÖVP, *Österreichische Zeitschrift für Politikwissenschaft* 21, no. 2, pp. 181–201.

Luther, K. R. and Müller, W. C. (eds), 1992, *Politics in Austria: Still a Case of Consociationalism?*, Frank Cass, London.

Müller, W. C., 1988, Conservatism and the Transformation of the Austrian People's Party, in B. Girvin (ed.), *The Transformation of Contemporary Conservatism*, Sage, London, pp. 98–119.

Müller, W. C., 1991, Die Österreichische Volkspartei, in H. Dachs et al. (eds), *Handbuch des politischen Systems Österreichs*, Manz, Vienna, pp. 227–46.

Müller, W. C., 1992, Austria (1945–1990), in R. S. Katz and P. Mair (eds), *Party Organisations*, Sage, London, pp. 21–120.

Müller, W. C., Philipp, W. and Steininger, B., 1992, Wie oligarchisch sind Österreichs Parteien?, *Österreichische Zeitschrift für Politikwissenschaft* 21, no. 2, pp. 117–146.

Müller, W. C. and Steininger, B., 1992, Party Organisation and Party Competitiveness: the Case of the Austrian People's Party, ECPR paper, Limerick.

Pelinka, A., 1983, Die Österreichische Volkspartei, in H. J. Veen (ed.), *Christlich-demokratische und konservative Parteien in Westeuropa*, Schoningh, Paderborn, pp. 195–265.

Plasser, F. and Ulram, P. A., 1992, Überdehnung, Erosion und rechtspopulistische Reaktion, *Österreichische Zeitschrift für Politikwissenschaft* 21, no. 4, pp. 147–64.

Plasser, F., Ulram, P. and Grausgruber, A., 1992, The Decline of Lager Mentality and the New Model of Electoral Competition in Austria, in K. R. Luther and W. C. Müller (eds), *Politics in Austria: Still a Case of Consociationalism?*, Frank Cass, London, pp. 16–44.

Reichhold, L., 1975, *Geschichte der ÖVP*, Styria, Graz.

Schneider, H., 1992, Kirche – Staat – Gesellschaft: ihre Beziehungen im Wandel, in W. Mantl (ed.), *Politik in Österreich*, Bohlau, Vienna, pp. 523–570.

Schulmeister, P., 1987, Konfliktlinien innerhalb des österreichischen Katholizismus 1987, *Österreichisches Jahrbuch für Politik*, pp. 401–26.

Sickinger, H. and Nick, R, 1990, *Politisches Geld*, Kulturverlag, Thaur.

Steger, G., 1985, ÖVP, Kirchen und politischer Katholizismus, in *Schwarz-bunter Vogel*, Junius, Vienna, pp. 64–94.

Stiefbold, R. P., 1975, Elites and Elections in a Fragmented Political System, *Sozialwissenschaftliches Jahrbuch für Politik* 4, pp. 119–227.

Stirnemann, A., 1980, Innerparteiliche Gruppenbildung am Beispiel der ÖVP, *Österreichisches Jahrbuch für Politik*, pp. 415–48.

Ulram, P. A., 1990, *Hegemonie und Erosion*, Bohlau, Vienna.

Welan, M., 1985, CV und ÖVP, in *Schwarz-bunter Vogel*, Junius, Vienna, pp. 170–77.

Zulehner, P. M., Denz, H., Beham, M. and Friesl, C., 1991, *Vom Untertan zum Freiheitskünstler*, Herder, Vienna.

6

THE CDU-CSU IN GERMANY: IS THERE ANY ALTERNATIVE?

David Broughton

One of the principal reasons for the publication of any book on Christian Democratic parties in Europe must be the prominent gap concerning such parties in the literature, despite their dominance of governments in a number of different countries since 1945. In Germany, this lacuna is particularly striking given the repeated success of the CDU-CSU (Christian Democratic Union/Christian Social Union) over most of this period. There is more academic interest in the problems of the Sozialdemokratische Partei Deutschlands (SPD), the 'dual' character of the Greens or even the recurrent internal tensions within the Freiheitliche Demokratische Partei (FDP) than in the Christian Democrats, who are simply taken for granted as part of the political furniture.

There have been useful and detailed studies in the past (Pridham, 1977; Irving, 1979; Mintzel, 1982; Weidenfeld, 1982) and more recent work by Chandler (1989, 1993); but in total this still gives little sense of the crucial importance of the Christian Democrats to the course of post-war German politics.

One reason for this neglect of the CDU-CSU is the difficulty in defining a Christian Democratic ideology which appears to be steeped in pragmatism rather than principle. Consequently, it is hard to relate such an ideology to other parties which can be defined and located much more easily using the left–right scale. This definitional problem has acted to shift the balance of attention too far away from the CDU-CSU when it was they who played the key role in settling the most important issues on the immediate post-war political agenda.

The historical origins and the development of the CDU-CSU

In its present form, the CDU-CSU was a new party after 1945. Its political roots can, however, be traced back to the Catholic Club in the Frankfurt Assembly of 1848, through to the Centre (*Zentrum*) party and the Bavarian People's Party represented in the Reichstag between 1871–1933.

The CDU-CSU's origins were therefore heavily Catholic in orientation, and a continuation of the Centre Party after 1945 was a possibility. However, the multiple traumas of the Weimar Republic's collapse and the need to establish an unequivocal rejection of the slaughter of the Third Reich ensured the emergence of a new type of party which could claim to represent Christian values in general and not just those of Roman Catholicism.

By explicitly straddling the denominational division which had been the source of considerable hostility in the past, the CDU-CSU opened itself up to Protestants and liberals. This broadened the party's base as a vital first step in the process of challenging the re-founded SPD for power.

The CDU-CSU became the main political force for integrating the various groups on the right via a process of absorption and amalgamation in the early 1950s. The Christian Democrats openly supported the new liberal democratic system (unlike the Catholics in the past) and they explicitly sought class reconciliation and solidarity between different groups. The CDU-CSU was also prominent in the initial moves towards European integration and transnational co-operation based on the accept- ance of a capitalist framework for running the economy. In addition, in terms of foreign policy, a united front against communism was maintained.

The CDU-CSU developed, therefore, as a 'hybrid' party which com- bined traditional ideas on religion and social values with an appreciation of the need for a strong, productive economy which permitted intervention and welfare state support for the disadvantaged. This kind of heterogeneity in outlook has meant that the Christian Democrats in Germany have often been difficult both to define and analyse. Above all, the Christian Democrats are a party for winning power and maintaining themselves in office rather than implementing a clearly set out ideological stance.

The values which underpin the party and which are contained in their policy statements and basic programmes are straightforward. Nevertheless, these values do not add up to more than a general and often undisputable set of precepts, since the perspective of power which drives the party forward ensures that ideology is rarely a matter of much import- ance, either internally or externally. The policy statements of the CDU- CSU tend to be defensive in orientation, largely intended to answer the question, 'what do we want power for?', a question regularly directed at many conservative and Christian Democratic parties throughout Europe. What is deemed to matter more than any prescriptive ideology by the CDU-CSU is their effectiveness in office in terms of the achievements and benefits provided for the German people.

It is this broad approach to politics which has lain at the heart of the CDU-CSU's strength since 1945. The electoral successes of the 1950s were grounded in spectacular economic growth and prosperity which filled the political vacuum of the immediate post-war years. These electoral rewards reached a peak at the 1957 federal election when the CDU-CSU won 50.2 per cent of the vote. This decade of dominance forced the SPD to re- evaluate its own position. The 1959 Bad Godesberg programme of the SPD saw the Social Democrats become noticeably less doctrinaire and less anti-clerical. Their attraction to liberal Catholics increased as a result, applying pressure on the loyalty of the progressive segment of the CDU-CSU's electorate.

Both inside and outside Germany, the initial evidence of deconfession-alisation and secularisation provided another challenge. The Second Vatican Council in the mid-1960s appeared to sanction moves away from exclusivity and separation between Catholics and non-Catholics which brought the instinctive support of the CDU-CSU by German Catholics further into question.

In addition, generational change in the late 1960s produced demands for radical change which went against the whole tenor of the CDU-CSU's approach to politics. The reaction of the Christian Democrats to these developments proved inadequate, and the CDU-CSU were ousted from power in 1969 by the SPD/FDP coalition. However, the vote share of the Christian Democrats did not decline by much. The consequent period in opposition saw the CDU-CSU re-evaluate its structure and organisation and regain its former strength by the mid-1970s. Despite winning 48.6 per cent of the vote at the 1976 federal election, the CDU-CSU stayed in opposition. The SPD/FDP coalition broke up in September 1982, allowing the Christian Democrats to re-form a coalition with the FDP by means of a 'constructive vote of no confidence'. This switch was legitimised by the March 1983 federal election.

Since 1982, the CDU-CSU/FDP coalition has remained in power, facing up to the very different world of the late 1980s, with the demise of Communism in Eastern Europe opening up the possibility, and then the reality, of German unification. The CDU-CSU and Helmut Kohl as Chancellor were closely identified as the party of German unity at the December 1990 federal election, particularly by the voters in the states of the former DDR. Kohl was widely seen as the *Kanzler für Deutschland* who promised prosperity for everyone (*Wohlstand für alle*).

The development of the CDU-CSU over the post-war period is therefore marked by a high degree of continuity. Its pragmatism has proven to be a potent form of appeal. The strong sense of moving with the times which the Christian Democrats have actively encouraged has seen their electoral and sociological base in German society remain both large and loyal.

The organisation of the CDU-CSU

The present party structure of the CDU-CSU can be traced back to developments in the immediate post-war period. When the parties were licensed by the Allies, the initial focus of political activity was at local and regional level. Differences at these levels within the nascent CDU-CSU, particularly between the Cologne and Berlin sections of the party, effec-tively precluded the option of a centrally organised party. The grip of Adenauer and Erhard, especially after the currency reform of 1948, how-ever, ensured that the commitment to a social market economy was entrenched throughout the party.

Adenauer's pro-Western stance and his conservative inclinations when

allied to Erhard's economic policies set the CDU-CSU firmly on a pragmatic course which encompassed not only a diverse electorate but also a
loose, decentralised, confederal party structure.

The party structure remained largely undeveloped for a number of years
as the task of governing Germany took precedence. The federal party was
only formally established in 1950 after Adenauer had become chancellor,
and the post of party general secretary was not created until 1967. The
main task for the party apparatus in the early years was to support the
CDU-CSU in power and to get it re-elected. Its role was largely seen to be
a *Kanzlerwahlverein* (a body to re-elect the chancellor), with much more
emphasis being placed on the development of the CDU-CSU as a party for
voters (*Wählerpartei*) than a party for members (*Mitgliederpartei*).
Decisions were taken by Adenauer himself, by the government as a whole
or by the CDU-CSU parliamentary group. The idea of an autonomous
party in the country remained stillborn.

Nowadays, the federal party conference meets at least once every two
years and it elects the federal executive committee. The conference lays
down the basic policy guidelines and the party programme.

As a new party after 1945, electoral success came very quickly to the
Christian Democrats. The first federal election of 1949 saw the party win
31.0 per cent compared to 29.2 per cent for the SPD. This secured the role
of the CDU-CSU as the most credible force capable of integrating the non-
SPD segment of the German electorate. By organising initially at the
regional level, the CDU-CSU was also well placed to adapt to the federal
structure of post-war Germany. It did mean, however, that the different
regional parties were largely autonomous, linked only by a general
obeisance to the principles of Christian Democracy. The leader of each
regional party (*Landesverband*) was akin to a baron who defended his own
autonomy with vigour but who simultaneously acknowledged the need for
a degree of loyalty to the feudal monarch of the time. Nevertheless, the
Land parties controlled candidate selection and finance. This strength was
reinforced by the important role of the Bundesrat which entrenched the
role of the regions as significant influences within the overall political
system. The leaders of the *Länder* (*Ministerpräsidenten*) were inevitably
influential figures in the national political elite as a result.

Their importance has been strengthened further by the tendency to
recruit nationally from the regions. Prominent post-war German politicians have often worked their way up the regional party ladder before
transferring to the national political stage in Bonn. Helmut Kohl is an
example of this, having started out as the *Ministerpräsident* of the
Rhineland Palatinate. Some such as Gerhard Stoltenberg have moved back
to the states from national politics as well. Few people ever doubted the
influence of Franz-Josef Strauss, even when he was 'only' the leader of the
Bavarian CSU.

The links between the CDU and the CSU are very important for
understanding the development of Christian Democracy in Germany. The
CDU and the CSU were formed as separate organisations after 1945 but
they have joined forces as a national parliamentary alliance in the

Bundestag since 1949. This alliance has certainly experienced rocky periods, particularly that following the 1976 federal election when the CSU threatened to put up candidates across Germany. This threat was dropped when the CDU retaliated by threatening to put up candidates in Bavaria. Such a ploy by the CSU would have been unlikely to succeed (Falter and Schumann, 1991).

The parties have retained a permanent alliance for contesting Bundestag elections, based on a recognition of separate identities and skilful bargaining between party leaders. Tensions between the two parties are nevertheless often apparent. Strauss was particularly hostile towards the role of the FDP in the coalition governments of the early 1980s but this has to be seen in a wider context of disagreement over strategy as well as personality clashes. The CDU tended to regard the FDP as an ally in its search for a 'natural' majority of the German electorate, whereas the CSU under Strauss saw the FDP as an irritant which should be dispensed with in favour of creating a conservative majority to the right of centre.

The CDU has moved towards an organisational structure more appropriate for a mass party since returning to power in 1982. This process was sparked off by the deliberations carried out during the years of opposition in the 1970s and it represents a major change in the party's structure from that prevailing during the Adenauer years. The party's central organisation in Bonn has in particular taken on a specifically integrative function. While the *Land* leaders are still influential members of the party's elite, the focus of power within the party has shifted markedly towards the parliamentary group and the national party apparatus.

The shock of opposition and organisational renewal also had a major impact on the CDU's membership. While the party remained based on a structure comprising regional notables and supporters of the chancellor, party membership did not appear important. While at the electoral level, the CDU was a broadly based party, in terms of membership, it was considerably narrower. The task of opposition forced a new role onto the party, with a consequently redefined role for the ordinary members.

The party's membership had traditionally been dominated by Catholics, males, the middle-aged and the occupations of the old middle class such as the self-employed and small businessmen. From 1969 to 1980, the party's membership more than doubled from 304,000 to 693,000 (Mintzel and Oberreuter, 1992, p. 568) and the social structure of the membership changed at the same time. The percentage of women members rose considerably and the traditional confessional imbalance between Catholics and Protestants narrowed. In occupational terms, more of the members are now employed in the white collar groups of salaried employees and public servants rather than being self-employed (twenty-nine per cent compared to twenty-one per cent) (Haungs, 1992, p. 193).

The membership of the CSU also doubled between 1969 and 1980 (77,000 to 172,000) (Mintzel and Oberreuter, 1992, p. 568) and it similarly saw a considerable increase to thirty per cent in its white-collar membership (Mintzel, 1992, p. 245). It remains though an overwhelmingly Catholic party (eighty-one per cent) (Mintzel, 1992, p. 243).

The membership of the CDU in 1991 was about 756,000, comprising 645,000 members in the former Federal Republic and 111,000 in the former DDR (Haungs, 1992, p. 193). The membership of the CSU is about 186,000 (Mintzel, 1992, p. 242).

There are huge differences between the CDU regional parties in terms of membership. The *Land* party of North-Rhine Westphalia had nearly thirty per cent of the total CDU membership in 1991. The next largest party was Baden-Württemberg with twelve per cent (Haungs, 1992, p. 193).

There are also clear differences in the membership between East and West. Far more workers are members in the East than in the West (thirty-four per cent compared to nine per cent) while white-collar members are more numerous in the West than the East (thirteen per cent compared to two per cent). There are more pensioners in the party in the East while there are more self-employed in the West (Haungs, 1992, p. 193).

Another aspect of the organisation of the Christian Democrats is their relationships with particular groups in German society. Four key groups can be identified – the churches, business, agriculture and labour.

With the division of Germany after 1945, the Federal Republic was confessionally balanced in numerical terms, unlike in the past. The bi-confessional nature of the CDU meant that the Catholic Church did not automatically get its way in terms of party policy. In an important sense, the Catholic Church had little choice but to urge its adherents to vote for the CDU-CSU as the main opponents of the SPD who were deemed to be *kirchenfeindlich* (hostile to the Church). As a result, there has normally been a broad organisational and policy affinity between the Catholic Church and the Christian Democrats. Practising Catholics have always comprised the core of the CDU-CSU's electoral support and therefore good relations on both a personal and professional level with the Catholic Church have always been important to the leaders of the CDU-CSU. Protestant influence upon the Christian Democrats is less obvious, but offices in the gift of the party are normally based on job quotas to ensure parity between the confessions.

Business groups tend to have stronger links with the CDU-CSU than with the SPD, with a considerable overlap between the membership of party committees and business associations such as the Federation of German Employers (BDA). There are also longstanding ties between the Christian Democrats and the Federation of German Farmers, although tensions do occasionally arise over reform plans for the EC's Common Agricultural Policy. The links between trade unions and the Christian Democrats are less well developed because the most salient common interests exist between the main industrial trade union federation (DGB) and the Social Democrats, although the DGB remains officially neutral in party political terms. There is, however, some influence for Christian trade unionists inside the DGB. Outside the DGB, white-collar unions in other federations are often closer in their outlooks to the CDU-CSU than to the SPD.

In addition to the relationships with interest groups mentioned above, the CDU-CSU has established a number of associations (*Vereinigungen*) such as youth groups, women's groups and local government associations. These groups provide the party with a means of opinion feedback to keep it in touch with differing views. It is however very difficult to ascertain how influential these associations are in terms of influencing the party's priorities and policies since such associations are essentially party support groups whose chief functions are to communicate, mobilise and recruit members for the party.

All political parties need substantial amounts of money to pursue their representative functions, but the amounts can vary considerably from year to year. This is particularly the case in Germany given the system of reimbursement of election costs by the state.

In 1989, the CDU had an income of just over 200 million DM made up of contributions from party members, donations, reimbursement of election expenses and miscellaneous contributions. Since the 1970s, the proportion of contributions from members to the CDU has increased, while other donations have declined. Today, the CDU is mainly dependent on the generosity of its membership, followed by election reimbursements and then donations. However, the federal party only receives a small percentage of the contributions from members. Out of roughly ten DM per month contributed by the members, the federal party only received one DM. This was changed in 1989 to 1.25 DM but this figure is still less than expenditure of between 2–3 DM per member per month. This situation has led to heated discussions within the party over the fairness of such a financial formula, since the costs of the federal party are rising in order to finance national election campaigns and to maintain the central organisation of the party. In addition, money must now be found to establish and maintain the party in the five new *Länder* of the former DDR (Haungs, 1992, pp. 200–202).

The CSU had an income of about 44 million DM in 1988, made up almost equally of membership contributions and other donations. The total sum available to the CSU has increased fourfold since 1968, but year on year there is considerable variation due to differing levels of donations from outside the party (Mintzel, 1992, pp. 243–7).

The Christian Democratic electorate

The first point to note about the CDU-CSU's electoral performance is its consistency. The range of its vote share at the eleven federal elections between 1953 and 1990 is just 6 per cent, between 44.2 per cent and 50.2 per cent. The first federal election in 1949 is ignored because it took place before the consolidation of the party system began and before the present two-vote electoral system was introduced. It is, however, the case that the three lowest vote shares for the CDU-CSU occurred in three of the last four elections (1990, 1987 and 1980 respectively), suggesting a failure to mobilise the German electorate as effectively as in the past.

In terms of the sociological base of the CDU-CSU within German society, the picture is clear. In many ways, the socio-structural basis of the CDU-CSU is the mirror image of the SPD. The Christian Democrats have a particular and long-term strength in the church-attending group of Catholics. The weaker the ties of Catholics to their Church, the stronger the SPD becomes (see Table 6.1).

Table 6.1 Religious and occupational bases of Christian Democratic electoral support (%) in the Federal Republic of Germany, 1976–90

Election year	1976	1980	1983	1987	1990
Catholics	59	55	64	54	54
Non-Catholics	45	37	46	39	46
Regular Catholics	82	74	78	70	75
Irregular Catholics	58	54	65	53	53
Non-attending Catholics	36	36	50	40	35
Union members	35	29	36	32	33
Non-union members	55	48	56	48	51
Unionised workers	35	29	34	29	37
Non-unionised workers	48	36	51	40	49
Unionised white collar	35	29	41	36	31
Non-unionised white collar	55	47	61	50	47
Catholic workers	57	52	58	47	52
Catholic white collar	65	51	67	58	55
Catholic unionists	53	49	48	41	41
Catholic non-unionists	61	52	66	53	57

Note: Regular Catholics: at least weekly church attendance
Irregular Catholics: at least annual church attendance
Non-attending Catholics: no attendance
White collar: clerical, office employees (*Angestellte und Beamte*)

Source: Calculated from Gibowski and Kaase, 1991, pp. 16–17

In terms of social status or class, the CDU-CSU are strongly supported by middle class groups such as the self-employed, executives and directors. They are noticeably less successful among the working class, particularly the unionised working class whose 'natural' tendencies have been to support the Social Democrats. However, among the non-unionised working class, the CDU-CSU has proven to be a serious competitor to the SPD. In the burgeoning white-collar groups of salaried employees and officials, the effect of union membership is again apparent, with the same pattern as for the working class. White-collar union members tend to see the SPD as 'their' party while white-collar non-unionists favour the CDU-CSU.

These general patterns have held true for most of the post-war federal elections, although there have been variations in the levels of support as set out in Table 6.1. It is also important to consider these support bases against the background of the changing structure of German society. In particular, there have been major changes in the size of religious and occupational groups. The number of practising Catholics and Protestants has declined sharply over the post-war period. According to Connor (1991, p. 90), the number of Catholics who attend church regularly (those who attend at least once a week) has decreased from 61 per cent in 1953 to 32 per cent in 1987. The group of Protestants who attend church regularly was always much smaller than the corresponding group of Catholics. The Protestant group of regular attenders has declined from 18 per cent in 1953 to only 4 per cent in 1987.

Simultaneously, there have been substantial changes in three key occupational groups. First, there has been a slow decline in the number of manual workers, from 51.0 per cent to 39.8 per cent in 1985. Second, there has been a rapid decline in the proportion of the self-employed within the work-force, from 28.3 per cent in 1950 to 11.8 per cent in 1985. Third, there has been a startling growth in the size of the 'new middle class' in the same period, from 20.6 per cent to 48.4 per cent (Connor, 1991, p. 94).

The main significance of this last development is that the milieu of the new middle class is particularly difficult to define. Unlike practising Catholics and unionised workers, who are the core supporters of the CDU-CSU and SPD respectively, the political cues which attract the new middle class are unpredictable because of the breadth and diversity of this category, which includes professional groups and high-ranking civil servants but also junior white-collar employees. This has meant that any distinctive pattern of voting from the new middle class has been difficult to establish. The assumption of group uniformity does not hold, given the group's heterogeneous composition.

The appeal of the parties to this group has therefore been uncertain and the group's reactions volatile and unpredictable. Research is continuing to try and break down this composite new middle class into its individual sectors but there is no doubt that the increasing size of this particular group has forced both major parties to reshape their appeals in the light of an increasingly 'functional' electorate which is well informed and which no longer uncritically accepts the political cues of a well-defined organisational milieu. This is a particular problem for the CDU-CSU as a self-proclaimed people's party trying to develop an integrated political programme.

Three other 'classic' social variables give us further indications of the bases of the CDU-CSU's support in German society. First, the Christian Democrats have always performed better among older rather than younger voters. The party has consistently underpolled among the two youngest age groups (18–24 and 25–34) while it has overpolled in the oldest group (60+ years) compared to its overall electoral performance. The two middle

age groups (35–44 and 45–59) tend to give support to the Christian Democrats similar to the party's overall level of support (Connor, 1991, p. 106).

Second, the CDU-CSU has often performed better among women
voters than among men. However, the 'gender gap' has diminished greatly
since 1972 in comparison with the 1950s and 1960s. For example, in 1965,
the gender gap in CDU-CSU support was 9.7 per cent; in 1987, it was only
2.6 per cent (Connor, 1991, p. 112). This could be due to the decline in
religious observance over the same period, which was particularly marked
among females. In addition, greater female support for the SPD in the
early 1970s was built as a result of the SPD's plans for abortion reform and
the popularity of Willy Brandt in general, producing a growth in the
number of women who did not automatically regard the CDU-CSU as
their natural political home (Rusciano, 1992).

Third, we should mention the regional basis of support for the Christian
Democrats. The topic of regional differentiation within Germany has often
focused on a putative north–south divide, with the CDU-CSU's support
appearing to be weakest in northern states such as Hamburg and Bremen
and strongest in the southern states such as Baden-Württemberg and
Bavaria. This division also reflects the religious composition of the
country, with the Protestants clustered in the north and the Catholics
concentrated in the south. It also fits with the socio-economic structure of
the country, with the CDU-CSU performing best in rural areas and small
towns and worst in the large cities and urban conglomerations.

The independent nature of regionalism can clearly therefore be questioned in the light of the above. It is the combination of denominational
and socio-economic characteristics which largely accounts for regionalism
in voting patterns, particularly since the concentration of the party system
in the 1950s which saw the demise of regionally based parties with the
exception of the CSU. The overall federal structure of Germany does,
however, continue to provide a clear focus for the articulation of regional
interests, particularly through the powerful position of the Bundesrat.
There is also some evidence of a revival of regional consciousness in the
mid-1980s in terms of economic restructuring and the question of EC
representation. For the future, however, it is more likely that regional
divisions within Germany will focus on the overall differences between the
states of the former Federal Republic and those of the former DDR.

The statistics mentioned earlier suggest politically important changes in
the social composition of the German electorate. These changes have
arguably not so much redefined the sources of political cues as seen the
decline of former certainties without replacing them with orientations to
politics of equal significance and import.

Models of German voting behaviour have therefore increasingly turned
away from socio-structural explanations towards giving greater emphasis to
political issues and the popularity of political leaders. This trend is widely
identified as beginning in 1972 with the prominence of the SPD/FDP's
policy of *Ostpolitik* and the popularity of Willy Brandt as chancellor. The
independent impact of political issues is notoriously difficult to ascertain
and the 'issue agenda' can and does change from election to election. The

party leader, particularly the incumbent chancellor, might over time become a key influence in overcoming fragile support among particular social groups, obtaining a *Kanzlerbonus* for his party.

Little support for the importance of the party leaders can be derived from the outcome of the last two federal elections. In 1990, Helmut Kohl was strongly favoured as chancellor over Oskar Lafontaine (fifty-six per cent compared to thirty-eight per cent) yet the CDU-CSU recorded its worst election result since 1953. In 1987, Kohl had the same percentage of preferences as his SPD opponent, Johannes Rau (forty-six per cent) and yet the CDU-CSU's support declined 4.5 per cent compared to 1983.

In the past, the image of the party leader may have been important. In 1972, Brandt's lead over Rainer Barzel (fifty-six per cent/twenty-four per cent) could well have contributed to the SPD's overtaking the CDU-CSU as the largest party for the first and only time in the post-war period (45.8 per cent/44.9 per cent). Four years later in 1976, Helmut Schmidt's lead over Helmut Kohl was clear (fifty-one per cent/thirty-nine per cent) but CDU-CSU support increased nevertheless by 3.7 per cent. In 1980, the candidature of Franz-Josef Strauss as the Union's chancellor candidate appeared significant when the CDU-CSU's vote share went down by 4.1 per cent. Schmidt's lead over Strauss as preferred chancellor candidate had been dramatic (sixty-one per cent/twenty-nine per cent) (Gibowski and Kaase, 1991, pp. 4, 14).

The effect of leaders on the popularity of their parties is certainly plausible but nevertheless inconsistent in effect. A leader who does not alienate voters may be a greater asset than one who can mobilise the electorate.

The policy positions of the CDU-CSU

Two factors in particular militate against the German Christian Democrats pursuing a clearly defined policy agenda. First, there is a lack of coherent doctrine within Christian Democracy as a movement which could give rise to specific policies, even given the existence of a number of ideas derived from Catholic social thought. Second, the decentralised nature of the party means that different emphases are usually subsumed beneath undisputed generalities such as the pursuit of the 'middle way' and a commitment to striving for consensus and solidarity.

In the early post-war years, the Ahlen programme of 1947 did address the question of values and policy direction but this proved to be an exception, particularly when the party's focus remained on the functions of government and the maintenance of political power. However, once in opposition, a much greater emphasis was placed on reconsidering the basic values of Christian Democracy. This coincided with the election of Helmut Kohl as party chairman in 1973 and a widespread recognition within the CDU-CSU of the need for a process of re-examination.

These internal discussions culminated in the publication of a set of

principles as a basic programme (*Grundsatzprogramm*) at a conference in
Ludwigshafen in 1978.

The basic goals of the CDU-CSU were defined as freedom, solidarity
and justice while the social market economy provided the framework for
the development of German society. While the 1978 programme was
clearly an attempt to set the Christian Democrats apart from the SPD, it
did not represent a break with the past as did the SPD's Bad Godesberg
programme of 1959. Instead, it largely represented a restating of party
positions established by practice, with its emphasis very much on
continuity rather than change. Despite the years in opposition, redefinition
led largely to restating what had already been tried and tested.

Both before and after 1978, there have been numerous policy documents
and statements from the CDU federal party conference, the federal executive committee, specialist party committees as well as the *Land* parties.
The central problem remains that of how exactly these ideas can be
implemented in government when the federal government is certain to be a
coalition. The marked tendency to retreat into vacuous generalities which
cannot engender internal party disputes is very tempting given this
constraint.

The best example of policy continuity occurred after the CDU-CSU
returned to federal power in 1982. It was assumed that Germany might also
be in line for a bout of 'neo-conservatism' similar to developments in
Britain and the United States in the 1980s. This was never likely in theory
and it has not materialised in practice although the 'economic liberal' wing
of the FDP is keen on reforms based on the theories of neo-liberal
economics. Once again, coalition constraints ensured that the CDU-CSU
could not implement any radically new agenda, even if it had developed
such policies and it possessed the necessary political will to do so (Grande,
1988). It would also have been difficult to push through such an agenda,
given the heterogeneous structure of the CDU-CSU and its claim to be a
people's party. Such a narrow and partisan approach to politics would
certainly have come up against opposition from within the party and would
have provided fresh sources of tension just when the party was turning its
thoughts once more to the problems of governing.

Nevertheless, some reforms have been pushed through in the last
decade, despite the institutional context of German policy-making which
discourages radical policy changes (Webber, 1992; see also a reply by
Leaman, 1993).

If we look in particular at the issue of privatisation, we can see how little
the CDU-CSU has pursued this policy in comparison with Conservative
governments in Britain. There have been largely symbolic privatisation
policies (Esser, 1988), which do not involve central political issues and are
more related to international competitiveness. Such a policy might also be
useful though to reduce the public debt. Privatisation has not been a major
concern within the German economic policy-making process, with the
obvious exception of the activities of the *Treuhandanstalt* in the former
DDR.

One potential concern has centred on legal questions over whether state-run enterprises could actually be sold off to the private sector. Combined with the moderation and pragmatism of the CDU-CSU and its continuing belief in the value of the public sector, it is not surprising that Germany did not go down the same path as Britain during the last decade.

This continuity with the past, with policy based on adjustment and adaptation, is also apparent in the latest draft of the CDU's new basic programme, prepared by the party's programme commission (CDU-Bundesgeschäftsstelle, 1993). The final version is due to be ready in time for the federal election in 1994. There are clear attempts throughout the document to update the 1978 basic programme but it seems nevertheless that continuity will remain the primary watchword.

The CDU is a people's party (the first sentence in the 1978 and also in the January 1993 draft), appealing to all classes and groups. The same three basic values – freedom, solidarity and justice – are retained within an overall striving to 'renew' German society. The most noticeable change is the explicit attempt to integrate ecological concerns with the running of the social market economy, the third chapter being entitled 'for an ecological and social market economy'. Yet the question will inevitably remain as to how exactly this synthesis will be achieved.

There is an expanded section on European integration, with an explicit call for the completion of European union. The longstanding enthusiasm of the CDU for European integration appears undiminished. Continuing the process of integration can be justified on the grounds that to mark time would be to send the wrong signal when nationalism and xenophobia are on the increase.

There is also a new chapter which takes a broader look at the environment, encompassing such matters as science, research and technology. The final page of the 1993 draft ends with a section on the 'politics of credibility' which concludes that 'paradise on earth' cannot be achieved but that the way forward must be based on justice, humanity, freedom and responsibility.

There is a clear attempt throughout this draft document to update the 1978 basic programme with newer concerns such as the protection of the environment but the language of the draft remains very similar to that of previous documents. The draft contains ideas expressed in general and contingent terms which provide no precise solutions, while setting out largely agreed problems and concerns.

The government record of the CDU-CSU

Even though the CDU-CSU has always (with the exception of 1972) been the largest party in the Bundestag, it has never formed a majority government on its own. Every federal government since 1949 has been a coalition and coalition changes have been implemented largely as a result of negotiations and bargaining which are subsequently legitimised at the polls, most notably in 1983. The emphasis on the value of coalition governments is

rooted in a broader search for consensus in German society as a whole and
the role of the FDP as a brake or third force between the CDU-CSU and
the SPD appears to be widely supported by the German electorate. At the
1990 federal election, two-thirds of the voters in the West and a similar
fraction in the East rejected the idea of an absolute majority for either
main party. Even among CDU-CSU supporters, this idea received the
backing of 55 per cent (Forschungsgruppe Wahlen, e.V, 1990, p. 69).

While all the parties constantly strive to maintain distinct identities and
profiles, the degree of overlap between all three of them has meant that
coalitions have been formed encompassing all possible combinations since
1949. The CDU-CSU formed coalitions with the FDP and minor parties
between 1949 and 1966, then the Grand Coalition between the CDU-CSU
and the SPD was in power between 1966 and 1969. The SPD supplanted
the CDU-CSU as the major party of government for the next thirteen years
until autumn 1982 when the initial post-war coalition pattern was renewed,
with the CDU-CSU joining up once more in federal power with the FDP.

The critical role of the FDP in these coalition configurations is clear. The
Free Democrats have spent more time in power over the post-war period
than either of the main two parties and they have often commanded key
cabinet posts as well. This has been a source of tension within the coalition,
particularly between the FDP and the CSU, with the former more con-
spicuously rewarded, while the latter contributed more Bundestag seats to
the governing coalition on a number of occasions.

In the present cabinet of 20, the CDU has 10 seats, the CSU has 5 and
the FDP also has 5, despite the fact that the FDP contributes 79 seats to the
coalition and the CSU 51. The FDP does, however, control two major
ministries, the foreign ministry and the economics ministry. The other
three it holds are justice, regional planning and education and science. The
CSU's major post is the ministry of finance but the other four are relatively
minor posts (food and agriculture, health, posts and communications, and
economic co-operation and development).

All the German parties have preferred to control cabinet posts in
accordance with their programmes and the interests of their supporters.
The cabinet posts which the CDU-CSU has controlled have depended on
their coalition partner of the time. They have always held the chancellor-
ship in office (even during the Grand Coalition with the SPD) but they
have had to allow their partners the foreign ministry, one of the two key
financial ministries (finance or economics) and some less important posts
such as agriculture or justice. This situation has nevertheless meant that the
CDU-CSU chancellor has been able to lay down the broad guidelines of
government policy within which the coalition's business is conducted.

These guidelines were clearer and more rigidly adhered to under
Adenauer than Kohl. The latter tends to hold the ring much more as a
party and coalition manager than the former who stamped his authority on
the various coalitions quickly. In key areas such as foreign policy, Kohl was
often content to let the FDP's Hans-Dietrich Genscher represent the
government's views. Kohl was, however, much more active in the process
leading up to German unification. Nevertheless, the apparent control of

foreign policy by Genscher (Kirchner, 1990) until his sudden resignation in May 1992 was a major contributory factor to coalition tensions amid growing complaints about a lack of leadership and direction from Kohl. This is hardly a new development within the CDU-CSU since complaints about leadership date back to at least the early 1960s when the question of Adenauer's successor as chancellor exposed a bitter struggle within the leading elite of the two parties. These tensions were also clearly apparent in the disputes in the 1960s between the 'Atlanticists' and the 'Gaullists' on key questions of foreign policy, disagreements which quickly assumed the mantle of personality clashes between Erhard and Schröder on one side and Adenauer and Strauss on the other (Broughton, 1992, pp. 59–60).

The CSU under Theo Waigel has its own problems to deal with at present and is therefore dependent on the success of the present government. While Germany as a whole has grown in size, Bavaria has not; other parties can now appeal to more voters but the CSU cannot. The challenge of the Republicans in Bavaria means that the old equation of the CSU equalling Bavaria no longer holds.

When Helmut Kohl became party chairman in 1973, he found a split leadership, with a different parliamentary leader and a different general secretary, all jostling for position in the strategic debates during the years of opposition. In addition, there were regular tensions between Kohl and Strauss over who should run as the CDU-CSU's chancellor candidate (Kohl in 1976, Strauss in 1980, Kohl since then) which only definitively ended with Strauss's death in 1988.

Kohl has appeared pre-eminent since then within the CDU-CSU, by retaining the party chairmanship while being chancellor and through the dismissal of Heiner Geißler from his post as CDU general secretary in 1989. Geißler had become one of Kohl's main critics within the CDU.

Nevertheless, Kohl's performance in the mid-1980s before unification led to yet another round of sniping about his leadership style. Much of this criticism became muted with the achievement of unification by the 'unity chancellor'. However, Kohl's style seems to enthuse fewer and fewer people despite his record in office, and the fact that there is no obvious successor to him suggests that the CDU-CSU will once more be confronted with a difficult transition period when the time comes to select a new leader.

One of the difficulties in renewing the CDU leadership has been the electoral losses in key *Länder* over the last five years, depriving poten-tial crown princes of experience and political clout. The growth in the number of political scandals and consequent resignations has been another problematic area for the CDU although this has affected the other parties as well.

Nevertheless, the overall record of the CDU-CSU in office is one based on very substantial achievements. They established and embedded within the German political culture a range of political actions and reactions based on the principle of continuity which had been unknown before 1945. They were the architects of the post-war consensus which has proven to be strong, adaptable and durable. They have legitimised the 'middle way' approach to politics which restored the country's economic strength and international reputation.

The challenges of unification will of course provide a quite different test from those of the past but the CDU-CSU still possesses the power to defend and adapt the present system. In some important ways, however, it will have to modify the prevailing consensus considerably, particularly in terms of distributional disputes between the old and the new states, which is most likely to involve long-term sacrifice in the West (something which Kohl initially denied would be needed). Changes will also be needed for reviving an economy which increasingly appears to be too regulated, subsidised and inflexible to maintain its competitive edge.

The task of bringing the West and the East together appears daunting. It cannot be achieved on the basis of shared Christian values since the vast majority of East Germans are 'post-socialist atheists'. It cannot be accelerated by promoting East Germans quickly to positions of responsibility since many could be compromised in public life by past links with the East German state.

Nevertheless, the approach of the CDU-CSU to these problems is much more likely to modify the consensus than to break with it.

Conclusion

It has been impossible in a chapter of this length to do justice to the dominant role of the CDU-CSU in post-war German politics. We have only been able to allude briefly to the major developments which have marked the hegemony of the CDU-CSU. However, we can still bring together a number of strands which together provide firm evidence as to the reasons why the Christian Democrats have proven to be so flexible in their outlook and so popular in their appeal to the German electorate.

First, the CDU-CSU established their dominance of post-war German politics in the early years of the Federal Republic. By inflicting three successive electoral defeats on the SPD, the CDU-CSU forced the Social Democrats to change. The SPD had no choice but to move towards the centre of a political spectrum which the Christian Democrats had defined, particularly in terms of the inviolability of the social market economy and integration into the transnational organisations of Western Europe.

Second, the very lack of ideology typical of the CDU-CSU has proven comforting to the German electorate in times of economic uncertainty. As the direct memories of the Weimar Republic and the Third Reich fade for more and more people, the CDU-CSU's idea of a 'new politics' grounded in pragmatism and continuity contains a vital sense of security for German voters at times of economic and social dislocation, as at present in the former DDR. This is something which the SPD will find very hard to combat in opposition. The SPD will equally find it difficult to establish its own economic competence and credibility, even when the present government is being forced to impose tax increases and spending cuts on the German electorate by the ballooning costs of unification.

Third, the FDP is hardly likely to jump ship back to the SPD when the present economic policies of the ruling coalition appear to be the only credible ones on offer. The SPD might well have been correct in its assessment of the true costs of unification, but in the present German party system, it would be risking a great deal if it appeared to be opposing 'consensual' policies for economic recovery. In addition, the danger for the SPD (currently on its third leader in six years) is that it will increasingly be drawn into a web of co-responsibility which holds the potential for little credit and much blame. This applies particularly to future appeals for national solidarity and for Germany to play a fuller international role.

It is common for Germans to worry about the health of their political system, even after more than forty years of continued success. The stability of the party system, the responsiveness of the parties to new concerns and the sheer extent of the task of truly unifying the country have all been debated at length, invoking fears that Germany might turn out to be a *Schönwetterdemokratie* (good weather democracy) but not one which can weather the storms of economic recession without major upheavals.

From outside, and with the benefit of hindsight, the first two of these issues appear entirely normal in a liberal democracy. In an important sense, then, such concerns reflect the final achievement of 'normality' in a country unused to favourable comparisons with others. The third problem is unique to Germany, but the approach of the CDU-CSU to its ultimate resolution is unlikely to be so. The pragmatism in power of the Christian Democrats to date suggests that their approach to the securing of German unity will explicitly eschew panaceas and prescription. Of course, pragmatism and modernity will not secure electoral success on their own, but the German voters seem very likely to be looking mainly for social and economic competence from the governing coalition.

Such an approach is consonant with the history, development and achievements of the German Christian Democrats. Such a route is also likely to prove to be the path to long-term success, even if slogans such as *'keine Experimente'* ('no experiments') and *'weiter so!'* ('more of the same') are unlikely to inspire many people. In a very real sense, there is no alternative at present to the CDU-CSU as it simultaneously grapples with the twin tasks of renewing itself and the country it has governed for so long.

References

Broughton, D., 1992, Elite Consensus and Dissensus in West German Foreign Policy, in Kirchner, E. J., Sperling, J. (eds), *The Federal Republic of Germany and NATO. 40 Years After*, Macmillan, Basingstoke, pp. 54–71.
CDU-Bundesgeschäftsstelle, 1993, *Im Gespräch: Ein neues Grundsatzprogramm der Christlich Demokratischen Union Deutschlands* (Diskussionsentwurf), CDU-Bundesgeschäftsstelle, HA Öffentlichkeitsarbeit, Konrad Adenauer Haus, Bonn, January.
Chandler, W., 1989, The Christian Democrats, in Merkl, P. H. (ed.), *The Federal*

Republic of Germany at Forty, New York University Press, New York, pp. 287–312.

Chandler, W., 1993, The Christian Democrats and the challenge of unity, in Padgett, S. (ed.), *Parties and party systems in the new Germany*, Dartmouth Press, Aldershot, pp. 129–46.

Connor, I. D., 1991, Social Change and Electoral Support: the Case of the CDU-CSU, 1949–87, in Kolinsky, E. (ed.), *The Federal Republic of Germany. The end of an era*, Berg, Oxford, pp. 83–118.

Esser, J., 1988, 'Symbolic privatisation': The politics of privatisation in West Germany, *West European Politics*, 11 (4): 61–73.

Falter, J., Schumann, S., 1991, Konsequenzen einer bundesweiten Kandidatur der CSU bei Wahlen. Eine in die unmittelbare Vergangenheit gerichtete Prognose, *Aus Politik und Zeitgeschichte*, B11–12, 8 March: 33–45.

Forschungsgruppe Wahlen e.V, 1990, *Bundestagswahl 1990. Eine Analyse der ersten gesamtdeutschen Bundestagswahl am 2. Dezember 1990*. Bericht no. 61, Mannheim, Forschungsgruppe Wahlen e.V.

Gibowski, W. G., Kaase, M., 1991, Auf dem Weg zum politischen Alltag. Eine Analyse der ersten gesamtdeutschen Bundestagswahl vom 2. Dezember 1990, *Aus Politik und Zeitgeschichte*, B11–12, 8 March: 3–20.

Grande, E., 1988, Neoconservatism without Neoconservatives? The Renaissance and Transformation of Contemporary German Conservatism, in Girvin, B. (ed.), *The Transformation of Contemporary Conservatism*, Sage, London, pp. 55–77.

Haungs, P., 1992, Die CDU: Prototyp einer Volkspartei, in Mintzel, A., Oberreuter, H. (eds), *Parteien in der Bundesrepublik Deutschland* (2nd edn), Bundeszentrale für politische Bildung, Bonn, pp. 172–216.

Irving, R. E. M., 1979, *The Christian Democratic parties of Western Europe*, Allen and Unwin, London, pp. 112–63.

Kirchner, E. J., 1990, Genscher and what lies behind 'Genscherism', *West European Politics*, 13 (2): 159–177.

Leaman, J., 1993, The Rhetoric and Logic of the *Wende* – A Reply to Douglas Webber, *German Politics*, 2 (1): 124–135.

Mintzel, A., 1982, Conservatism and Christian Democracy in the Federal Republic of Germany, in Layton-Henry, Z. (ed.), *Conservative Politics in Western Europe*, Macmillan, London, pp. 131–59.

Mintzel, A., 1992, Die Christlich Soziale Union in Bayern, in Mintzel, A., Oberreuter, H., 1992 (eds), *Parteien in der Bundesrepublik Deutschland* (2nd edn), Bundeszentrale für politische Bildung, Bonn, pp. 217–65.

Mintzel, A., Oberreuter, H., 1992 (eds), *Parteien in der Bundesrepublik Deutschland* (2nd edn), Bundeszentrale für politische Bildung, Bonn, pp. 217–65.

Pridham, G., 1977, *Christian Democracy in Western Germany*, Croom Helm, London.

Rusciano, F. L., 1992, Rethinking the Gender Gap. The Case of West German Elections, 1949–1987, *Comparative Politics*, 24 (3): 335–357.

Webber, D., 1992, Kohl's Wendepolitik after a Decade, *German Politics*, 1 (2): 149–180.

Weidenfeld, W., 1982, The German Christian Democrats, in Morgan, R. and Silvestri, S. (eds), *Moderates and Conservatives in Western Europe. Political parties, the European Community and the Atlantic Alliance*, Heinemann Educational, London, pp. 73–93.

7

CHRISTIAN PARTIES IN SCANDINAVIA: VICTORY OVER THE WINDMILLS?

Lauri Karvonen

Religion and politics: Scandinavia as an extreme case

One of the features that sets Scandinavia apart within a comparative West European perspective is the religious homogeneity of the region. Well over 90 per cent of the religiously affiliated population belong to the Lutheran Established Church. Even if the religiously non-affiliated population is included, around 90 per cent or more of Scandinavian citizens are Lutheran Church members. At the same time – and this might be called the first paradox of Scandinavian religious life – this extreme church fidelity is connected with a singularly low level of religious activity. Merely a couple of per cent of the population attend church services regularly each week; for the overwhelming majority church attendance is limited to the Christmas Mass – that is, if they go to church at all (Gustafsson, 1985, pp. 238–65).

Scandinavia stands apart in another respect as well. The Lutheran Established Church is formally 'stronger' in the governmental apparatus than in most other parts of the Western world. The church as an institution is well integrated into the state machinery; its economic position is secured through appropriations in the government budget and via the direct church tax, and it performs a number of functions which cannot strictly speaking be regarded as religious. Nevertheless – and this might be the second paradox of Scandinavian religion – the church as an institution has very limited influence in politics. The church has rarely been able to spearhead important political debates. The few instances when it has attempted to do so have evoked criticism concerning the proper place of the church in social life: *sutor, ne supra crepidam*!

Against this Nordic backdrop it is easy to understand why the real strongholds of European Christian parties are to be found outside Scandinavia. Religious conflicts are necessary for the rise to prominence of religiously based political organisations. In countries where the relationship between church and state was a central bone of contention over long periods of time, Christian parties have established themselves to defend the church's point of view. In Central Europe, separate parties originally emerged as representatives of the Protestant and Catholic populations.

This cleavage has, however, in several cases been bridged during recent decades; instead of representing Catholicism or Protestantism, these parties today promote general Christian values in politics. Nevertheless, their historical background is to be found in important contradictions involving church, state and religious affiliation; as for Scandinavia, the region largely lacks experience of these kinds of political conflicts (Madeley, 1977; Madeley, 1982, pp. 149–53; Flanagan and Dalton, 1990, p. 233; Lijphart, 1990, p. 259).

This being the case, it is somewhat surprising that two of the four Nordic countries, Finland and Sweden, today have Christian parties in government positions. In Denmark Kristeligt Folkepartiet participated in Poul Schlüter's four-party cabinet from 1982 until 1988. Norway, finally, has the electorally strongest Christian party in Scandinavia; the Norwegian Kristelig Folkeparti can scarcely be characterized as a minor party in the Scandinavian multiparty context. Are we witnessing a breakthrough for the Christian parties in Scandinavian politics? If that is the case, what is the background to this development? Have the Christian parties managed to activate a politically relevant cleavage based on religiously defined values? From where does their popular following originate? And finally, what are the prospects of continued growth of the Christian element in the Scandinavian party setting?

From nil to small to medium-sized?

The religious parties are latecomers in the party political arena of Scandinavia. When they emerged the population had already to a large extent been mobilised by the older parties. The Christian parties have faced major difficulties in gaining a foothold among the electorate as a result (see Table 7.1).

The Norwegian party constitutes a special case among the Nordic Christian parties due to its long history and its relatively strong electoral position. Kristeligt Folkepartei was established in 1933 in West Norway, and during its first ten years it was largely a regional party for the Hordaland area. In the first post-war election, however, the party rose to national significance, a position which it has been able to maintain and even to some extent strengthen since then. The Suomen Kristillinen Liitto (SKL) in Finland has never gained comparable shares of the vote. Nevertheless, in 1970 the party won its first seat in Parliament, and it has managed to maintain parliamentary representation ever since. The Swedish Kristen Demokratisk Samling (KDS) also remained a peripheral party over a long period; its chances of exceeding the 4 per cent threshold required for representation in the Riksdag seemed decidedly poor. In the 1985 election the KDS joined forces with the Centre Party; this electoral alliance gave the Christian Party leader Alf Svensson a seat in Parliament. In the following elections, however, the two parties again ran on separate tickets, and Svensson failed to maintain his seat. The 1991 election result was all the more sensational. The KDS had no trouble exceeding the 4 per cent

Table 7.1 The Christian Parties of Scandinavia in Parliamentary Elections, 1933–91 (percentage of valid votes)

Norway		Finland		Sweden		Denmark	
Year	%	Year	%	Year	%	Year	%
1933	0.7	1958	0.2	1964	1.8	1971	2.0
1936	1.3	1962	0.8	1968	1.5	1973	4.0
1945	7.9	1966	0.4	1970	1.8	1975	5.3
1949	8.4	1970	1.1	1973	1.8	1977	3.4
1953	10.5	1972	2.5	1976	1.4	1979	2.6
1957	10.2	1975	3.3	1979	1.4	1981	2.3
1961	9.6	1979	4.8	1982	1.9	1984	2.7
1965	8.1	1983	3.0	1985	2.5*	1987	2.4
1969	9.4	1987	2.6	1988	2.9	1990	2.7
1973	12.3	1991	3.1	1991	7.1		
1977	12.4						
1981	8.9						
1985	8.3						
1989	8.5						

Notes: The parties are:
Norway: *Kristelig Folkeparti*
Finland: *Suomen Kristillinen Liitto (SKL)*
Sweden: *Kristen Demokratisk Samling*, since 1991 *Kristdemokratiska Samhällspartiet (KDS)*
Denmark: *Kristeligt Folkeparti*
*KDS share of ballots cast for the electoral alliance with the Center Party.

Source: Wörlund, 1988, p. 80.

barrier clause on its own; the party suddenly commanded twenty-six seats in Parliament. As for Kristeligt Folkeparti in Denmark, its electoral peak seems to have occurred in the 1970s; nevertheless, the party has managed to stay above the 2 per cent limit required for representation in the Folketing, and it presently holds four seats in the Danish Parliament.

Frame of reference: the question of critical thresholds

Mogens Pedersen (1982, pp. 6–9) has drawn attention to several critical thresholds that political parties must pass in order to be able to gain significance. At each instance, the party's character and position is moulded by the circumstances that prevailed when the party passed the threshold in question. The 'threshold of declaration' – the moment when the party is 'declared into being' – is likely to influence its orientation for many years to come. The 'threshold of representation' means that a party has established a sufficient foundation in terms of electoral support; these social, geographical and ideological voter constellations are a source of strength as well as a limiting factor for the future course of the party.

Finally, the 'threshold of relevance' implies that certain requirements must be fulfilled by a party in order for it to quality as a coalition partner.

'Declaration': the emergence of the Christian parties

Kristelig Folkeparti in Norway is not only the oldest and electorally strongest Christian party in Scandinavia, its emergence and activities also came to influence the rise and orientation of the three other parties. In Chapter 8 the emergence of the Norwegian party is discussed in detail. Here, it is sufficient to note that the immediate impetus behind the creation of the party had the moralist stamp typical of Christian politics in Scandinavia in the years to come. Essentially a regional party in the west of Norway during the first decade of its existence, Kristelig Folkeparti rose to national significance immediately after World War II (Lomeland, 1971, pp. 19–43; Johansson, 1985, p. 72; Saeter, 1985, pp. 8–10).

As frequently happens in comparative Nordic studies it is necessary to take into account the phenomenon of diffusion (Karvonen, 1981) when studying the character and background of the Christian parties in Scandinavia. The second oldest of the four parties, Suomen Kristillinen Liitto (SKL) in Finland, was founded in 1958 with considerable inspiration and influence derived from the Norwegian Christian movement. The first program of the SKL in fact turned out to be more or less a verbatim translation of the corresponding Norwegian document (Arter, 1980, p. 46). The political and historical context in which the Finnish party came into existence displayed, however, some special features. It would appear that the general political background was of greater importance in Finland than in the case of the other three parties. The entire post-war era had been a strong period for the Finnish Communists. In the second half of the 1950s they experienced a clear upward trend among the electorate, which was to result in their best electoral performance ever in 1958: 50 seats in the Eduskunta, a result which made them the largest party in Parliament. The Communists and their allies the People's Democrats took a clear 'system critical' policy line, meaning that the concept of an established Church as well as the strongly conservative profile of the Church itself were subjected to severe criticism. Withdrawals from Church membership increased markedly towards the end of the 1950s and had a clear relationship with Communist electoral strongholds (Sundback, 1991, pp. 277–8). The fact that the Christian activists chose to establish a separate Christian party instead of trying to work through existing bourgeois parties was related to the social foundation on which the party was based (Johansson, 1985, p. 24). The strong position of atheist Communism in the labour movement had evidently alienated Christian workers and smallholders. It was primarily to these people that the SKL wished to appeal; they could not be expected to rally strongly behind the established bourgeois parties. Generally speaking, perhaps the most important impetus behind the creation of a Christian party was the proliferation of politically motivated secularism and atheism. In the course of the 1960s, the party gradually attained a clearer image of a 'moral vigilante' as various scandals became topical on the political agenda, and important issues concerning religious instruction in schools for example were to be decided (Arter, 1980, p. 48; Arter, 1987, p. 32).

The emergence of Kristen Demokratisk Samling in Sweden is closely associated with several heated debates on religion and morality. At the beginning of 1964 there was a debate around what was known as the Petition of the 140 Doctors, a document signed by professors of medicine as well as by practising physicians. The petitioners expressed their concern about increasing promiscuity and the proliferation of venereal diseases; according to them, the sexual instruction given at schools and the cultural and sexual policies of the government bore a major responsibility for this state of affairs. The ensuing debate became highly polarised; the 140 doctors received strong support from Christian organisations and commentators. Parallel to this, a memorandum from the National Board of Social Affairs about a religious sect known as Maranata gave rise to additional friction between religious activists and the government. The Board had deemed it necessary to advise all municipalities to take proper measures to prevent children under sixteen years of age from attending 'ecstatic meetings' (Johansson, 1985, p. 80). In nonconformist circles this was seen as an attempt to limit the freedom of religion. The question of religious instruction at schools was another incentive behind the decision to create a political organisation based on explicit Christian values. A plan aimed at reforming the curriculum of secondary schools proposed a reduction in the share of religious instruction. Moreover, the subject itself was to have the character of an objective social science only loosely connected with confessional Protestantism. Those who protested against this plan decided to launch a mass petition in order to stop it from being implemented. This turned out to be a highly succesful enterprise, as all of 2.1 million people (out of some five million adult citizens) signed the petition in the course of a few months. This rapid mobilisation represented a hopeful sign from the point of view of those who argued for the establishment of a separate Christian party. Yet another debate on morality caused by the film *491* helped mobilize the Christian opinion. This film, which among other things contained explicit sex scenes, was first prohibited altogether by the Government Motion Picture Agency; later, however, the cabinet decided to lift the ban after certain scenes were cut. Christian activists were at the forefront of this debate, and several of them later underlined the importance of this question for the decision to create the KDS in 1964 (Johansson, 1985, pp. 90–95).

The early history of Kristeligt Folkeparti in Denmark is in many ways very similar to what has already been said about the KDS above. The 1960s had witnessed such a considerable radicalisation, especially relating to issues related to sexuality and morality. This process included the liberalisation of legislation on pornography and abortion. 'Danish sin' became a widely known concept throughout the world. Parallel to this, school reform plans proposed a steadily decreasing share for religious instruction in school curricula (Riis, 1985, p. 29). Kristeligt Folkeparti was established in

1970 as a direct and explicit reaction against these tendencies in Danish society. The struggle against liberal abortion policies seems to have been particularly important. Moreover, the programme presented by the party stressed the importance of continued confessional religious instruction at all levels of the school system; sexual instruction was to be 'marriage oriented'; 'border control of hippies' was to be made tougher; both private and public consumption was to be cut back; and tax and inheritance legislation was to encourage people to save (*Nordisk kontakt* 1971: 10, p. 615).

To summarise then, the emergence of Christian parties in Scandinavia can be characterised in the following way:

1 The Norwegian party became the archetype which largely set the standards for the programmatic orientation of the parties, and it inspired the establishment of the other parties.
2 The parties acquired the character of 'protest parties' from the beginning; they capitalised on negative reactions to current social phenomena and gathered strength from debates on these questions.
3 The parties at no time represented the 'official standpoint of the Church' or some sort of average opinion among church members. The centre of gravity at all times lay among nonconformist and revivalist groups and among the lay activists of the Lutheran State Churches. There were some clearly negative reactions on the part of the Church against the formation of the parties. This was at least in part explicable in terms of the support the Church had traditionally received from the conservative and agrarian parties, which were now presented with competition. Seen from the point of view of the average voter or church member, the Christian parties can be said to have stood out as an exclusive society. In contradistinction to the Christian Democratic parties on the continent, the Nordic Christian parties represented a demonstratively and aggressively Christian posture within their national settings.

Representation: sources of strength and weakness

Electoral law and the Christian parties

Since 1945, when the Norwegian party launched its first nation-wide electoral campaign, it has never had less than ten seats[1] in the Storting. The peak was reached in 1973 with twenty-one seats; after the 1989 election the party was represented by fourteen MPs. The absence of an electoral barrier which stipulates a minimum share of the vote necessary for parliamentary representation from the very beginning made Kristelig Folkeparti a realistic alternative for the electorate.

The Finnish SKL has also benefited from the liberal electoral laws. To be sure, the d'Hondt Method which continues to be applied in Finland (the other three countries have switched to the Saint Laguë variety) to a certain extent favours the largest parties. On the other hand, there is no barrier in

Finland either. Moreover, the parties are entirely free to form electoral alliances with each other, and this is decided at the constituency level depending on the regional relationships among the parties. The Finnish Christian League received its first seat in Parliament in 1970 through an electoral alliance with the Centre Party despite the low Christian share of the total vote. Since then, the party has been one of the most active and successful participants in electoral alliances (Noponen, 1988, p. 111). After the 1991 election the Christian League had eight seats in the 200 seat Eduskunta, a result of highly favourable electoral alliances.

It is in Sweden that the electoral law has created a major obstacle for the Christian party. The first electoral result of the KDS, 1.8 per cent in 1964, was far from impressive; still, it brought the party reasonably close to its first seat in Parliament. Four years later, after a thoroughgoing constitutional reform, the prospects seemed hopeless despite the fact that the KDS had maintained its share of the vote. The 4 per cent barrier clause which had been introduced seemed at once to put parliamentary representation far beyond the reach of the Christian Democrats (Johansson, 1985, pp. 221–41). The electoral alliance between the KDS and the Centre Party, which gave the Christians their first seat in the Riksdag, was criticised by the social democrats as being unlawful. The 1991 election finally lifted the KDS easily over the threshold and made the party a factor to be taken into account even from the point of view of electoral arithmetic.

The Danish party in 1971 barely reached the 2 per cent limit required for representation, but it fell a few hundred votes short of gaining a seat in the Folketing. In elections since then, it has managed to gain and maintain parliamentary representation; in a few instances, its share of the vote has fallen dangerously close to the 2 per cent threshold. The 1990 election saw the party winning the same number of seats (four) as at the previous election.

Electoral peaks: Christian parties as a 'system protest'

The 1970s brought the greatest electoral success ever for the Danish, Norwegian and Finnish parties. In the first two countries, the rise started in 1973 and reached its peak in the following elections (1975 and 1977, respectively). The Finnish party followed suit a couple of years later. In Sweden, by contrast, the comparable rise of the KDS came considerably later. There was, to be sure, a weak but noticeable upward trend through the 1980s. However, this trend is dwarfed by the electoral success of the KDS in 1991.

The fact that the Swedish party suddenly managed to surpass the electoral threshold without the help of any electoral alliances, can only be understood in terms of a more general electoral protest against the 'system'. It can, however, be argued, that the best electoral results of Scandinavian Christian Democracy are (in all cases) an expression of such protest. The ascendancy started in 1973 in Norway and Denmark, in the wake of a heated debate about EC membership; parallel to this, the dominant Social Democrats met with their greatest electoral disasters in the entire post-war era. Danish Social Democracy plunged from 37 per cent of the vote to 25 per cent two years later; in Norway, the Labour Party lost eleven percentage points as compared to 1969 and wound up with 35 per cent of the vote. When Sweden repeated the pattern in 1991 the Social Democrats did not suffer quite as dramatic a loss: from 43.3 per cent in 1988 to 37.6 per cent. Nevertheless, this was the poorest electoral perform-ance for the Social Democrats since 1928. The election was preceded by a number of 'scandals' and debates about betrayed promises in which the Social Democratic Party was portrayed in a very poor light. The dominant atmosphere surrounding the election was one of disillusionment with the prolonged social democratic rule in the country.

The Finnish party system lacks a clearly dominant party comparable to the social democratic parties in the other three countries. Nevertheless, the Christian electoral peak in 1979 can be interpreted in terms of a similar protest against the political 'establishment'. The year before, the position of President Urho Kekkonen as the real power centre in Finnish politics had been manifested visibly as all major parties rallied behind him at the presidential election. The Christian League had, however, nominated its own candidate for the presidency, the party leader Raino Westerholm. His campaign was generally deemed to be competent and serious, and his share of the vote was more than double that of the Christian vote in the 1975 parliamentary elections. A major part of the protest against the lack of real alternatives in the 1978 presidential elections had apparently been ex-pressed through votes for Westerholm (whom nobody expected to really challenge Kekkonen). In the 1979 election, the Christian League evidently managed to hold some of the extra votes its presidential candidate had secured the year before.

The electoral successes of the Scandinavian Christian parties seem to confirm Fisher's proposition (1980, p. 610) about the connection between the proliferation of minor parties and the decline of major parties. In Denmark, Norway and Sweden, the Christian electoral peak coincides with protests against the dominant party. Generally speaking, these elec-toral successes can be explained with reference to the fact that the parties managed to capitalise – in addition to the original moral appeal – on a more general political protest.

Electoral geography

The electoral geography of Scandinavian Christian Democracy is stable over time, but one cannot really speak of an unambiguous Scandinavian pattern (see Figure 7.1). The strongholds of the Norwegian party have always been the western and southern parts of the country, particularly Hordaland county in the west. Large portions of the narrow coastal strip in central and northern Norway have also seen Christian voting above the national average. The weak spots of the party are equally easy to pinpoint: east Norway, i.e. Oslo and the counties surrounding it in the north and the east, has consistently displayed Christian shares of the vote below the national average. The exception has been the Östfold county in the extreme southeast. In Stein Rokkan's classic conceptual map of Norwegian politics (1967, pp. 367–444), Kristelig Folkeparti is undoubtedly a party of the 'cultural periphery' in the west and the south.

A look at the electoral geography of the Finnish SKL may at first glance point in the opposite direction: it is in the southern half of the country that the party's electoral support has reached the highest level. In the real periphery of the north and the east it has been considerably more difficult for the SKL to gain an electoral foothold. In particula, Oulu and Lapland counties in the north have been difficult to conquer electorally; this is notable, since these are the strongholds of Leastadianism, one of the most important revivalist movements inside the Finnish Lutheran Church. Still, it would be an exaggeration to depict the SKL as a party of the centre. Its main strongholds have been the Kymi and St Michael counties; although situated in the southern half of the country, they certainly do not belong to the core of urban Finland. Rather, the electoral geography of the Finnish Christian Party might be characterised as 'semi-peripheral'.

Over a long period, the electoral geography of the KDS bore a striking resemblance to the map of Swedish nonconformism: the counties of Västerbotten and Jönköping in the north and in central south Sweden, respectively, were the main strongholds of both. This means that electorally the party relied more on the periphery than on the centre, although Jönköping at least can not be considered as a part of the extreme periphery. The 1991 election brought about a major change, as the party advanced strongly and uniformly across the country, including such previously weak spots as Stockholm and the areas surrounding it. Nevertheless, the greatest growth occurred in the traditional stronghold in Jönköping county. In this electoral district, the KDS is now the third largest party, quite comparable to the Conservatives; only the Social Democrats are stronger within this region.

The Danish Christian Party has consistently had its strongholds on the west coast of Jutland. The island of Bornholm in the Baltic Sea has also given support above the national average. In other parts of the country, particularly in the Copenhagen area, Kristeligt Folkeparti has met with little success. The Danish party clearly repeats the Norwegian and earlier Swedish pattern with strongholds in the nonconformist and revivalist areas of the periphery.

In sum, it appears as if the Norwegian and Danish parties face the greatest difficulties in the populous areas in and around the national capitals. Until the last election, this was true of the KDS in Sweden as well. The Finnish party has, by contrast, had higher shares of the vote in the southern half of the country than in the northern periphery.

Voters and sympathisers

When it comes to individual-level data Norway once again occupies a special position thanks to the fact that Kristelig Folkeparti is large enough

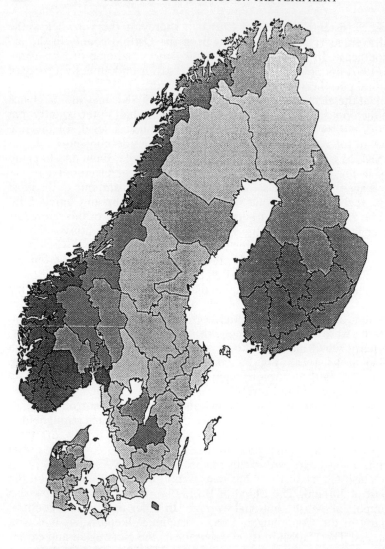

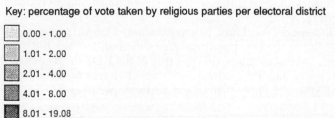

Key: percentage of vote taken by religious parties per electoral district

	0.00 - 1.00
	1.01 - 2.00
	2.01 - 4.00
	4.01 - 8.00
	8.01 - 19.08

Figure 7.1 The electoral geography of Scandinavian Christian Democracy

Source: Norwegian Social Science Data Services, Bergen.

to be represented by a sufficient number of respondents in a normal sample survey. Generally, access to individual-level data has been best for Norway and Denmark and most limited in the case of Finland. Since identical data sets do not exist for the four countries, no strictly numerical comparison will be presented here. Instead, characteristic features of Christian party voters and sympathisers will be presented in a less stringent form for each country separately.

Data for Norway are from electoral surveys in connection with the 1973 and 1989 parliamentary elections. Table 7.2, summarises some characteristic features of Christian party sympathisers. The continuity over the decade and a half covered by table 7.2 is striking. The archetype of a Christian party supporter in Norway is still an elderly woman in western Norway, married or a widow. She frequently speaks the more 'peripheral' *nynorsk* variety of Norwegian. By the same token, one would not expect to find a Christian party sympathiser who is a younger industrial worker, divorced and living in eastern Norway.

Table 7.2 Christian party sympathisers in Norway, 1973 and 1989: characteristic features

Variable	1973	1989
Sex	Women over-represented	Women over-represented
Age	50 and older over-represented	50 and older over-represented
Marital status	Married and widowed persons overrepresented	Married and widowed persons over-represented
Occupational distribution	Fairly even, industry under-represented	Fairly even, industry under-represented
Level of income	Lowest brackets over-represented	Medium
Region	South and west over-represented	South and west over-represented
Dialect	*Nynorsk* over-represented	*Nynorsk* over-represented
Political interest	Medium	Medium
Second party	Center Party over-represented	Conservatives, Center Party over-represented
Attitude towards EC membership	'No' strongly over-represented	'No' over-represented
Attitude towards alcohol	Teetotalism strongly over-represented	Teetotalism strongly over-represented

Source: Norwegian Election Studies 1973, 1989 N: 1973=177, 1989=107

On moral questions – here represented by the attitude towards alcohol – the followers of Kristelig Folkeparti are in a category of their own. By contrast, they hardly differ from national averages concerning socio-economic characteristics or general political and social views. They are least numerous in industrial occupations, and especially in 1973 they were over-represented in the lower income brackets. Generally speaking, however, their distribution over occupational groups and social classes came close to the national averages. Moreover, as regards class identification, political interest and attitudes towards immigration, Christian party sympathisers choose a middle course; unfortunately, longitudinal data are not available on all these questions. The deviations in moral questions and those concerning age, sex and regional identification do not spill over into general political attitudes. In the light of this empirical evidence it seems reasonable to characterise Kristelig Folkeparti as a party of the political centre.

The Danish surveys which are available contain only a limited number of Christian party voters. In the 1981 Danish Election Study only twenty-five respondents said they had voted for Kristeligt Folkeparti. The survey data for 1988 contain sixty-three Christian party voters. Even given these limitations it seems clear that the Danish party is also a 'women's party', and that particularly the youngest age groups (those under thirty years) are clearly under-represented. In the 1981 sample western Jutland and the island of Lolland seem somewhat over-represented; the 1988 survey points to an under-representation for Zealand including the Copenhagen area and for the island of Funen, whereas northern and western Jutland again are over-represented. Also in Denmark, married and widowed people are over-represented among Christian party voters. As to occupation and income level, there is some over-representation in 1988 for officials and pensioners; in 1973 as well as fifteen years later, Christian voters represented the lower rather than the highest income brackets. Again, as for political interest and attitudes towards social and economic policies, Christian voters came close to national averages.

As for Sweden, Göran Johansson's dissertation (1985, pp. 221–279) contains data for all elections from 1964 until 1982. However, only two variables are included: occupational group and previous party choice. Sample size is limited: between thirty-five and sixty KDS voters depending on the election. In one respect, nevertheless, the results are unambiguous. The largest single group of KDS voters during this period consisted of mid-level officials. This group was consistently over-represented among KDS voters. A survey conducted by Swedish Television in connection with the 1991 election shows that the KDS has managed to make inroads into all occupational categories. The percentage change was greatest among farmers, but in absolute figures the greatest KDS gains came from officials (ValU91/STV). It was noted above that in 1991 the KDS made a general breakthrough in the geography of Swedish elections. The survey results indicate that the party has managed to break some barriers in a socio-economic respect as well.

Finnish survey data are scarce and the small size of the samples troublesome if one wishes to study SKL voters. The number of respondents who say that they vote for the SKL is usually twenty to thirty in a normal survey. This being the case, questions pertaining to socio-economic or attitudinal correlates of SKL voting are difficult to analyse in a statistically reliable way. Even with these limitations in mind one may note that SKL voters in both 1973 and in 1991 came closer to national averages than the supporters of any other party as to occupational distribution. In 1973 the majority (64 per cent) of Christian League voters were workers, in 1991 officials were the largest category (54 per cent) (Sänkiaho, 1991, pp. 38). This corresponds to general social change in Finland. For class identification and income categories there was some over-representation for a working class identification among Christian voters. In 1991 this was no longer the case; Christian League voters had a class identification corresponding to averages among voters at large. A constant feature found in 1983, 1987 and 1991 is the over-representation of voters who describe themselves as low-wage earners (Sänkiaho, 1991, p. 41). What there is of survey data for Finland indicates that Christian voters in Finland are to be found somewhere in between the working class and the lower bourgeoisie.

From what parties have Christian parties in Scandinavia gained votes? Unfortunately there are no data concerning, for instance, the important period immediately after World War II in Norway. Data for more recent periods are, however, available to a certain extent. The Norwegian Election Studies for 1973 and 1989 show that the electorate of Kristelig Folkeparti has been highly faithful to the party. Mobility has concerned the two parties which are closest to the Christian Party in general political terms: the Centre Party and Venstre. These are the two parties who have lost voters to the Christian Party. As for Finland, there are transition matrices for 1979–83 and 1987–91. As for the 1983 election the main conclusion is that the SKL lost votes and that the remaining voters had voted for the party already in 1979. There is greater mobility in the 1991 election; the Christian League seems mainly to have attracted previous non-voters but also some voters from minor parties, including the populist Rural Party (Risbjerg Thomsen et al., 1990, pp. 60–61; Berglund, 1991, p. 338). As for Sweden, Johansson (1985, pp. 221–73) demonstrates that the KDS gained votes from other centrist parties, while at the same time an important part of the KDS vote originated from newly enfranchised voters and previous non-voters. The 1991 election again brought about a change, as practically all parties seem to have lost votes to the KDS. The percentage loss was greatest for the liberals and the Centre Party. Of roughly equal importance to the KDS were, however, the voters it won from the Social Democrats (ValU91/STV). In Denmark, finally, Christian voters have normally originated from the Radical Liberal Party and to some extent from the populist Progress Party (Risbjerg Thomsen et al., 1990, pp. 52–3). A common feature of the four countries is that they have normally not won votes from the major parties, especially the Social Democrats. In this respect, the 1991 Swedish election represents a change. Nevertheless, the typical loser to the Christian parties has been a small or medium-sized party in the political centre. Fisher's thesis that the decline of major parties has been conducive to the proliferation of minor parties is of course true for the Christian parties as well; this decline has made it easier for minor parties to gain an electoral foothold. In terms of direct voter mobility, however, the flows between major parties and the Christian parties have, nevertheless, been limited.

The Christian voter in Scandinavia is naturally primarily singled out through his or her attitudes to questions of morality and ethics, be they related to alcohol, sex, marriage or school. In Norway and Denmark, the Christian party supporters have a clearer regional identity than in Finland; the Swedish party has recently managed to become genuinely nationwide in its electoral appeal. Women and older age cohorts are over-represented among Christian party sympathisers, but in socio-economic or general political terms they are not particularly different from the national average. Typically, the Christian electorate consists of the lower bourgeoisie plus some farmers and non-industrial workers. The traditional representatives of these groups, the centrist parties, have most clearly felt electoral competition from the Christian parties.

Relevance: the Christian parties in coalition politics

The relevance of parties is determined by their numerical strength and their utility. Numerical strength is easy to pinpoint and measure; 'utility' defies every attempt at exact definition. The stronger a party is, the more difficult it becomes to ignore. Being big is, however, of little use if a party is not useful, if ideological and programmatic abysses separate it from other parties or if it in other respects represents unwelcome competition for other parties.

Nordic parliamentarianism at large has drifted increasingly farther away from the classic Anglo-Saxon ideal of alternating majorities. This has in fact never been a reality in Finland. During recent decades, Finnish politics has made a virtue out of the necessity of coalitions, which has made for considerable stability in cabinet politics. The other three countries, by contrast, have moved towards increasing instability with a stronger element of minority parliamentarianism and temporary coalitions in individual policy sectors and around separate issues. The process at large has increased the potential significance of minor parties as coalition partners or as allies for parliamentary oppositions (Damgaard, 1990b, pp. 176–90).

Kristelig Folkeparti in Norway is the only one of the four parties which at no time has been a *quantité négligeable* in the parliamentary game. In the entire post-war era, the party has been one of the central actors of the divided non-socialist camp in Norway. As the prolonged social democratic reign ended in 1963, the Christian Party entered into the short-lived bourgeois minority coalition led by John Lyng. Since then, the party has participated in five out of the six bourgeois cabinets; the exception was Kåre Willoch's conservative one-party cabinet in 1981–3. In 1972–3 the Christian party leader Lars Korvald headed a bourgeois coalition formed by non-socialist opponents of EC membership after the majority of the

voters had turned down full Norwegian membership in the Community (Rommetvedt, 1990, pp. 51–4).
The central factor in the arithmetic of Norwegian coalition politics has been the predominance of the left. Up until 1961, the Social Democrats commanded a majority of their own in Parliament. Even after that, they have more often than not been able to count on the support of Socialistisk Venstreparti on the extreme left. In all situations, the co-operation of the Christian Party has been a necessary but normally not sufficient condition for a non-socialist majority cabinet. Two such cabinets have appeared: the first one led by Per Borten in 1965–71, the second led by Kåre Willoch in 1983–6.

Up until the crisis created by the EC referendum the distances between Norwegian parties were clear indeed: all bourgeois parties stood closer to each other than to Social Democracy in terms of voting behaviour in Parliament. Since about 1972–3 these distances have been blurred; among other things, there has been a *rapprochement* between the Social Democrats and the Christian Party (Rommetvedt, 1990, p. 88). Among non-socialist parties, European integration and regional policies are some of the important issues that have given rise to new conflicts. The conservative stands on these issues differ widely from those of the centrist parties, particularly Kristelig Folkeparti. Simultaneously, the emergence of the populist Progress Party has split the non-socialist front further and made the coalition puzzle even more complicated. Today, the crucial question of Norwegian policies *vis-à-vis* the European Community constitutes a watershed right across the non-socialist camp. Christian policies are clearly more restrictive than those of the conservatives and the Progress Party. Another topical issue which may develop into a deep conflict around the very core of Christian ideas is the fact that the conservatives have signalled their readiness for a programmatic reorientation concerning the relationship between Church and State.

The relevance of the Norwegian Christian Party in coalition politics seems to be decreasing. Their parliamentary strength has declined since their heyday in the 1970s; at the same time, their utility has also been called into question owing to conflicts around central political issues.

Danish coalition politics were shaken even more thoroughly as a result of electoral protest of the early 1970s. The Danish party system has since had a 'Finnish appearance'; in contrast to Finnish politics, however, broad coalitions bridging the socialist-non-socialist divide have been all but absent in Denmark.[2] The power centre of Danish politics has increasingly been found in Parliament itself. More and more, Danish politics have been based on deals and agreements inside the Folketing on individual issues and policy sectors; varying constellations of parties have supported such deals (Damgaard, 1990a, pp. 15–17).

The entry of Kristeligt Folkeparti into the Danish parliament in 1973 was itself an element in the dramatic loss of political stability in the country. The party at once became a player in a highly complicated political game, where the main goal was to create temporary majorities for individual decisions. Up until 1982, the Christian Party actively participated in such deals with both non-socialist and Social Democratic minority cabinets. In 1982, the conservative party leader Poul Schlüter managed to form a cabinet including his own party, the Agrarian Liberal Venstre, the Centre Democrats and the Christian Party. This was formally a minority cabinet, but in 1983–7 it commanded a *de facto* majority in the Folketing. In certain important policy areas, including defence policy, however, the cabinet must rely on 'alternative majorities'. The electoral success of the populist Progress Party in 1988 once again complicated the party pattern further and the four-party coalition resigned (Damgaard, 1990a, pp. 23–4). The 1990 election points in the direction of a renewed Social Democratic ascendancy; together with the increased complexity of the party pattern on the non-socialist side this may render it very difficult to achieve broad bourgeois coalitions. Consequently, it may come to limit the role of the Christian Party in coalition politics as well.

Finnish parliamentarism has run counter to the development elsewhere in Scandinavia. The fractionalisation of the party system has, to be sure, increased in Finland as well. The response has, however, been radically different from that in the neighbouring countries. Instead of unstable minority parliamentarism, the past two decades have seen rule by cabinets based on considerable majorities in Parliament. Cabinets across the socialist-non-socialist gap have been the norm rather than the exception in Finland. A major impetus behind the process leading to an overarching political consensus was the entrance of protest parties into the Eduskunta in the early 1970s. These consensual mechanisms among the major parties have naturally restricted the potential of the Christian League to exert parliamentary influence by tipping the balance in favour of one of the blocs (Anckar, 1990, pp. 141–8).

Finnish parliamentarianism displays a greater number of critical thresholds than normal majority parliamentarianism. This is due to the constitutional stipulations which provide a minority of one-third of the MPs with effective means of obstructing legislative work. A minor party can therefore be pivotal in three different ways: it can provide a cabinet with an absolute majority, it can help give it a two-thirds majority, or it can help the opposition to reach the necessary minimum required to obstruct legislation.

The Christian League has had the possibility of playing a pivotal role only once during its parliamentary era. In 1979–82 Mauno Koivisto led a cabinet which was one seat short of a two-thirds majority in Parliament. However, there was very little in the way of an effective opposition in Parliament despite the fact that the parties outside the cabinet commanded the necessary minority of sixty-seven seats. For instance, these parties did not issue one single joint declaration (Anckar, 1990, pp. 154–5). One main reason was the fear of the small non-socialist parties that such co-operation would give them the image of mere appendages of the largest opposition party, the conservatives (p. 156). In sum, the Christians have normally been unable to play a pivotal role in opposition; when it was arithmetically possible they did not wish to play that role.

Moreover, even the entrance of the Christian League into government in

1991 emphasises the supplementary role of the party. Cabinet majorities normally require the participation of at least one of the minor parties in Finland. In order not to give a minor party (normally the Swedish People's Party, which is a more or less permanent cabinet participant) dispro- portionate influence, the larger parties frequently include two minor par- ties in the cabinet. These balance each other out, since one of them is, strictly speaking, superfluous. Consequently, when Esko Aho included a Christian League minister in his cabinet, a major motive was to make sure that they toe the line. To be sure, this gave the Christians an opportunity to influence policy in the field of development aid, where they presently hold a cabinet post. Nevertheless, they are now expected to toe the line in all important issues in order not to risk being ousted from government.

The KDS in Sweden became relevant overnight in 1991. Before that, the party had been a *quantité négligeable* in Swedish parliamentary politics. The entrance of the KDS into the bourgeois coalition led by Carl Bildt was not, however, sufficient to give the cabinet a majority status. Bildt must rely on the support of either the left or the controversial populist party New Democracy for parliamentary majorities. The KDS is clearly stronger in the cabinet than its Finnish counterpart. Its parliamentary strength makes it an equal partner to both the Centre Party and the liberals. Only the Conservatives clearly carry more weight in the cabinet. The three posts held by the Christians – communication, the interior and development aid – do not belong to either the most prestigious or the most peripheral ministerial posts. The KDS road to parliament and cabinet was character- ised by an energetic attempt to change the profile of the party; it no longer wished to stand out as a Christian single-issue movement but a humanist and liberal party with a pronounced interest in social welfare questions (*Nordisk kontakt* 1991: 9, pp. 84–6). In the negotiations preceding the formation of the cabinet, the KDS displayed great flexibility avoiding all stands which might endanger the party's entry into cabinet politics.

In sum, the role of Christian parties in Nordic coalition politics does not constitute a clear pattern. The Norwegian party has in several instances in the post-war era played the role which the Swedish KDS assumed in 1991. At the same time, there are features in Norwegian politics today which may render the position of Kristelig Folkeparti more difficult in the future. In Denmark the Christian Party carries limited parliamentary weight, but it has been able to play a role thanks to the complicated parliamentary arithmetic. The Finnish SKL participates in the cabinet 'at the mercy' of the larger parties; its role is clearly supplementary. The rapid rise of the KDS to government position rests on one single election result; it is too early yet to judge whether this reflects a passing electoral protest or a more permanent change in the attitudes of the Swedish electorate.

Concluding remarks

The Christian parties of Scandinavia emerged as parties of moral protest, and they have more or less retained this image through the years. To be a Christian party voter in the Nordic countries has meant a stand which goes beyond conformist church membership or an identification with general Christian values. The Christian parties in Scandanavia have been far more deviant than their Continental counterparts in their national settings. Church and religion contain little political potential that might be exploited by parties in Scandinavia; the Christian parties lack the natural historical and structural preconditions on which Christian Democracy further south has thrived. The threshold created by the active stands taken by the Scandinavian parties on moral questions continues to be too high for the average voter.

The Scandinavian Christian parties have largely retained their characteristic voter profiles: over-representation for women and elderly side by side with average distributions in relation to socio-economic groups and general political attitudes. How clear and definite the recent Swedish change may be is uncertain at the moment.

The traditionally strongest of the four parties, Kristelig Folkeparti in Norway has gathered strength from the classic coincident cleavages of Norwegian politics; religious revivalism, economic structure and language make for dynamic 'politics of cultural defence' outside the dominant eastern part of the country, particularly in western Norway. The Swedish and Danish parties have also had their geographic strongholds, but these have not been as extensive and socially dynamic as the western and southern peripheries in Norway.

While the core of Christian party support has always consisted of moral protest, the parties have reached their electoral peaks thanks to more general waves of political protest. The turbulence created by the EC membership controversy in Denmark and Norway in the early 1970s paved the way for the best electoral results of the Danish and Norwegian parties. The protest against the dominant position of President Kekkonen and against the lack of real political alternatives largely explains the best results of the Finnish SKL at the end of the 1970s. Similarly, it is difficult to understand the rise of the KDS in Sweden without reference to the general political protest in Sweden at the beginning of the 1990s.

As for coalition politics, the best days of the Norwegian and Danish parties may be over. The complex party structure which has in itself been a precondition of their 'relevance' has acquired traits which make it more difficult for the Christians to play a pivotal role. The cabinet participation of the Finnish party is not necessary for the survival of the government coalition; the Christian League is in every respect supplementary in the present coalition. The KDS is, to be sure, more important in the parliamentary game in Sweden; nevertheless, it is not able to provide the present government coalition with the necessary majority.

It would therefore be greatly exaggerated to speak of a general upswing in Christian politics in Scandinavia. On the contrary, three of the parties face considerable difficulties in trying to reach beyond their traditional supporters; the combination of fundamental religious homogeneity and the image of the parties as moral vigilantes is a definite disadvantage in this regard. By and large, the Danish, Finnish and Norwegian parties lead a defensive struggle against increasingly difficult odds.

Against this background, the recent success of the KDS in Sweden is all the more noteworthy. In connection with the 1991 campaign, it seemed as if the party had indeed managed to define a political line beyond the traditional moralist message. The general humanistic approach offered by Alf Svensson and his party appears a new element in the Swedish political debate. Could it become a source of lasting success for the KDS?

The electoral record of the non-socialist parties in Sweden certainly calls for caution in this regard. The Conservatives, the Centre Party and the Liberals have had considerable ups and downs during recent decades. The Environmentalist Party fell from the Riksdag in 1991 after a rise largely similar to that of the KDS today. The non-socialist parties are each other's major rivals in electoral terms; in this competition, the KDS may soon find itself on the losing side. The electoral wind which blew in favour of the KDS this time is no different from the relatively recent but already vanished successes of the other parties. If and when the wind turns against the KDS we will suddenly be reminded of the fact that 7 per cent of the vote lies only three percentage points above the most critical of all thresholds.

Acknowledgements

Part of the data used in this publication originates from *Norwegian Election Studies* 1973 and 1989. Data in anonymised form have been made available through *Norwegian Social Science Data Services* (NSD) in Bergen, Norway. The material was originally gathered and processed by the *Norwegian Central Bureau of Statistics*.

Individual-level data on Denmark originate from *Danish Election Studies* 1981 and 1988. These were also made available through the NSD with the kind permission of the *Danish Data Archives* (DDA) in Odense, Denmark.

Data and cartographic material on regional variations in Christian party support originate from the *Nordic Database for Regional Time Series* (NDRT) created and made available by the NSD.

While all these institutions and their staffs deserve my warmest thanks for their valuable assistance, they bear no responsibility for the analyses and interpretations of the data in this study.

The study was carried out while the author was a Visiting Research Fellow at the Instititute of Comparative Politics at the NSD in Bergen. Special thanks are due to Jostein Ryssevik, Bjarne Öymyr, Lars Holm, Dag Kiberg, Atle Alvheim and Björn Henrichsen.

An earlier version of this article was published in *Scandinavian Political Studies* Number 4/1992.

Notes

1 The number of seats in the Storting was 150 until 1973, 155 in 1973–85 and 157 in 1985–89; in 1989 it was increased to 165.

2 The exception is the 1978 coalition between the Social Democrats and Venstre; this was also a minority cabinet.

References

Anckar, D., 1990, Finland, dualism och konsensus, in Erik Damgaard (ed.), *Parlamentarisk forandring i Norden*, Universitetsforlaget, Oslo.
Arter, D., 1980, The Finnish Christian League, party or 'anti-party'?, *Scandinavian Political Studies*, 3 (2): 143–162.
Arter, D., 1987, *Politics and policy-making in Finland*, Wheatsheaf Books, Worcester.
Berglund, S., 1991, The Finnish parliamentary election of March 1991, *Scandinavian Political Studies*, 14 (4): 335–342.
Damgaard, E., 1990a, Parlamentarismens danske tilstande, in Erik Damgaard, (ed.), *Parlamentarisk förändring i Norden*, Universitetsforlaget, Oslo.
Damgaard, E., 1990b, Parlamentarisk forandring i Norden, in Erik Damgaard (ed.), *Parlamentarisk förändring i Norden*, Universitetsforlaget, Oslo.
Fisher, S. L., 1980, The 'decline of parties' thesis and the role of minor parties, in Peter Merkl (ed.), *Western European party systems*, The Free Press, New York.
Flanagan, S. and Dalton R. J., 1990, Models of change, in Peter Mair (ed.), *The West European party system*, Oxford University Press, Oxford.
Gustafsson, G., 1985, Utvecklingslinjer på det religiösa området i Norden – en jämförelse, in Göran Gustafsson (ed.), *Religiös förändring i Norden*, Liber, Stockholm.
Johansson, G. V., 1985, *Kristen demokrati på svenska. Studier om KDS tillkomst och utveckling 1964–1982*, CWK Gleerup, Lund.
Karvonen, L., 1981, *Med vårt västra grannland som förebild. En undersökning av policydiffusion från Sverige till Finland*, Åbo Akademis Förlag, Åbo.
Lijphart, A., 1990, Dimensions of ideology in European party systems, in Peter Mair (ed.), *The West European party system*, Oxford University Press, Oxford.
Lomeland, A. R., 1971, *Kristelig Folkeparti blir til*, Universitetsforlaget, Oslo.
Madeley, J., 1977, Scandinavian Christian democracy, throwback or portent?, *European Journal of Political Research*, 5: 267–286.
Madeley, J., 1982, Politics and the pulpit. The case of protestant Europe, in Suzanne Berger (ed.), *Religion in West European politics*, Frank Cass, London.
Noponen, M., 1988, *Suomen kansanedustusjärjestelmä*, WSOY, Juva.
Nordisk kontakt (official bulletin of the Nordic Council) 1971:10.
Nordisk kontakt (official bulletin of the Nordic Council) 1991:9.
Pedersen, M., 1982, Towards a new typology of party lifespans and minor parties, *Scandinavian Political Studies*, 5 (1): 1–16.
Riis, O., 1985, Danmark, in Göran Gustafsson (ed.), *Religiös förändring i Norden*, Liber, Stockholm.
Risbjerg Thomsen, S. et al., 1990, Assessing the validity of the logit method for ecological inference, in Sten Berglund and Sören Risbjerg Thomsen (eds), *Modern political ecological analysis*, Åbo Academy Press, Åbo.
Rommetvedt, H., 1990, Norge: fra konsensuspreget flertallsparlamentarisme til konfliktfylt mindretallsparlamentarisme, in Erik Damgaard (ed), *Parlamentarisk förändring i Norden*, Universitetsforlaget, Oslo.
Rokkan, S., 1967, Geography, religion and social class, crosscutting cleavages in Norwegian politics, in Seymour Martin Lipset and Stein Rokkan (eds), *Party systems and voter alignments, cross-national perspectives*, The Free Press, New York.

Saeter, O. 1985, *Samling om verdier. Kristelig Folkepartis Historie 1933–1983*, Valo Forlag A. S., Oslo.

Sundback, S., 1991, *Utträdet ur Finlands lutherska kyrka. Kyrkomedlemskapet under religionsfrihet och sekularisering*, Åbo Akademis Förlag, Åbo.

Sänkiaho, R., 1991, Puolueiden kannattajakunnan rakenne, *Riksdagsmannavalet 1991. Statistikcentralen, Val 1991*, 2. Helsingfors, 37–45.

ValU91/STV. Unpublished electoral survey of 1991 election conducted by Swedish Television.

Wörlund, I., 1988, The election to the Swedish riksdag 1988, *Scandinavian Political Studies*, 12 (1): 77–83.

8

THE ANTINOMIES OF LUTHERAN POLITICS: THE CASE OF NORWAY'S CHRISTIAN PEOPLE'S PARTY

John T.S. Madeley

It is the principal purpose of this chapter to examine the impact of the religious factor on Norwegian politics by paying particular attention to the Christian People's Party (CPP) and the circumstances which gave it birth (Madeley, 1991, pp. 34–5). The Norwegian party was the first, and continues to be the most significant, of the four parties which exemplify the Scandinavian species of the genus Christian Democracy[1] and as the prime exemplar it presents a particularly interesting case of what might be called the antinomies of Lutheran politics: the articulation of contradictory doctrines and impulses with which any Christian political movement must come to terms but which in the context of Lutheranism almost takes on the form of a collective neurosis. In tracing the roots of this phenomenon, it is hoped that the specifically religious aspects of the party will come into focus in a way that previous treatments of it have tended to obscure or misrepresent.

In his article 'Geography, religion and social class: crosscutting cleavages in Norwegian politics', Stein Rokkan provided a classic account of the development of the Norwegian electoral cleavage system from which it is possible to extract a brief genealogy of the CPP over the four political generations or phases prior to the party's actual birth in the 1930s (Rokkan, 1967). In the first phase, which culminated with the first emergence of mass parties in the early 1880s, the forerunners of the CPP ranged themselves with urban radicals and nationalist intellectuals in the great Left Party coalition which prosecuted the struggle for parliamentary supremacy against the crown. In the second the same forerunners, constituting a moderate wing of spokesmen for traditional religious and moral values, split from the pure majority of the left in 1888, only four years after it had achieved its great victory (Rokkan, 1967, p. 391). In the third, spanning the period from national independence in 1905 to the 1920s, the earlier division between Pures and Moderates subsided as the core of the 'Left' party united in defence of the rural counterculture, an amalgam of prohibitionism, lay activism and support for the rural linguistic standard (pp. 391–4). Finally in the fourth the fundamentalists of the west found it increasingly difficult to stay within the old party as the repeal of prohibition and the rise of the secularist Labour party set the stage for the formation of a distinctly religious party. A Christian People's party first appeared in 1933 (p. 399).

Rokkan argued that the regional bias of this religious-political tradition, reflected in its disproportionate strength in the south and west of the country, could only be explained in cultural terms although part of the variance could be accounted for by that region's peculiarities in terms of community structure and the nature of the primary economy (p. 415). In addition to being a stronghold of the rural language movement and fertile soil for the prohibition movement, the south and west had long constituted a bulwark for defence of Lutheran orthodoxy and pietistic fundamentalism agains the radicalising and secularising influences of the cities. Although the three related movements did not always pull together, their net impact on national politics was unmistakable: they all stood for the defence of rural values against the centralising forces triggered off through economic development and the strengthening of governmental agencies (pp. 415–7). So far as the religious component in this countercultural mix was concerned the tradition of resistance went back to the refounding of the nation in the early nineteenth century.

Religious life in Norway has ever since 1814 been marked by a polarisation between government-appointed clergymen and activists in revival movements, mission organisations and 'Free Churches'. The conflict between the established church and the fundamentalist organisations paralleled very closely the conflict between the King's officials and the old Left: there was the same rejection of central authority and the same assertion of the values and traditions of rural life against the corruption of the cities. (p. 419)

It is the starting point of this paper that this brief sketch of the origins and character of the CPP, which Rokkan never expanded on significantly, is open to considerable misinterpretation by readers who are not familiar with the peculiarties of the Lutheran tradition as it exists in Norway. Rokkan was translating for an English audience when he adopted the now common usage of the Anglo-American term 'fundamentalist', a term the denotative meaning of which does not accurately describe the dissident Lutheran tradition to which he refers. Similar caution is necessary in construing the term 'orthodox', the application of which to the more radical pietist groups associated with the origins of the CPP is, to say the least, controversial. More substantively the connection crucial in Rokkan's analysis between particular religious values and the values and traditions of rural life in Norway is open to serious question.

Mixing and matching religion and politics

For some, notably their political opponents, the Christian Democratic parties of Scandinavia have always been the illicit offspring of a *mésalliance* between religion and politics; for others, in particular their religious critics, they were the product of theological error rather than some crude miscegenation. Between the two conceptions of the proper relationship between the spheres of religion and politics, the one deriving predominantly from classical liberalism, and the other from Lutheran orthodoxy *proprie dictu* there are areas of both agreement and contradiction. The points of agreement arise from one of the few points of intersection and coincidence between the rival world views and concern the notion that the two spheres of religion and politics are distinct and should not be confused. The points of contradiction arise from all the other more fundamental considerations about the relevant political and religious concerns at issue in terms of which the relationship between liberalism and orthodox Lutheranism resembles more an ideological war of the world views than a simple area of disagreement. Implicated in this confrontation are many of the contrasts which make for a tension between tradition and modernity in Lutheran Scandinavia.

For the CPP's defenders meanwhile both types of objection were always argued to rest on mistaken premises regarding, at a general level, the question of the appropriate relationship between religion and politics in the context of liberal democracy and, in more particular terms, the issue of the nature and aims of the party itself. Properly understood and conscientiously practised, it is claimed, religion cannot but have implications for *all* aspects of an individual's life, including the public, political aspects; in a liberal democracy the natural vehicle for working out such implications and acting on them is the political party. It is accepted that, as both liberal and Lutheran critics insist, such a party should not become a vehicle for promoting unwarranted privileges for church institutions or for whipping religious adherents to act in accordance with the dictates of clerical authorities. Hence no attempt should be made to copy the patterns of confessional or clerical politics which were thought to be typical of many post-war Christian Democratic parties on the Continent. On the other hand, while it might be quite legitimate (if mistaken) for individual Christians to eschew the option of supporting a properly constituted religious party in favour of other parties which made no particular claim to religious inspiration – as in Fogarty's Anglo-Saxon type of Christian Democracy (Fogarty, 1957) – this carried no implication that a religious party as such was illegitimate. Thus, avoiding the Scylla of Continental confessional politics and the Charybdis of individual immersion in non-religious parties of the Anglo-Saxon variety, Scandinavian Christian Democracy ended up pioneering its own distinctive pattern of party politics. Unlike the Continental type they have no straightforward denominational ties and unlike the Anglo-Saxon type they take the organisational form of overtly religious parties (Madeley, 1977, p. 268).

Despite the lack of overt denominational ties, Norway's CPP and its Scandinavian sister parties cannot however escape the historic fate of being religious parties in overwhelmingly Lutheran societies where the orthodox view that religion and politics ought to be kept radically apart was long propounded. The non-denominational form the parties adopted helped to avoid one sort of objection, while it also had the advantage of being well suited to the religious situation in countries which, despite the high degree of inclusiveness of the national Lutheran churches, have become character-ised particularly among the activist minority by considerable religious pluralism.

As compared to the other principal confessional forms of Christianity in the modern world the Lutheran tradition is in fact notable for the historic weakness of its capacity to generate political activism out of religious commitment (Lipset, 1968, p. 219; Madeley, 1982, pp. 153–60). Thus Weber described Lutheranism as relatively indifferent to the world when contrasted with the active involvement and concern typical of Calvinism: Lutheranism lacked any motivation toward revolutionary attitudes in social or political relationships and any inclination toward rational reformist activity. Its teaching required one to maintain, both within the world and against it, the substance of salvation promised by one's faith, but did not require one to attempt a transformation of the world in any rationalised ethical direction (Weber, 1966, p. 199). In similar vein, Troeltsch wrote of Lutheranism's social impotence reflected in the fact that the Lutheran church concerned itself only with the question of the family and the household, which it felt ought to constitute the chief sphere for the development of the ethical virtues of Christianity. The regulation of the whole society is left to the government, which, strongly supported by Lutheranism, takes supreme control (Troeltsch, 1960, p. 562).

The distinctive doctrine which reinforced this intrinsically apolitical aspect of orthodox Lutheranism, the doctrine of the two realms or regi-ments, states that the Church (the spiritual realm) must confine itself to its allotted tasks and govern the soul and the conscience alone. The magistrate (the secular realm) rules over the other areas of human existence and for this realm the Church has no right to legislate. Lutheran theologians have emphasised the autonomy of the State. Certain fields of human activity have their own laws with which the Church has no right to interfere (Molland, 1959, p. 197). The attempt to return the Church to its primary spiritual tasks and remove the scandal of its entanglement with secular affairs was of course a princial aim of Luther's Reformation. For Roman Catholics from the Counter-Reformation on of course the cure was, at least until recently, seen as worse than the disease in that it effectively undermined, where it did not destroy the spiritual power of the Church and its officials, leaving it and them completely at the mercy of the temporal power.

In the areas such as Scandinavia, where it was unilaterally imposed virtually without opposition, the Lutheran Reformation did bring about a radical shift, a great declension, in the status of the Church; it was demoted from its former standing as the perfect society founded by Christ, the core of a great international ecclesiastical civilisation whose laws were held to be absolutely binding on all members of society of whatever station. In its place, under Luther and his successors the true church of the believers came to be presented as little more than the heavenly enclave of grace in the midst of the state which surrounds her on all sides with its might and right (Keller, 1936, p. 152). In the Lutheran view the invisible, true Church was to be distinguished from the temporal shell of the church institution, which had become corrupted under the papacy; the former, the mystical body of Christ, was constituted not by a priestly hierarchy charged with the administration of the means of divine grace but instead by the collectivity of the believers.

On one view indeed, so absolutely did Luther distinguish between the spiritual and the temporal that the realm of the spiritual vanished from sight. Every earthly manifestation of the spiritual life of Christians, words, deeds or institutions, are temporal things and within the jurisdiction of the temporal magistrate. Any visible and organised church that is soundly based on the Scriptures is, in a secondary sense, a true church. But so far as it is visible, it is a temporal thing. It is the duty of all secular princes to establish and maintain such churches. In doing this righteous work the prince may organise the church as he thinks fit in relation to all needs that are earthy and temporal (Allen, 1928, p. 24). The consequences of this new dispensation for the monarchies of the north was not only that they benefitted from the eclipse of a wealthy and powerful instititic which had been their principal rival for a millennium, and from the takeover of its enormous resources; they were also elevated and celebrated in the new climate of ideas which sacralised the state as much as it secularised the church.

In Lutheran thinking the state was not then presented as a secular power inherently hostile to the claims of the church, rather it was held to be a divine order instituted by God to maintain life and law and to prevent the world from being delivered into the hands of the devil and from falling into chaos (Keller, 1936, p. 165). The need for law was understood to arise in part out of natural law requirements for the maintenance of order. On the other hand, the law was also held to serve religious as well as temporal purposes. Both the law and the gospel derive from God and are the word of God. The gospel brings the tidings of salvation, while the law is to prepare man by making him conscious of his sins and evoking in him the deep despair which is necessary for the effectiveness of the gospel (Molland, 1959, p. 195). The Lutheran state was thus to be a Christian state with important pedagogical functions and a responsibility as much for the spiritual as for the material welfare of its subjects.

If the responsibility of the state authorities has typically been held to span very widely in respect of the interests of its subjects, the exclusive role of the latter is taken in orthodox Lutheranism to be that of obedient subjects submitting to the powers that be in a spirit of patient resignation. Even princes who neglected their duties to the extent of persecuting the Church were to be obeyed except in so far as they commanded actions which were contrary to the word of God. At no point was the common subject accorded a role of attempting to reform the state, let alone the world. The Lutheran churches cherish a deep-rooted conviction of the incorrigibility of the world. The Kingdom of God is always conceived as transcendent; according to the Lutheran view, it is hopeless to try to apply the laws of God's Kingdom to the world. It is not the concern of the

Church to solve the problems of human society; its task is rather to preach the consolation of forgiveness and to prepare believers for eternal life (Molland, 1959, p. 196).[2] This combination of transcendentalism and resignation in Lutheranism provided, as Troeltsch, Weber and others realised, no basis for generating a culture of activist commitment in politics.

The active ingredient: pietism

Nor at first did pietism depart from the orthodox view of the appropriate attitude to be taken to temporal authority in church and state. A dissident movement which arrived in Norway in the eighteenth century, it represented the Lutheran equivalent of Methodism in the Anglican, and various forms of puritanism or precisionism in the Calvinist, religious context (Berger, 1969, pp. 156–7). It did not even dispute the orthodox Lutheran view that the institutional church rightly belonged to the secular realm of law and obedience. True, from the time of Hauge on there was always an element of lay religious anti-clericalism based upon a rejection of the more rationalist clergy, but very few of the more radical revivalist elements rejected the order of the state church.[3] And since the state authorities were eventually unwilling to pay the cost of preserving the use of the more repressive church laws against the pietists, the latter were able, unlike their Anglican and Calvinist equivalents, to avoid the rigours of church discipline and remain within the ambit of the state church. Thus established, they were free despite the opposition of the more traditional clergy to build a network of powerful and independent lay organisations, a sort of church within the Church, dedicated to spreading their own version of the gospel both abroad, through foreign missions, and at home, through the so-called Inner Missions.

It is these lay Lutheran organisations, thrown up by successive waves of revivals between approximately 1840 and 1920, that have collectively constituted the opposite pole to that of the official church in modern Norwegian church life. Rokkan calls them fundamentalist organisations although, since they tend to follow orthodox Lutheran teaching in their view of bibilical inspiration at least, this label is not entirely apposite.[4] Nor on the other hand can they be labelled orthodox without heavy qualification. As their conservative clerical critics pointed out, from the time they first arose the organisations' very existence defied orthodox doctrine relating to church order in so far as it short-circuited the requirement that those who preach should be properly called. In the light of such an interpretation even the more churchly wing of the pietists could scarcely claim to be orthodox. It is true that the pietists generally have typically insisted on defending core church doctrine against rationalist, modernist or liberal deviations although their other insistence, on personal conversion experience as the mark of authentic Christianity, marks them as dissident rather than orthodox.

Weber pointed to a marked divergence between pietism and Lutheran orthodoxy arising from the former's rejection of the posture of patient resignation toward the world's institutional structures (Weber, 1966, p. 197).[5] It is not surprising therefore that the lay pietist movement was sometimes criticised by Lutheran commentators as a Calvinist, and by the same token foreign, infection (Jonassen, 1947). The Calvinist cast of Lutheran pietism is however only one of the features in terms of which its distance from, and antagonism towards, the traditional rural culture of Norway can be measured. As Bjørklund has argued the lay revivalist movement, like the prohibition movement with which it has long been associated, took hold in areas which were subject to considerable social and economic change. The typical Haugian leader started out as a peasant boy and ended up in trade in a town; the pietists were the first to found voluntary associations and exploit the use of the printed pamphlet for mass communication; and it was usually from among the prayer-folk that the campaigns were mounted which aimed at the reform of manners and the suppression of colourful folk traditions (Bjørklund, 1979).

It was however in their approach to politics that the more anti-clerical leaders of the pietist movement eventually demonstrated their most signal departure from the posture of Lutheran orthodoxy. There were two occasions in the nineteenth century when the pietist movement, despite its ostensible mission to concentrate on the one thing necessary (individual salvation), became embroiled in national politics. The first occasion, in the early part of the century, involved the entry into political life of individual Haugians, usually laymen who were trusted as much because they were natural leadership figures as because they were pietists. Only in connection with the struggle for the repeal of the Conventicle Ordinance and, shortly after, *against* a measure of toleration for dissenters did they particularly mark themselves out, however.[6] The second occasion was during the great constitutional struggle which culminated with the victory of the Left in 1884. This was the time when the parties of the left and right were founded and the more radical (or anti-clerical) pietists aligned themselves with the left, while leaders of the more churchly tendency based in the capital identified themselves with the right. Shortly afterwards, as Rokkan's account indicates the Left party split between the predominantly pietist Moderate, and the more national-liberal Pure, Left in 1888.[7] As with the Haugians before them, the Moderates adopted a distinctively pietist set of concerns which conflicted with the secularist liberal attitudes prevalent among the Pure Left. In particular, they insisted on the binding character of the clauses in the constitution which entrenched the position of the Lutheran-Evangelical religion and required all parents to bring up their children the same.

When the CPP finally emerged in the province of Hordaland in 1933, the core concerns remained essentially the same although by then the commitment to alcohol prohibition had been firmly added to the more exclusively religious ones. The proximate causes for the launching of the party that year was the coincidence of a challenge and an opportunity such as had not occurred over the previous decade when the idea of such a party had been mooted. The challenge came from two blasphemy cases, one involving a prominent leader of the Labour Party who toured the country with a speech to student audiences entitled 'Christianity: the Tenth Plague'. The opportunity arose when the general secretary of one of the main lay organisations, a rather radical one with its headquarters in Bergen (the unofficial capital of western Norway), was controversially passed over in the nominating convention of the Hordaland Left Party. Within a matter of weeks the CPP was launched and, exploiting its opportunity to use the ramified networks of the pietist movement to mobilise support, managed to get their man elected.

The CPP's manifesto opened with the preamble:

There are strong tendencies toward secularisation in today's society. These tendencies are at war with the Christian view of life, our Christian heritage and morals, which together provide the only sure foundation for a strong and healthy national way of life. Since these secularising tendencies are more and more joining together and organizing themselves it has become necessary for those who wish to protect our Christian heritage to do the same. The foundation of the Christian People's Party is an initiative in that direction. (Kristelig Folkeparti, 1963, p. 33)

In accordance with this overriding emphasis on the importance of defending the country's Christian heritage, the first of the programme's six points announced that the party would work to protect Christian and national values in the church, school, work and in our cultural life as a whole. Other points called for social justice based on Christian principles, a number of specific demands in connection with temperance legislation, relief for farmers and fishermen and the unemployed, and calls for peace in the fields of industrial and international relations.

The accompanying appeal, explicitly directed at rallying the *kristenfolk*,[8] addressed a number of the anticipated objections which were much debated during the campaign, not least in the pages of the Christian daily paper published in Bergen. It opened with the claim that it had become more and more difficult for Christian-interested (*kristeleg interesserte*) people to vote in Storting elections with a good conscience because party politics was more and more diverting attention from the welfare of the whole society. It went on to acknowledge that Christianity is first and foremost a personal matter and does not as such belong to political life; but no one can be blind either to the fact that the authorities can provide the various views of life (*livssyn*) with either good or less good conditions within which to work. When it was a matter of confronting the forces which were laying siege to Christianity it was essential then that those in authority should be people of Christian conviction (Kristelig Folkeparti, 1963, p. 34).

It was however in 1945 that the CPP finally emerged as a national party. In the last months of the occupation a number of prominent individuals associated with the Oxford Group (later renamed Moral Rearmament [MRA], started to lay plans for the reassertion of the country's Christian traditions after the barbarism which had been visited on Norway during the Nazi occupation. These centred on plans for a Christian daily newspaper and permanent conference centre, but when the CPP was launched as a national party the MRA also became involved in party activities in and around Oslo. The party's campaign was also supported by many other religious leaders, including representatives of other denominations as well as of the major lay Lutheran organisations, the official church leadership itself however remaining aloof. This and the party's success indicated that it had quickly become more than the spokesman for the radical pietist tradition of the south and west which it had been in the 1930s; the election, for example, of one of the leading Oxford Group men on the party's ticket in the Oslofjord area was symptomatic of a new reality, namely that the CPP had not only finally transcended the old tensions which had divided the *kristenfolk* and the members of other minority religious traditions.

The socially elitist Oxford Group movement had in fact scarcely been accepted as Christian before the war by many of the *kristenfolk*'s leaders; now the CPP's programme called for moral rearmament in all areas of national life. More significantly still in the context of a century of triangular Church–political tension between radical and churchly revivalism and the official Church, the party programme also called for reforms to give the state church greater internal freedom, although it balanced this with the demand that the Christian organisations and societies must continue to be given full freedom and the right to work in accordance with their traditions. The common denominator which bound the divergent tendencies together was indicated in the following passage from the main national election brochure:

It is our conviction that nothing will benefit the nation more than that the spiritual power of Christianity should have free and favourable conditions to do its cleansing and creative and constructive work through the schools, the church and the other organs which have influence over our people. (Folkets Framtid, 1945)

Underlying this and many other representative statements lay the characteristically Lutheran conception of the critical but essentially passive role of the state in the spiritual realm, as facilitator of the work of divine grace and frustrator of the work of the devil.

Dilemmas and ambiguities

In Lutheran thinking it is for the state in a Christian society (or even a Christian state) to use the medium of law and order to create conditions which facilitate divine and frustrate diabolical forces. As the party's election propaganda put it in 1945:

At a time when bewildered people swing from one paganism to another, from worshipping the Leader to worshipping themselves, it is time that the only real source of authority should be held aloft. . . . The law is holy, something in the deepest sense God-given which neither the individual nor the majority must make themselves masters over. The heart of all law-giving must be the laws of life which God has laid down in His creation, the clear commandments he has revealed and the clear guidelines which can be derived from the gospel. (Folkets Framtid, 1945)

All but the last of these statements can be seen as being quite in keeping with the classic Lutheran doctrine of the two realms referred to above;

the last however involves a crucial shift from Lutheran to Calvinistic emphases.

The idea that guidelines derived from the gospel should be relevant to the ordering of the temporal realm departs clearly from orthodox Lutheran doctrine. It was however one of the central ideas promoted in a collective volume called *Christian Responsibility*, planned in 1943 and published in 1946, not least in the contribution of Ragnvald Indrebø, a minister in the state church who had already associated himself with the CPP in the late 1930s. Looking forward to the restitution of legitimate state authority after the war he argued: 'it cannot be a matter of indifference (for Christians) who shall govern, or what principles shall inform that government. The state has an enormous capacity either to frustrate or promote that which must for Christians be the aim of all prayer and effort in so far as it concerns existence in this temporal dispensation: that God's kingdom be realised as fully as is possible, that as many as possible be won for the kingdom and that human life be marked as completely as can be managed by the spirit of God's kingdom and *ruled by its laws*' (Wisløff, 1946, pp. 81–2, emphasis added). He went on to argue that by contrast with conditions under absolutism (let alone occupation) the means of influence were no longer restricted to prayer or preaching, since divine providence provided a third way via direct political involvement.

The CPP continues periodically to wrestle with the ambiguities of its political philosophy which derive from the attempt to accommodate divergent impulses and doctrines. The issues are only rarely addressed in terms of classical Lutheran teachings and even then the bearing of such fundamental principles upon practical political issues is typically as loose as it is in most political movements (Seliger, 1976). As Barnes points out, however, occasional practical issues do directly activate the dilemmas of pietist politics. He mentions as a case in point the 1960s debates within the CPP branch in the small island community of Bremnes in western Norway over the matter of state aid to private religious schools: some members argue that the secular state has no authority to discriminate in religious matters and that, to be fair, if it subsidises the schools of one religious persuasion it must subsidise all; others argue that the state should aid only those citizens who preach the word of God and not those who preach false doctrines (Barnes, 1971, p. 4).[9] Similar dilemmas have exercised and occasionally divided the party in connection with the EC issue in the 1970s, where the country's moral-religious heritage was held by some to be at stake, and the abortion issue in the 1980s, where the CPP has through membership of coalition governments had to bear the stigma of operating a law which it regarded as being at variance with Christian principles.

Bremnes represents precisely the sort of community which Rokkan and the Norwegian school of electoral research identify as CPP home territory; Barnes argued that their support for the Christian People's Party is an expression of support for the dominant culture in the face of increasing local attack and erosion (p. 5), a statement redolent both of the notion of territorial-cultural defence and of the perception that the enemy is at the gate. As has been argued here, however, the party's motivation and character is to be found not in the defence against the state or urban corruption of tradition rural culture, or of modern North Atlantic fundamentalism, or of orthodox Lutheranism, or even some mix of these which has managed to achieve local dominance in places like Bremnes. Rather, its inspiration is to be found in the confessionally and politically ambiguous heritage of revivalist pietism, Lutheranism's internal opposition with its contradictory drives – activism and quietism, national inclusiveness and socio-religious exclusivity, individualism and collectivism, resistance to state interference on the one hand and promotion of the state's role as guardian of the nation's spiritual and moral welfare on the other.

Notes

1 I attempted to establish the identity of an independent and distinctive strain of Scandinavian Christian Democracy, as distinct from Fogarty's Continental and Anglo-Saxon species, in Madeley, 1977. Fogarty's own typology is to be found in Fogarty (1957). It might be argued that since the 1991 election in Sweden, when it achieved its parliamentary breakthrough and went on to join the Conservative-led Bildt coalition, the Christian Democratic Union (KDS) is more significant. For KDS and the other Nordic Christian democratic parties see Chapter 7.

2 Molland adds: 'This form of Christianity differs radically from the current in the English-speaking world, both in the Anglican and the Free [Calvinist] Churches. They represent an active type of Christianity which wishes to reform the world and to apply Christian principles to international and social problems. Their aim is to be found in some approximation at least to the Kingdom of God on earth.'

3 Indeed one of the peculiarities of the Norwegian case is that it is the leaders of the more 'radical' lay organisations such as the West Country Inner Mission League who have been the most consistent defenders of the state church system on the precise grounds that, since it cannot claim to be a true Church, it cannot legitimately interfere with the activities and claims of the independent lay organisations.

4 Christian fundamentalism in its strict sense insists on the plenary inspiration of the Bible in its entirety. Turner, Molland's translator, argues that the (in English) unfamiliar term Biblicist is more appropriate and notes: 'While Biblicism is often found in combination with Fundamentalism, this is by no means always the case. It is rather concerned with a way of using the Bible rather than with a doctrine of Biblical inspiration.' (Molland, 1959, pp.1-90ff).

5 Weber continued: 'In this teaching of resignation, Lutheranism presents a striking contrast to those religions, especially those forms of Protestantism, which required for the assurance of one's salvation either a distincitve methodological pattern of life or a demonstration of good works, which was known as *fides efficax* among the Pietists.'

6 The Conventicle Ordinance of 1741 forbade the holding of unlicensed religious meetings. It had been used to restrict and occasionally to penalise the work of Haugian preachers but was repealed in 1842. The ambiguity of the Haugian position on orthodoxy and religious freedom is well illustrated in their opposition to the Dissenter's Law passed only three years later.

7 Among the issues which precipitated the split was the granting of a state bursary to an author who was notorious among the pietists of the southwest for attacking their most prominent leader. When that same leader shortly after was exposed

for a scandalous relationship with a maid, many who had warned about the corrupting effect of involvement in politics felt themselves vindicated.

8 Literally Christian folk, a term of the pietists' own coinage well understood as referring to the membership of the lay religious organisations.

9 Barnes also points out that some party members in Bremnes hold that the sole function of their representatives should be to preach the word of God in parliament to their colleagues in other parties (pp. 14–15). It can be argued that for the most pietistical section of the *kristenfolk* the proper function of the CPP is not so much to engage in discussion of difficult and divisive policy matters, which seem to have little bearing on the spiritual state of the country, as simply to constitute a sort of mission group in the central political arena of the nation.

References

Allen, J. W., 1928, *A History of Political Thought in the Sixteenth Century*, Methuen, London.

Barnes, J., 1971, The Righthand and Lefthand Kingdoms of God: A Dilemma of Pietist Politics, in Beidelman, T. O. (ed.), *The Translation of Culture. Essays to E. E. Evans-Pritchard*, Tavistock, London, pp. 1–17.

Berger, P., 1969, *The Social Reality of Religion*, Faber, London.

Bjørklund, T., 1979, Motkulturar i Motvind, *Syn og Segn*, 8, 9.

Fogarty, M. P., 1957, *Christian Democracy in Western Europe 1820–1953*, Routledge and Kegan Paul, London.

Folkets Framtid, 1945, *Valgavis for Kristelig Folkeparti i Oslo og Akershus*, Kristelig Folkeparti, Oslo.

Gustafsson, G. (ed.), 1985, *Religiös Förändring i Norden 1930–1980*, Liber Forlag, Malmö.

Heidenheimer, A. J., 1983, Secularization Patterns and the Westward Spread of the Welfare State, 1883–1983, in Tomasson, 1983, pp. 3–38.

Jonassen, C. T., 1947, The Protestant Ethic and the Spirit of Capitalism, *American Sociological Review*, 12, pp. 676–86.

Keller, A., 1936, *Church and State on the European Continent*, Epworth, London.

Kristelig Folkeparti, 1963, *Kristelig Folkeparti, 1958–63*, Kristelig Folkeparti, Oslo.

Lipset, S. M., 1968, *Revolution and Counter-Revolution*, Basic Books, New York.

Madeley, J., 1977, Scandinavian Christian Democracy: Throwback or Portent, *European Journal of Political Research*, 5: 267–286.

Madeley, J., 1982, Politics and the Pulpit: the Case of Protestant Europe, in Berger, S. (ed.), *Religion in West European Politics*, Frank Cass, London, pp. 149–171.

Madeley, J., 1983, Religion and the Welfare State, in Tomasson, 1983, pp. 43–49.

Madeley, J., 1991, Politics and Religion in Western Europe, in Moyser, G. (ed.), *Politics and Religion in the Modern World*, Routledge, London, pp. 28–66.

Martin, D., 1978, *A General Theory of Secularization*, Blackwell, Oxford.

Molland, E., 1959, *Christendom: The Christian Churches, their doctrines, constitutional forms and ways of worship*, Mowbray, London.

Rokkan, S., 1967, Geography, Religion and Social Class: Crosscutting Cleavages in Norwegian Politics, in Lipset, S. M. and Rokkan, S., *Party Systems and Voter Alignments*, Free Press, New York.

Seliger, M., 1976, *Ideology and Politics*, Allen and Unwin, London.

Tomasson, R. F. (ed.), 1983, *Comparative Social Research: The Welfare State, 1883–1983*, JAI Press, London.

Troeltsch, E., 1960, *The Social Teaching of the Christian Churches*, Harper, New York.
Weber, M., 1966, *The Sociology of Religion*, Methuen, London.
Wisløff, H. E. (ed.), 1946, *Kristent Ansvar*, Indremisjonsforlaget, Oslo.

9

CHRISTIAN DEMOCRACY IN FRANCE: THE POLITICS OF ELECTORAL CONSTRAINT

Robert Elgie

Christian Democracy and the Fifth Republic

Christian Democracy first became an effective party political force in France following the Liberation of the country in 1944 (Irving, 1973). At this time, the Mouvement Républicain Populaire (MRP) was formed as a centrist Christian Democratic party, seeking a third way between capitalism and socialism. During the Fourth Republic (1946–58), the MRP played a major role in the political system, with its representatives frequently occupying senior ministerial posts as well as holding the position of head of government on a number of occasions.

However, by the time of the creation of the Fifth Republic in 1958, the MRP was already a party in decline. The pervasive influence of de Gaulle and the institutional dynamics of the new Republic hastened this decline. In 1963, the MRP agreed to merge with other democratic forces, so as to form a wider movement, whose aim would be to challenge the dominant position of the Gaullist party. The first manifestation of this new movement came in 1965 with Jean Lecanuet's bid for the presidency. Lecanuet formed a new party, the Centre Démocrate (CD), consisting largely of Christian Democrats, but which also included centrist politicians and voters who had not previously been identified with the MRP.

Although Lecanuet performed well at the 1965 presidential election, winning 15.8 per cent of the vote, the CD failed to establish itself as a major political force. Indeed, following further disappointments at the 1967 and 1968 legislative elections, the CD split. A large proportion of its members left to form a new party, the Centre Démocratie et Progrès (CDP), which joined the Gaullist majority in government.

In 1971, Lecanuet made one final bid to create a wide-ranging, Christian Democratic-inspired centre grouping when he allied with the small Radical Party to fight the 1973 legislative elections as the Mouvement Réformateur (MR). However, the MR failed to make a major impact and, thus, it was

with great relief and without hesitation that the MR agreed to support
Giscard d'Estaing's presidential campaign in 1974. Once elected it was
natural that Giscard should ask the leaders of the MR, including Lecanuet,
to join the government. The offer was gratefully accepted.

The decision to ally with Giscard and enter government paved the way
for a reconciliation between the two parts of the Christian Democratic
family, the CD and the CDP. This reconciliation took place at the
Congress of Rennes in May 1976. This date marks the beginning of the
current manifestation of Christian Democracy in France, the Centre des
Démocrates Sociaux (CDS).

The ideology of the CDS

The creation of the CDS in 1976 was an attempt to recreate a centrist
party, based upon avowedly Christrian Democratic principles, which
would be attractive in themselves to a large electorate (Dreyfus, 1988, p.
379). To date, these ambitions have largely been frustrated. The CDS has
failed to win the support of a large number of voters. Moreover, it does not
have a distinct political existence, since, in 1978, the party agreed to
become one of the founder members of the UDF confederation of parties,
alongside Giscard's Parti Républicain (PR), the Radical Party and several
smaller groupings. Nevertheless, the CDS has tried to elaborate a distinctive Christian Democratic ideology for itself, which marks it out it from the
other components of the UDF and from the Gaullist Rassemblement pour
la République (RPR).

The latest reworking of French Christian Democratic thought came at
the party's special convention in Saint-Malo, in October 1990. At this
convention, a new ideological document was approved. The document
consisted of four separate sections: 'Democratic reawakening and the
revival of justice'; 'Equality of hope, quality of life'; 'A shared prosperity';
and 'The United states of Europe'.

Many of the traditional themes of Christian Democracy were to be found
in the document: the promotion of the family unit; the importance of self-
fulfilment of the person; state intervention to encourage individual saving
and investment as well as to help trade and industry; and closer European
integration. In addition, much of the first section of the document was
devoted to the political system of the Fifth Republic and to the changes
which the party considered to be necessary so as to create a better and
fairer set of political institutions.

Although it is evident throughout the document that the Catholic faith is
the party's main inspiration (there are references, for example, to Pope
Paul VI), it is nevertheless specifically stated that the party welcomes
people whatever their religious or philosophical outlook, as long as they
share the party's belief in 'democratic humanism'. Indeed, the party's two
main convictions are that, 'The human person is unique, but not alone' and
that, 'The aim of politics is to allow the human person to bloom' (Barrot
and Bayrou, 1990, p. 1).

Elections, geography and sociology

The electoral performance of Christian Democracy in France has been uneven (see Table 9.1). The heyday of Christian Democracy was in 1946 when the MRP was the largest party in France, winning 28.2 per cent of the vote. However, support for the MRP quickly declined and, by 1958, it was a party in crisis. Irving gives three reasons for the MRP's decline: its failure to support de Gaulle in 1946 and 1958; its connections with Catholicism in a country with a strong anti-clerical tradition; and its failure to establish a popular, national press (Irving, 1973, p. 86).

Table 9.1 The performance of Christian Democracy in elections since 1945[a]

Election	Year	Party label	Score (%)[b]
Constituent Assembly	1945	MRP	23.9
Constituent Assembly	1946 (June)	MRP	28.2
Legislative	1946 (November)	MRP	25.9
Legislative	1951	MRP	12.6
Legislative	1956	MRP	11.1
Legislative	1958	MRP	11.1
Legislative	1962	MRP	8.9
Presidential	1965	Jean Lecanuet	15.8
Legislative	1967	CD	13.5
Legislative	1968	CPDM	10.3
Legislative	1973	MR	13.1[c]
Presidential	1988	Raymond Barre	16.5
European	1989	Centre	8.4

Notes:
[a] Figures from 1945–1968 inclusive are taken from Irving, 1973. In national elections from 1978–1988 the CDS was part of the UDF confederation of parties. As a result, it is impossible to separate out the CDS vote from the score of the UDF as a whole.
[b] Where applicable, these figures represent the percentage of votes cast at the first ballot.
[c] This figure represents the score of the Mouvement Réformateur, one component of which was the Christian Democratic party. Therefore, the total exaggerates the Christian Democratic vote.

The creation of the Centre Démocrate was Jean Lecanuet's personal attempt to counter the second of Irving's reasons for the MRP's decline. However, in his attempt to extend the appeal of Christan Democracy beyond the Catholic world so as to incorporate other organisations and parties, Lecanuet only succeeded in diluting the movement's distinctiveness, until it became a 'ragbag' (Hanley, 1991, p. 208) of ideas. Moreover, there was no 'compensatory electoral gain' for the CD and, in the eyes of at least one observer, Lecanuet's strategy was a failure (Hanley, 1991, p. 214).

Now, the CDS can count on the support of only a hard core of electors,

representing between 8 and 15 per cent of the vote. Moreover, these
electors are concentrated in diverse geographical areas, which are traditionally associated with Christian Democracy. In the 1989 European
elections, support for the Christian Democratic centre list was significantly
higher than the national average in five regions: Alsace, Bretagne, Ile-de-
France, Pays-de-la-Loire and Rhône-Alpes (Le Gall, 1989, p. 14). These
regions largely correspond to the bastions of MRP support in the 1950s and
to the areas where Lecanuet's support was greatest in the 1960s. It must be
noted, however, that there are people who identify with the Christian
Democratic tradition, but who do not necessarily vote for the CDS. In this
sense, the movement is larger than the party.

Sociologically, the CDS electorate demonstrates characteristics which
set it apart from its rivals. This distinctiveness can be seen in the sociological profile of Raymond Barre's electorate at the first ballot of the 1988
presidential election (see Table 9.2). Although Barre refused to be classed
as the candidate of the CDS, he was certainly closer to the party than any
other candidate and the party embraced him as one of their own. The
sociology of Barre's electorate was different from that of the candidate of
the right in 1988, the Gaullist Jacques Chirac, and from that of the
candidate of the extreme right, Jean-Marie Le Pen. Barre won the support
of a higher percentage of lower middle-class voters than either Chirac or
Le Pen, while Chirac won the support of more managers and Le Pen the
support of more small businessmen.

Not surprisingly, the CDS also wins the support of a higher number of
practising Catholics than any other party. A 1978 study showed that
practising Catholics made up 43 per cent of the CDS's electorate. This
figure compares with 27 per cent for the Giscardian PR and 21 per cent for
the Gaullist RPR (Dreyfus, 1990, p. 848).

The electoral strategy of the CDS

During the Fifth Republic, the electoral dilemma for Christian Democracy
has revolved around the issue of whether or not the movement should exist
as an independent party, or whether it should engage in electoral alliances
with other such forces. If it follows the first strategy, the movement's
ideology is kept intact, but it risks electoral annihilation. If it follows the
second, its principles are diluted, but it stands the chance of sharing power.
Since 1958, the strategies of both independence and alliance have been
pursued. In fact, in terms of electoral strategy, it is possible to divide the
Fifth Republic up into three distinct periods: 1958–69; 1969–88; and 1988
to the present.

From 1958–69, the movement's strategy was broadly one of independence. Although the MRP was in government between 1959–62 and
although both the MRP and the CD were often reliant on the votes of
other parties in order to elect deputies to the National Assembly, nevertheless, there was a desire to stress the distinctiveness of Christian Democratic
principles through the medium of an independent party. For example, in

Table 9.2 Sociological profile of Raymond Barre's electorate, 1988

Category	Barre (17% of first ballot vote)
Gender	
Men	15
Women	18
Age	
18–24	19
25–34	16
35–49	15
50–64	17
65+	17
Occupation	
Farmer	16
Small businessman	23
Professions libérales	16
Senior manager	22
Teacher, doctor	16
Middle manager	17
Office worker	15
Shop worker	21
Manual worker	7
Personnel de service	10
Employment	
Public sector	11
Private sector	19
Self employed	17
Unemployed	10
Retired	18

Source: Taken from Dreyfus, 1990, p. 856.

1962, MRP representatives resigned *en masse* from the government in protest at what they considered to be de Gaulle's negative attitude towards the European Community.

From 1969–88, the movement's strategy was broadly one of alliance. This point can be illustrated by the creation of the CDP in 1969; the formation of the MR in 1971; the CD's decision to support Giscard in 1974; the formation of the UDF in 1978, the CDS being one of its major components; and with the party's decision to enter Jacques Chirac's right-wing coalition government in 1986. On these occasions, the Christian Democratic message was to be heard from within a larger organisation, rather than as a separate force.

After 1988, the CDS tried to follow a strategy of semi-independence. That is to say, it remained a member of the UDF confederation and still considered itself to be in opposition to the socialist government. However, it took steps to differentiate itself from the UDF in the National Assembly and its policy towards the government was, in the words of the party leader, Pierre Méhaignerie, one of 'constructive opposition'.

There are two main reasons why the CDS's electoral strategy shifted from one of alliance to semi-independence in 1988. First, in the early 1980s, ideological tensions increased between the CDS and its partners on the right. The main disagreement was between the people in the CDS who were still largely committed to emphasising the social aspect of economic management and those in other parties, especially the PR, who had been converted to neo-liberal economics as a result of its apparent success in the US and the UK.

Second, these tensions were increased by the CDS's period in government in 1986–8. The party was perturbed by the reforming zeal of the Chirac administration. Much of the government's economic policy, as well as certain aspects of its social policy, in areas such as immigration, education and broadcasting, proved to be difficult for the party to swallow. Moreover, the eagerness with which certain Gaullist ministers appeared to want to court the National Front's electorate was anathema to the CDS.

As a result of these problems, there was a growing feeling within the CDS that the party should change its electoral strategy. Therefore, following Mitterrand's re-election as president and the subsequent legislative elections in June 1988, the party attempted to reassert its identity by forming its own parliamentary group, separate from the wider UDF group in the National Assembly. A large majority of the party's forty-nine deputies voted to join the new group, the Union du Centre (UDC). The creation of the UDC in June 1988 marked the beginning of the third period of the CDS's electoral strategy, namely, a change to semi-independence.

The decision to create a separate parliamentary group was an important step for the CDS. In the first place, it gave the party the automatic right to speak in parliamentary debates alongside the other parliamentary groups. As such, it provided the party with a greater opportunity for its voice to be heard than before, as part of the larger UDF group. Moreover, it was an important financial step for the party to take, in that parliamentary groups are eligible to receive public monies. Given the parlous state of the party's accounts, the financial support that the group would receive was most welcome. In addition, it was also a clear sign to the public that the party was a distinctive force within the UDF and that the pro-European, social market values of Christian Democracy were different from those traditionally propounded by the parties on the right of the political spectrum.

The CDS's strategy of semi-independence was followed up by the party's decision to put up its own separate list at the European elections in June 1989. During the campaign period various party representatives set a target for the percentage of votes that the list would have to receive in order for it to be considered a success. For example, Pierre Méhaignerie arrived at a figure of 13 per cent, while Jean Lecanuet said that anything less than 16 per cent would be considered a failure (Charlot and Charlot, 1989; Le Gall, 1989; Lodge, 1990, pp. 126–44). In the end, the list scored 8.42 per cent of the votes cast. For most outside observers and for most people within the party, therefore, the results of the European elections were a great disappointment for the CDS.

For the party, the score registered by the list was not only disappointing, it was also a signal that the strategy of semi-independence from the UDF was a failure and that it had to be abandoned. By default, therefore, the party started to reforge its links with its right-wing partners and, consequently, a series of inter-party intiatives were taken. As early as the summer of 1989, it was agreed that there should be closer co-operation between the UDC, UDF and RPR party groups in the National Assembly. The CDS also agreed to take part in a series of round table policy debates, alongside the RPR and the UDF, collectively known as the *états généraux de l'opposition*. Furthermore, the CDS was part of an electoral coalition with the RPR and UDF which fought the March 1992 cantonal and regional elections. Consequently, the post-1988 strategy of semi-independence was put to one side, at least temporarily.

The question which arises from this analysis of the electoral strategies of successive Christian Democratic parties, therefore, is why has it consistently proved to be impossible for the Christian Democrats to exist independently, or even semi-independently of the parties of the mainstream right? Why is a party with such a distinctive message obliged to follow a strategy of electoral alliances?

The institutional constraints of the Fifth Republic

In this section, it will be argued that the institutional constraints imposed upon the French party system by the primacy of presidential politics and, in particular, by the effects of the two ballot majority electoral system have together encouraged successive Christian Democratic parties to ally with the parties of the traditional right.

The presidentialisation of the political system of the Fifth Republic began under de Gaulle in 1958. It was then consolidated and even extended under the presidencies of Pompidou, Giscard d'Estaing and Mitterrand. Presidential control of the policy-making process has been one of the enduring features of the Fifth Republic's political system to date. The president's control of the political system is derived from his election by universal suffrage. In France, the outcome of the presidential election is the key moment in the political process.

The centrality of presidential politics to the political system ensures that parties organise their activities around presidential elections. The goal of each party is to see the election of its leader as president. The consequence of such a system, however, is that it is only possible for parties to thrive if they are headed by a figure who realistically aspires to winning the highest office (*un présidentiable*). By way of their personal appeal, such figures are able to attract a greater level of support for their political grouping than would otherwise have been the case. In the Fifth Republic to date there are two very striking examples of this 'coat-tails effect': General de Gaulle, whose Gaullist party benefited from its mentor's popularity, and Giscard d'Estaing, whose popularity rubbed off onto the PR and also onto the UDF as a whole in the late 1970s.

By contrast, parties which do not enjoy the presence of a *présidentiable* among their number are only able to operate independently of those which do with great difficulty. In practice, parties without presidential candidates are obliged to attach themselves to the political groupings which do possess them, otherwise they run the risk of being marginalised in the political system as a whole. It is noticeable, for example, that for much of the period when the Christian Democrats were able to operate independently of the major party blocks in the 1960s, they also possessed their most likely presidential candidate to date, Jean Lecanuet. His popularity was such that the CD was able to gain enough support, so as to operate as an independent political force over a prolonged period. However, by 1974, when Lecanuet's personal appeal had diminished and when Giscard d'Estaing had become the undisputed candidate of the non-Gaullist right, the CD was obliged to join the presidential majority and to sacrifice its independence.

The importance of presidential politics to political parties can also help to explain some of manoeuvres in the CDS's recent history. For example, the party's decision to support Raymond Barre in the 1980s, even though he was not a member of the party, but was just close to the movement, was an attempt to produce more coat-tails benefits for itself. Unfortunately for the CDS, this attempt proved to be unsuccessful. Similarly, the fact that the CDS did not possess a credible presidential candidate after 1988 was one of the reasons why the party's strategy of semi-independence had to be shelved. The party did not possess a figure around whom a major centrist force could coalesce. Instead, the party was obliged to rejoin its traditional right-wing partners, the RPR and the UDF, both of which, in Jacques Chirac and Valéry Giscard d'Estaing, had potential presidential candidates around whom the political debate on the right was centred.

In addition to the importance of presidential politics, the other main influence on the party sytem of the Fifth Republic has been the impact of the country's electoral system. In France, presidential elections take place under a two ballot majority electoral system, as indeed do legislative, municipal and cantonal elections. The institutional constraints of the two ballot majority system have to a large extent determined the patterns of inter-party alliances under the Fifth Republic and have led to the situation where successive Christian Democratic parties have had to abandon their strategy of electoral independence, in favour of joining a broader right-wing coalition.

There is a clear institutional dynamic to the French two ballot majority electoral system, to which parties and candidates have to conform. Taking legislative elections as an example, at the first ballot all parties are able to stand. If a particular party wins an absolute majority of votes at this ballot, then its representative is elected. However, if no party is able to win such a majority, then a second ballot is held. At the second ballot, only the parties that won more than 12.5 per cent of the registered electorate at the first ballot are allowed to stand again. In the resulting contest, the candidate of the party that wins the largest share of the vote will be elected.

The importance of the two ballot system lies in the fact that parties (and candidates in the case of presidential elections) are obliged to form alliances at the second ballot in order to be elected. Indeed, it is often beneficial for parties to form such alliances before the first ballot, in order to receive enough support to avoid being eliminated at the first ballot and so be able to contest the second.

This coalitional dynamic is the single most important determinant of the French party system. Parties, such as the CDS, which do not enjoy mass support, will perish under the two ballot system, unless they ally with other political groups. The effects of this coalitional dynamic could be seen, for example, in the alliance between the CD and the Radical Party in 1971 and in the creation of the UDF in 1978. It was also another of the reasons why the CDS abandoned its strategy of independence and reforged its links with the RPR/UDF in the run-up to the recent 1993 legislative elections. Alliances were reforged in order for the CDS to safeguard its parliamentary representation.

This coalitional dynamic has had a bipolarising effect upon the French party system as a whole. The parties which were closest together ideologically tended naturally to ally with each other. As such, the party system split into two opposing left- and right-wing blocks of parties. In seeking electoral alliances, the Christian Democrats were obliged to belong to one or other of these blocks. In practice, this situation meant that the CDS was inclined to look to the block of parties on the mainstream right for its electoral partners. There were two main reasons as to why the party sought out its electoral allies on the right. First, for much of the Fifth Republic, allying with the left meant allying with the Communists. Such a prospect was abhorrent for Christian Democrats. Second, there was also a reluctance to ally with the Socialists, because, for the most part, they were considered to have a different, less humanistic conception of the relation between the individual and the society than the one which was shared by Christian Democrats.

In addition to the points mentioned above, the existence of presidential politics and of a two ballot majority electoral system have together had a further consequence for centrist parties in the Fifth Republic's political system. Both of these elements encourage centripetal, rather than centrifugal politics. Although there has been a bipolarisation of the party system since 1958, both candidates at presidential elections and parties at legislative and local elections have nevertheless been obliged to fight for votes at the centre of the political system rather than at the extremes.

For example, in order for candidates to win an absolute majority of votes at the second ballot of a presidential election, they have to appeal to a wider electorate than can be found within their own left- or right-wing blocks. This move to the centre can clearly be seen during the Mitterrand campaigns of 1974, 1981 and 1988. On each occasion, Mitterrand tried to extend his support base out from the Socialists and Communists, so as to include the centrist electorate as well. In 1974, he was unsuccessful. In both

1981 and 1988, he was successful. In fact, one of the reasons for Mitterrand's failure at the 1974 election was that Giscard d'Estaing was able to mobilise the centrist vote behind his campaign more effectively.

The consequence of this centripetal dynamic, however, is that the ideological space previously claimed by a centrist party becomes crowded. As other political parties and candidates move to the centre in the search for votes, so the party which occupies the centre loses its distinct message and at least part of its electoral appeal. This situation was particularly noticeable at the 1988 presidential elections, as the Barre electorate was squeezed, when both Chirac and Mitterrand moved to the centre. It was also noticeable at the 1989 European elections, when there was little to choose between either the UDF/RPR list, the Centre list, or indeed the Socialist list. In such a situation there is neither the incentive, nor the opportunity, for centre parties to exist independently of the larger party blocs.

Local politics

In addition to the institutional dynamics which have operated at the national level, there are also the dynamics of local politics to take into account. In France, local politics are of great and, arguably, ever increasing importance. In particular, mayors exercise considerable powers of patronage in local municipalities, placing them in a very influential position. Often one of the beneficiaries of the mayor's powers of patronage both directly, in terms of money, and indirectly, in terms of votes, is the party to which s/he belongs.

Traditionally, in France, Christian Democracy has been been particularly well entrenched at local level. At present, there are CDS mayors in a number of large towns and cities throughout the country. These include municipalities such as Toulouse, Angoulême, Lourdes, Saint-Malo and Annecy. Given that the two ballot majority system also operates for municipal elections, the party at the local level has to choose which party bloc it wishes to support. For similar reasons to those at national level, most CDS politicians at the local level have consistently allied with the right.

The co-operation which already takes place at the local level between Christian Democrats and the parties of the right has a knock-on effect at national level. After all, if the party were to break with its right-wing allies at the national level, it would be bound to face repercussions at local level. The CDS could not afford to lose its representation in the municipalities, yet this would be the result if the RPR and the UDF withdrew their support for the party in local elections. The link between the alliances at the local level and the alliances at the national level is reinforced by the fact that senior mayors often hold the post of deputy as well. This situation makes it impossible for the national party apparatus to force the local party apparatus to assume an independent strategy, because the same people are in control at both levels. Undoubtedly, the impact of the local political situation was a further reason why the CDS's strategy of independence after 1988 was soon reversed.

It can be seen, therefore, that Christian Democratic parties have not been free simply to choose from any of the possible electoral strategies available to the party. Over the years, the institutional characteristics of the Fifth Republic have effectively obliged the party to follow a certain course, namely that of allying with its larger partners on the right of the political spectrum. However, it would be wrong to suggest that the CDS will be condemned to follow this logic for ever. No political system is permanently fixed. Indeed, there is evidence to suggest that the Fifth Republic is evolving and that the opportunity structure in which the CDS operates is changing concomitantly. In the next section, the evidence pointing to the recent evolution of the political system of the Fifth Republic will be examined and the effect that this evolution might have on the CDS will be considered.

The evolution of the Fifth Republic's political system

There are several good reasons for believing that the French political system may undergo a transformation in the near future. In the first place, the rise of the Front National (FN) has had a profound effect upon the previously bipolarised party system. In addition to the traditional left- and right-wing blocs, there is now a party on the extreme right whose candidate won 14.4 per cent at the 1988 presidential election. The presence of the FN has caused severe problems for the parties of the traditional right. In particular, it has created a new cleavage between those people who are willing to work with the FN, either formally or informally, and those people who are not willing to do so under any circumstances. In the main, the CDS has distanced itself from its right-wing partners by refusing to contemplate any alliance with the FN.

This situation has helped to create the conditions for what Parodi has called, 'a new political space' (Parodi, 1989). That is to say, the possibility of the formation of a large centrist group, whose motivation would be to ensure that the FN is excluded from power. Such a group would still have to work within the coalitional dynamic of the Fifth Republic, which, in this case, would entail an alliance between the Christian Democrats and the Socialists. Although such an alliance failed in 1988, there is evidence to suggest that such an alliance is not unthinkable. For example, there are ideological differences between the Christian Democratic electorate and the electorate of the traditional right, particularly on issues such as Europe and immigration (Ysmal, 1988, p. 32). At the same time, there are similarities between the Christian Democratic electorate and the Socialists, particularly with reference to the importance the CDS places on social issues (Hanley, 1991, p. 218). An alliance with the Socialists would become more realistic if either Raymond Barre, or Jacques Delors were to be elected as president or appointed as prime minister.

Unfortunately for the CDS, even if such a scenario were to come about, it is not at all clear that an alliance with the Socialists could ever be successfully launched. There is still a strong ideological bond between the CDS and the parties of the traditional right. Undoubtedly, the CDS feels more at home with the right than with the left. At its Saint-Malo convention, the party placed great emphasis on the inviolability of the person. It stated that neither race, social class, nation, state nor any other organisation was more important than the individual person. As such, the party was distancing itself from its interpretation of the Socialist view, which it saw as being one of the subordination of the individual to wider social forces. At the same time, the party emphasised the importance of the market economy as the system which created the best conditions for economic growth, employment and prosperity. While the role of the state was acknowledged as being necessary so as to compensate for the deficiencies of the market economy, the emphasis which was placed on the market would be unacceptable for most Socialists. It is perhaps not coincidental that these principles were formulated after the 1989 European elections and during the period when the party was once again working closely with the RPR and the UDF.

Ideally, the CDS would still prefer to be able to exist independently of either of the two left- and right-wing blocs. This situation is not entirely implausible for two reasons. First, the party has a number of young (40+), high-profile politicians, one of whom could assume the mantle of a *présidentiable*. Most notably, the highly popular Dominique Baudis, the Executive President of the party and mayor of Toulouse might prove to be in the position to contest a presidential election in the near future. Such a challenge would be likely to create coat-tails benefits for the party, which might allow it to operate independently once more.

Second, it is possible that there may be constitutional changes to the Fifth Republic in the near future. If the country were to operate as a true parliamentary regime, especially if it were to select a form of proportional representation as its electoral system, or if a US-style presidential regime were to be set up then the country's political system would be rendered less rigid. In such a case, there would be more room within which the CDS could manoeuvre. It is noticeable that senior politicians from all parties have argued that constitutional reforms along these lines are necessary.

Whatever course the evolution of the political system of the Fifth Republic may take, Christian Democracy will have an important role to play. It may be that it will be able to act as '*un pôle de rayonnement*' for all democratic, centrist forces. It may be that it is forced to act as '*une roue de secours*' for a larger political grouping. In either case, it will continue to be a major current in society and one which will play a pivotal role in the political system.

Note

1 The changes outlined below were suggested by Jacques Barrot in an interview with *Esprit*, no. 143, octobre 1988, p. 61.

References

Barrot, J. and Bayrou, F., 1990, *Actualité de la pensée démocrate chrétienne*, CDS, Convention de St. Malo, 19–21 october, pp. 1–7.

Charlot, J. and Charlot, M., *Electoral Studies*, 8: 3, 246–253.

Dreyfus, F-G., 1988, *Histoire de la démocratie chrétienne en France, de Châteaubriand à Raymond Barre*, Albin Michel, Paris.

Dreyfus, F-G., 1990, Place et poids de la démocratie chrétienne, *Revue Française de Science Politique*, vol. 40, no. 6, 845–862.

Hanley, D., 1991, Christian Democracy in France, 1965–1990: Death and Resurrection?, in N. Atkin and F. Tallet (eds), *Religion, Society and Politics in France*, Hambledon, London, pp. 203–219.

Irving, R.E.M., 1973, *Christian Democracy in France*, Allen & Unwin, London.

Le Gall, G., 1989, Un triple avertissement: pour l'Europe, la démocratie et les Socialistes, *Revue Politique et Parlementaire*, no. 942, 11–20.

Lodge, J., ed., 1990, *The 1989 Election of the European Parliament*, Macmillan, London.

Parodi, J-L., 1989, Le nouvel espace politique français, in Y Mény, (ed.), *Idéologies partis politiques, groupes sociaux*, FNSP, Paris.

Ysmal, C., 1988, Barre: la persistance du tempérament centriste, in P. Habert and C. Ysmal (eds), *L'Election présidentielle 1988*, Figaro/Etudes politiques, Paris, pp.17–18.

10

THE BRITISH EXPERIENCE: CHRISTIAN DEMOCRATS WITHOUT A PARTY

Joan Keating

It may seem strange to talk of Christian Democracy in a British context. But there have been Christian Democrats active in British political life in the twentieth century: various groups and individuals, in some ways very different from one another, have styled themselves as such. This will come as no surprise to those familiar with the work of John H. Whyte. His analysis is that something approaching what he terms 'closed Catholicism' existed in Anglo-Saxon as well as continental European countries (Whyte, 1981, pp. 8–9). A moment's reflection on the nature of the papacy of the late nineteenth and twentieth centuries (with ultramontanism triumphant) tells us that there is no reason to expect Catholics in Britain to have been immune to the message of the social encyclicals and the call for Catholic Action.

The decision by some British Catholics to call themselves Christian Democrats raises questions as what exactly people were laying claim to when using this label. Do we in the British context have, as William Rauch has suggested in his study of French Christian Democracy, to talk about Christian Democracies rather than Christian Democracy? (Rauch, 1972, p. 10). British Catholic Christian Democrats were certainly not a homogeneous group and reflected the marked class division among the British faithful. At times all Catholic Christian Democrats (with a few maverick exceptions) supported the same party, the British Labour Party; but in the 1950s there were a number of defections to the British Liberal Party, where, such people believed, Christian Democratic ideas stood a better chance of getting an airing. Their action in leaving the Labour Party has to be differentiated from the actions of those who left the party believing it to be heretical. Those Christian Democrats who left, while wary of some of the developments within Labour, did so in no spirit of moral condemnation. They did not suggest that those continuing to support the Labour Party were endangering their souls.

It can also be observed that some British Christian Democrats did not see themselves primarily as political activists, but rather were committed to the advancement of what could loosely be termed humanitarian ideas:

policies advocated by the League of Nations Union for example. Out of this arises the question of whether Christian Democracy has as much to do with a style of politics as with political content.

In this chapter I will describe some British Christian Democrats and examine their relationship to both Labour and Liberal parties. I will do this chronologically, looking at the various groups and individuals active over the period 1910–60. In covering fifty years the chapter has necessarily to be concise. However, enough idea of the people and organisations is given for me to be able, in the conclusion, to discuss what such activities say about the nature of Christian Democracy in Britain.

The emergence of the Labour Party and the Catholic Social Guild

The Catholic population in Britain at the turn of the century was largely working class and of Irish descent. These were the people who received the impact of the social teaching of Leo XIII. They encountered a developing labour movement which, unlike its European counterparts, was not characterised by a great deal of anti-clericalism. In Britain, becoming involved in the existing organisations of the labour movement did not necessarily mean a rejection of the Church and what it stood for. However, there was still the question of just how safe the Labour Party was for Catholics. In the second decade of this century the British Catholic hierarchy, and some lay people, were preoccupied with asking whether or not the Labour Party was socialist. Socialism was to be condemned on four grounds: its idea of equality, its dangerous concept of the state, its rejection of private property (all of these three were in contravention of natural law) and its atheism. Some Catholics felt very strongly that the Labour Party was socialist and to be condemned, particularly after the adoption by the party in 1918 of Clause IV which called for the 'common ownership of the means of production, distribution and exchange'. One Manchester layman, John Burns, felt this so strongly that he established a political party which held Labour Party values but excluded Clause IV. Yet, his Centre Labour Party died a quick death having achieved very little in the way of support (Fielding, 1988, p. 288). This was hardly surprising since it has to be remembered that only around 5 per cent of the population of England and Wales at this time was Catholic (Cleary, 1960, p. 4). Such demographics meant that an explicitly Catholic party was never a viable option.

An authoritative ruling on Catholics and the British Labour Party was slow to come. The British hierarchy taught that until it did Catholics were free to support the party. By the mid-1920s this negative permission had been replaced by a positive one. Catholics could join and vote for the Labour Party: their role would be one of permeation and damage limitation. They would be organised into groupings via which they would learn how to keep the party 'straight', i.e. limit socialist influence within it. Out of this arose the development of a whole network of Catholic organisations with this aim in mind, the most important of which was the Catholic Social Guild (CSG). Founded in 1909 this set out to warn Catholics of the dangers of socialism, propagate the Catholic alternative to the workers' question and develop skills among its members which would enable them to take part in political activities.[1]

The Catholic Social Guild is interesting in that its founders were all middle-class professionals, many of them converts. They were hardly representative of the main body of the faithful. What kept the CSG from simply being a talking shop for Catholic middle-class reformers was the development of study circles. These were groups of Catholic working men and women who met to discuss social issues. The CSG provided an umbrella for them to operate under, providing books, pamphlets and reading lists. Membership of study circles had a profound effect on those who became involved. Often semi-literate at the outset, a considerable number of them ended up as executive members of their trade union and Labour Party branches. Some of the most talented were encouraged to embark on a two year course of full-time study at the Catholic Workers' College, Oxford, which was established by the CSG in 1921.

The CSG played an influential part in encouraging British Catholics to act within the Labour Party *as* Catholics. What did this mean? It meant support for a particular set of values, familiar from the social encyclicals (particularly *Rerum Novarum*, published in 1891) and defined by the CSG as Christian Democratic. From 1921 the Guild published a monthly journal, the *Christian Democrat*. In the first issue its editor, Henry Somerville, laid out the political philosophy of the Guild: 'We call ourselves Christian Democrats, for we are of the people, working by and for the people. Our first name is Christian, because there is no other name under heaven given to men whereby individuals or societies may be saved, but the name which is Christ.' He went on to set out the social platform of the Guild and *Christian Democrat*. This was fourfold: the maintenance and defence of the Christian family, the establishment of a living wage as the universal minimum, partnership (rather than class antagonism) in industry and the diffusion of property. These were the ideas which the CSG was to campaign for within the Labour Party, and to a limited extent the Liberal Party, throughout its lifetime.

Europe comes to London: the People and Freedom Group

The CSG had good links with Christian Democrats in mainland Europe. While from the early 1920s the Catholic paper *The Tablet* was vociferous in its support for Mussolini, the *Christian Democrat* championed those opposing him. In 1924 the most important Italian Christian Democrat, Don Luigi Sturzo, founder of the Parti Popolare Italiano (PPI) was forced into exile when the Vatican decided its best interests lay in co-operating with Mussolini (Molony, 1977, p. 167). Luckily for British Catholics Sturzo settled in Notting Hill, London, where he was to remain for sixteen years. In these years of exile he sought to encourage those gathered around him to consider Christian Democracy in a British context. Among his most loyal supporters in this period was one of the founders of the CSG, Mrs

Virginia Crawford. She was important in what was to be Sturzo's major contribution to British Christian Democracy, the People and Freedom Group.[2] This organisation was founded in 1936 as a result of the confusion and pain felt by British Catholics in the face of the Spanish Civil War. Its members were largely middle class and already committed to the CSG. People and Freedom was to spawn a regular news sheet published between 1938 and 1953. And in 1939 the group published its manifesto, in book form, *For Democracy*.

Sturzo and his collaborators in the People and Freedom Group spent much time advancing the idea that it was perfectly acceptable for Catholics to be democrats, certainly not a superfluous message in the times in which they lived. They focused in particular on the 1931 encyclical *Quadragesimo Anno* which, Sturzo maintained, did not support Fascism, as had been suggested, but rather advocated what he termed 'corporativism'. People and Freedom not only opposed the activities of Mussolini and Franco but also those of Dollfuss in Austria. It was, however, less certain of how to view Salazar's Portugal.

Sturzo was on the left of the Christian Democratic spectrum. Speaking in 1905 he had stressed that, 'the new Catholic party must have a social democrat content, inspired by Christian principles: outside of these limits it will never have the right to a life of its own, it will become an appendix of the moderate party' (Molony, 1977, p. 33). This was in line with what the CSG had been teaching as comprising Christian Democracy. CSG members did not have to do any major rethinking to accommodate the ideas which Sturzo was advancing during his stay in London. What his arrival (and its circumstances) did was to make British Christian Democrats more sure of the importance of their beliefs and of the validity of their views. It made them acutely aware of the terrible turn of events in Europe and of the need to counter these. In fact, while Sturzo maintained that Catholics in Britain should concern themselves with events at home, individual members did this largely through their continued membership of the CSG. The *People and Freedom News Sheet* in its early years focused instead on events in continental Europe, particularly in France and Italy. This was however not the case in the post-war era and particularly not at election times, when, as we shall see, interest turned to events at home.

Christian Democrats and the Labour Party in the 1930s

The debate about the appropriateness of the Labour Party as a vehicle for Catholic support never wholly went away. The year 1935 saw the birth of another forum in which this was discussed, the *Catholic Worker*. This was a popular monthly tabloid newspaper edited by former students of the Catholic Workers' College. It was in existence in time to debate the Spanish Civil War, traumatic for all Catholics, but particularly difficult for those active in the Labour Party and trade union movement. Certain other issues, notably the attitude of the Labour Party to the funding of Catholic schools also caused problems. And in this decade fears were frequently raised, because of the popularity of 'United Front' arrangements, about the role of Communists in the Labour Party. In Liverpool, Catholics put up an independent candidate for one by-election as a protest against the Labour candidate's 'pro-Communist' activities (he sold Left Book Club publications) (*Catholic Worker*, April 1938). Even Sturzo, long intent on eulogising the British labour movement for its respect for the religious conscience of its members, questioned in 1938 whether the party had now 'gone socialist' (Sturzo, 1938, p. 40). Nor was it just a question of asking whether the Labour Party was doing anything which rendered it unacceptable to Catholics. Some were asking whether something better was possible, a more authentically Catholic political option. Catholic organisations elsewhere were very visible. Even those who did not support the so-called Catholic corporatist states of Portugal and Austria had a model to envy in Ireland (*Catholic Worker*, June 1937). But British Christian Democrats were realistic about what was possible in their own country and remained generally supportive of the Labour Party at this time.

Post-war events: disenchantment with Labour

The 1945 election saw the first majority Labour government in Britain. There was a good deal of loyalty towards this government on the part of working-class supporters. Christian Democrats were no exception to this; supporters of the middle-class People and Freedom as well as the largely working-class *Catholic Worker* welcomed the Attlee government. But such unanimous support did not last. What is noticeable is the movement, in the course of the next ten years, on the part of some Christian Democrats towards support for the Liberal Party. One prominent example of this was Michael Fogarty, Labour Party activist of the 1930s and 1940s, who went on to be a vice president of the Liberal Party. Fogarty was certainly not alone; the People and Freedom Group also grew dissatisfied with Labour and supportive of the Liberals. The next two sections of this chapter chart this process of disenchantment with Labour on the part of some Christian Democrats. The first looks at the serious concerns Catholics had at the way the Labour Party was developing in these years. The second looks at the attempts, in particular by People and Freedom, to get Labour to view itself as related to the Christian Democratic tradition.

The post-war Labour Party: a safe place for Catholics?

British Catholics in the post-war period were very aware of the plight of their co-religionists in communist-controlled Eastern Europe. An outcome of this was their heightened concern at the threat of communist involvement in the British Labour Party. In the immediate aftermath of the war Labour Party membership was expanded by many who had previously belonged to the Communist Party and the ILP but now believed, to quote Fenner Brockway, that 'the best work for socialism and for peace could be done within the [Labour] Party' (Schneer, 1988, p. 104). Many Catholics did not differentiate between communists and the membership of the wider left. All represented a threat to Catholic values, particularly in their support of wide-ranging nationalisation.

British Catholics did not condemn all nationalisation. In September 1945 the *Catholic Worker* had concluded that the plans for nationalisation in *Let Us Face the Future* (the Labour Party manifesto) could not be condemned on moral grounds. The following year the *Christian Democrat* declared that indiscriminate nationalisation was wrong but that selective nationalisation was acceptable. The fears of wider nationalisation came to focus on one man, Aneurin Bevan. If he gained ascendancy, the *Catholic Worker* warned in November 1953, there would be 'nationalisation for nationalisation's sake'. The one Catholic Labour MP who strongly supported Bevan, Hugh Delargy, was viciously attacked by the Catholic press (e.g. *Catholic Herald*, 26 March 1954). The extent of the vitriol poured upon him was an illustration of his uniqueness. Catholics were more often to be found on the right of the party and the obvious question to ask is whether any easy equation could be drawn between the philosophy of Christian Democracy and that of Labour Party revisionism.

There continues to be much debate over the exact nature of Labour Party revisionism. For the purposes of this paper a simple view of it must be taken. One feature of it was its anti-communism. With this, Catholic Christian Democrats obviously concurred. People and Freedom voiced in print its support for the revisionist publication *Socialist Commentary*, produced by the Socialist Vanguard Group. They were particularly supportive of its views on Russia (it was strongly anti-communist) (*People and Freedom*, Jan. 1946). But Catholic support for revisionist thought did not stem purely from a shared anti-communism. Christian ideas of 'fellowship' were strong within the revisionist movement, deriving in part from the influence of the Christian thinker, R. H. Tawney. This sits well with the Christian Democrat emphasis on a particular style of politics.

Of most importance in revisionism was its view of nationalisation as merely a possible means to achieving the goals of socialism, not a goal in itself. Leading revisionists such as Douglas Jay advocated limited nationalisation of national monopolies (Foote, 1985, p. 201). There was nothing here for Catholic Christian Democrats to reject. While some Catholics, e.g. the convert from Communism Hamish Fraser, told their co-religionists that membership of the Labour Party was incompatible with their Catholicism, Catholic Christian Democrats did not agree.[3]

One Catholic who loudly supported Labour until shortly before his defection to the Liberals was Michael Fogarty. In 1950 he wrote an article in the *Christian Democrat* describing how he saw the Labour Party developing. He suggested that it was moving from 'Socialism to Personalism; from grand scale planning to looking direct at individual human beings. This all implied a move from an emphasis on central planning and public ownership to small groups. The prominent Catholic Labour MP Frank Pakenham (later Lord Longford) wrote an article for the *Catholic Herald* some five years later suggesting that while this move had not yet happened there was a chance that it still might (*Catholic Herald*, 10 June 1955). Such an approach, defined by Pakenham as personalist, would 'put nationalisation and other State techniques in their proper place as methods among other methods of giving back each individual the chance to realise his infinite possibilities'. But Pakenham was pessimistic about the possibilities of such thinking gaining ascendancy in the party. A similar reading contributed to Fogarty's ultimate split from Labour.

Another element of the questioning of Labour Party acceptability to Catholics was the debate about the welfare state. Discussion about this had started with the publication of the Beveridge Report in 1942. It became particularly heated after the publication in 1954 of the pamphlet *Welfare and Taxation* by Colin Clark. Clark, a convert to Catholicism and long-time friend of the Catholic Workers' College and CSG, had been influential with Labour Party leaders in the 1930s. But by the 1950s he had moved to the right. Such was his political journey that one obituarist could perceptively describe him as the man whose name – rather than Hayek or Friedman – should be associated with 'proto-Thatcherism' (*The Guardian*, 6 September 1989). Clark's pamphlet, linking the welfare state with totalitarianism, was not popular among Christian Democrats (*Catholic Worker*, May 1954). The CSG, publisher of Clark's pamphlet, had by this time temporarily fallen under the control of Catholic conservatives. The most prominent, Paul Crane, had associations with the strongly reactionary wing of the anti-communist organisation Common Cause and with the right-wing Conservative MP Pat Wall. The outcry from the rank and file of the CSG at Clark's pamphlet showed the continuing support among Christian Democrats for the welfare state, a support strongly expressed in 1951 by Michael Fogarty in an article called 'I Love the Welfare State' (*Christian Democrat*, Nov. 1951). Labour's stand on the welfare state, while occasionally provoking fears, was not a major contributory factor to the decision by some Christian Democrats to leave the party. Their main gripe, dealt with in the next section, was the failure of the Labour Party to embrace fully the ideas of Christian Democracy, in particular support for a united Europe.

The attempt to portray Christian Democracy as of the left

As I have shown, British Catholic Christian Democrats worked to push the Labour Party onto the Christian Democratic track. People and Freedom believed that the way to do this was through familiarising British political activists with the programmes and policies of European Christian Democrats. They were not alone in this. John Eppstein of the CSG was keen to disseminate the programmes of the various European Christian Democratic parties but failed in his attempt to get them translated and published by a mainstream publisher.[4]

People and Freedom was better placed than Eppstein to make things happen. It had close friendships, developed in the 1930s and war years, with leaders of the European parties, Alcide de Gasperi, Maurice Schumann and Georges Bidault among others. It was particularly interested in portraying European Christian Democratic parties as of the left and so natural allies of the Labour Party. In 1948 it defended the Italian Christian Democrats against attacks from the British Labour politician Richard Crossman (*People and Freedom*, May 1948). He claimed de Gasperi's victory to be due to the support of big business, the Vatican and big landowners. In 1952 *People and Freedom* quoted de Gasperi's description of the Italian Christian Democrats as 'a party of the centre going towards the left' (*People and Freedom*, Dec. 1952). Labour's suspicion of Christian Democracy extended, unsurprisingly, to the German variety. It strongly distrusted Frank Pakenham's close friendship with Adenauer. Pakenham was appointed in April 1947 as Chancellor of the Duchy of Lancaster with responsibility for the British zone of both Austria and Germany. The leader of the German SPD Kurt Schumacher called Pakenham 'a pseudo-socialist' and claimed that by collaborating with Adenauer and his 'clerical bourgeois party' he had betrayed the working class (Craig, 1977, pp. 75–6). Britain's Foreign Secretary, Ernest Bevin, was similarly unhappy. In contrast one contributor to *People and Freedom* went as far as to suggest that Christian Democracy was inseparable from Social Democracy (*People and Freedom*, Feb. 1950). This was the line the group liked to propagate.

People and Freedom was very keen to get the Labour Party involved in the international machinery of Christian Democracy. The birth of the Nouvelles Equipes Internationales (NEI) took place in 1947, a development strongly encouraged by Sturzo who had kept alight the prospect of such liaison throughout the war years. It was in fact not a grouping of parties. Rather, those represented in it were individuals interested in Christian Democratic politics and (what was to become its more specific work) in international co-operation. As Michael Fogarty has explained, in reality it did consist of political parties where these existed but the membership formula allowed involvement by British delegates (i.e. the People and Freedom Group), exiled Spaniards and the like (Fogarty, 1957, p. 340).

The attempt by People and Freedom to get Labour to accept Christian Democracy as related to itself and become involved in the NEI came to nothing. Its frustration at this was on occasion palpable. A 1947 article listed the European Christian Democrats who would support Labour 'if they were Englishmen' (de Gasperi and Bidault among them). It continued:

Yet British Socialists (the Christian Socialist parliamentary group as vehemently as any) spurn Christian democracy as 'of the Right' and utterly alien. . . . Christian Democrats and personalist socialists, supported by true liberals and by progressive conservatives who believe in human rights, are fighting for the soul of Europe. Gladly would they accept the leadership of Britain. But Britain cannot assist their cause by promoting division rather than healing it, by blanketing in hostile incomprehension the axial force on which the whole battle depends – Christian democracy. (*People and Freedom*, Dec. 1947)

This failure to understand the nature of Christian Democracy was also a theme of Michael Fogarty. In his 1957 book, *Christian Democracy in Western Europe, 1820–1953*, he attempts to explain the Christian Democratic position on the State in terms which those brought up in the British tradition would understand. He concludes that the problem lies in the fact that Christian Democracy does not put the state at the centre of its thinking in the way that the British tradition does: 'Christian democrats are not looking outwards from the State. They are looking at the social structure as a whole and trying to bring the State, among other groups, into its proper perspective' (Fogarty, 1957, p. 99). Those in Britain best positioned to understand this are the 'social democrats' or 'social conservatives'.

People and Freedom continued to lament the British public's ignorance of Christian Democracy. In the one hundredth edition Barbara Barclay Carter, a People and Freedom founder member, was stressing the role of the group in trying to break this down, a task, 'urgently needed if the battle of freedom is to be won, in a framework of both political and social democracy, through the working, on the political and social plane, of the Christian leaven without which civilisation will cease to be' (*People and Freedom*, Jan. 1948).

Despite all these efforts the only Labour representative present at the January 1948 NEI Congress was George Catlin. Catlin, later to edit *People and Freedom*, had contested seats as a Labour candidate in 1931 and 1935. His general views are perhaps best expressed in a letter he wrote to his wife, Vera Brittain, in 1946. For him, 'significant living' meant 'to express effectively the ideas within one's self, to promote the rule of peace, the restoration of Christendom, the Union of the West'. In her memoirs his wife described him as standing 'to the right-centre of the Labour Party' (Brittain, 1971, p. 419).

Catlin's attendance at the Luxemburg NEI made him unpopular with Labour Party chiefs. Not only was it a meeting of Christian Democrats; it was a meeting about European co-operation. This conference was quickly followed by the Hague Conference of the NEI which in fact merged with the conference of all of the European movement, including Churchill's United Europe Movement. Significantly, with hindsight, Catlin took his daughter Shirley (Williams) to it. In his memoirs, published in 1972, he mentions her subsequent career as chairman of the Labour Party's Parliamentary European Group (Catlin, 1972, pp. 371–2). Williams' membership of the founding 'gang of four' of the British Social Democrats (the SDP) would seem a logical development from her father's ideas.

Catlin's attendance at The Hague earned him further disapproval from Labour Party chiefs. He was angered by this and reserved special venom for the Parliamentary Christian Socialist Group maintaining that their anti-Christian-Democrat stance was 'attributable to the influence of certain Socialist neophytes concerned to show ultra Socialist orthodoxy' (*People and Freedom*, Mar. 1948). The historian David Ormrod has suggested that the Parliamentary Christian Socialist Group, with its one hundred Labour MPs, 'exercised a powerful influence in maintaining the post-war Labour government's commitment to a socialist programme' (Ormrod,

1987, p. 448). This was hardly likely to endear them to supporters of the Christian Democratic programme.

Further objection to the Christian Democrats came from Labour's Stafford Cripps, a committed Christian, who maintained an opposition to specifically Christian political parties. His grounds were that they were just as rationalistic and no more religious than any other parties (*People and Freedom*, Mar. 1949). His 1945 book, *Towards Christian Democracy*, embodied many of the views favoured by Christian Democrats. It placed a strong emphasis on the sanctity of the human person and expressed the commonplace Christian Democratic belief that 'democracy is the practical application of the Christian teaching to the governance of society' (Cripps, 1945, p. 77). However, his views were unacceptable to Catholic Christian Democrats because of his stance on private property. The same was true of the platform of the Common Wealth Party, otherwise a possible home for British Christian Democrats. In the case of Common Wealth, the *Catholic Worker* valued its passionate belief in democracy and the need for morality in politics but commented on its basic programme of 'common ownership of almost all the means of production'. 'This programme', it stated, 'keeps many Catholics out of Common Wealth' (*Catholic Worker*, Mar. 1950).

Labour's attitude to People and Freedom endeavours such as the NEI did nothing to encourage support among this group for Labour policies. The news sheet had expressed reservations about the party as early as 1945 calling for a bolder approach, particularly in the area of workers' partici-pation in management (*People and Freedom*, June 1945). In the same article it spoke kindly of the Liberals hoping that the 1945 election would see a Labour victory but with a strong showing by the Liberals, an important party because of its stress on liberty and the rights of minorities. By March 1950 the reservations about Labour had grown much stronger. In an editorial dealing with the general election of that year the editors questioned whether the welfare state could avoid degenerating into the servile state as conservative Catholics had long been predicting. Praise was reserved for the Liberal Party (which had just polled disastrously in the election), seen by People and Freedom to be adopting Christian Democratic ideas. A few months later George Catlin was expressing the view that a Christian Democratic party might become a necessity in Britain since the current government did not pay enough respect to 'freedom as well as planning, to personal dignity as well as "welfare"' (*People and Freedom*, June 1950). Even in its death throes in 1953 the paper was still preaching the danger that Britain might 'soon cease to be a Christian Democratic country' (*People and Freedom*, Mar. 1953).

The People and Freedom Group were not the only ones to become disillusioned with Labour. Michael Fogarty was never involved with People and Freedom. Fogarty, a cradle Catholic, was educated at Christ Church, Oxford, where he was taught by Frank Pakenham. From 1938 to 1944 Fogarty was a prospective parliamentary candidate for the Labour Party but by the mid-1950s he was moving towards the Liberals. By this time, he said, he felt the Liberals to be much closer to Catholic social teaching and also in some ways a more exciting party where new ideas were coming through.[5] This was certainly the case in the late 1950s when the party was under the leadership of Jo Grimond. Grimond saw the Liberal Party as a party of the left – much as the British Christian Democrats of People and Freedom viewed Christian Democracy. Fogarty must have been very much at home in a Liberal Party espousing such ideas. This was a Liberal Party which could contain 'The Radical Reform Group' which sought to, 'reconcile individual freedom with that measure of wise planning which maintenance of our welfare society demands' (Watkins, 1966, p. 17).

Post-war Liberals gained further laurels from Catholics because of their stand on Europe. This was an issue to which British Catholic Christian Democrats attached great importance. The idea of an integrated Europe had (and continues to have) a profound appeal to those steeped in Catholic social theory.[6] In fact, one reason for British suspicion of the concept was an instinctive linking of the idea of European unity with that of a rebuilding of the Holy Roman Empire, i.e. a victory for Catholicism. The Labour Party itself certainly had no time for the idea of a united Europe, tainted in its mind by association with Churchill. In discussion in 1990 Michael Fogarty stressed the hopelessness of the attempts in this period to interest Labour in the European project. This played a big role in alienating him from the party. In contrast the 1951 Liberal manifesto *No Easy Way* stressed the Liberal commitment to a rapid development of the Council of Europe. It was Liberals such as Lord Leyton and Lady Violet Bonham Carter who had been original members of, and heavily involved in, the United Europe Movement (Watkins, 1966, p. 53).

Conclusion: who were the true British Christian Democrats?

This chapter has shown that in the case of Britain it is necessary to talk of Christian Democracies rather than Christian Democracy. Supporters of People and Freedom had a different conception of Christian Democracy from those of the *Catholic Worker*. The Catholic Social Guild had a wider constituency and contained elements of both. It is not possible to imagine a mass defection to the Liberals on the part of readers of the *Catholic Worker*. Their class base kept them too closely tied to Labour for this. Their concern was to keep Labour 'pure'. The editors assumed that their readers would vote Labour and were only concerned to ensure that when doing this they would be supporting a Labour Party which was not heretical. Their Christian Democratic project such as it was – limits to nationalisation, anti-Marxism and a feeling for their fellow man – was to be achieved within the Labour Party.

In contrast, supporters of People and Freedom and people like Fogarty and Eppstein represented a constituency close to that of the European Christian Democratic parties. This was certainly true of their class position. Hanson has pointed out that European Christian Democrat voters were often progressive Catholics of the middle classes (Hanson, 1987, p. 57). British middle-class progressive Catholics were set apart from what the up market Catholic weekly, *The Tablet*, was prone to call 'the parish

Irish' (Gallagher, 1987, p. 45). They failed to be interested in the issues which concerned this much larger group: trade unionism and Labour Party politics. In a sense they were anti-political. They enthused about democracy, taking much of their understanding of its relationship to Christianity from reading the work of Jacques Maritain.[7] They supported humanitarian ideas like the UN Charter on Human Rights rather than a specific political policy. This feature of Catholic activism has long been attacked: some European Christian Democratic parties have been criticised on such grounds, particularly the MRP (Rauch, 1972, p. 199). Support for Christian Democratic politics was a support for a style of politics as much as for a political programme. It is tempting here to recall the rhetoric of the Limehouse declaration of the British Social Democratic Party (SDP) with its emphasis on mould breaking politics.

The influence of middle-class lay Catholics, and the extent to which their values were shared by the British hierarchy (itself drawn from the same social strata), is shown in decisions taken by the latter. Organisations such as the Catholic Social Guild and the Association of Catholic Trade Unionists (founded in 1944) received little in the way of Church resources. While proclaiming an interest in working for a safe political home for its members, the British Catholic Church failed to put its money or even pulpit time into the project. The Church hierarchy did show an interest in the activities of the Labour Party, particularly in the post-war era but only actively lobbied it when the Church's interests (e.g. its schools or hospitals) were directly threatened. It encouraged political involvement on the part of its members since it realised that this was the best way to gain influence, the value of which had become clear during the years of World War II. It sought to discredit the separatist stance advocated by the Distributist movement of Hilaire Belloc and G. K. Chesterton. But those wishing for more hierarchical interest and direction in shaping the Labour Party, the natural home for the vast majority of British Catholics, were to be disappointed. The hierarchy and influential middle-class lay Catholics were just not interested in this.

The small group of People and Freedom supporters could, I believe, genuinely be called Christian Democrats in the sense of European developments. Their decisions to leave the Labour Party arose from a feeling that Christian Democratic ideas were failing to be heard, or to have any possibility of achieving prominence within that party. When they decided that the politics they believed in were being better expressed in the Liberal Party they were able to move their support without too much trauma, for they were not bound to the Labour Party in the way that working-class Catholics were. In contrast, those involved in the *Catholic Worker* were not about to leave the Labour Party. Their fight was to keep the party acceptable and to portray it as such in the face of attacks from Catholic conservatives. What both groups had in common (with the odd exception in each camp) was an awareness that a specifically Christian Democratic party was not a viable option in Britain. Then, as now, those calling themselves Christian Democrats had instead to concentrate their energies on getting their ideas accepted within existing British parties.[8]

Notes

1 The activities of the CSG are covered in Cleary, 1960. The archives of the Guild are held at Plater College, Oxford (formerly Catholic Workers' College). See Keating, J. E., 1992, *Roman Catholics, Christian Democracy and the British Labour Movement, 1910–1960*, Ph.D. Thesis, University of Manchester.
2 Crawford's papers, held in the Churchill Archives, Churchill College, University of Cambridge, contain much material relating to Sturzo and People and Freedom.
3 For Fraser's views see his autobiography published in 1954, *Fatal Star*, John S. Burns, Glasgow.
4 Eppstein correspondence, June–July 1946. Plater College Archives.
5 Author's interview with Fogarty, Oxford, August 1990.
6 For an analysis of this see Hanson, 1987, p. 53; Alan White OP, Memory, Nostalgia and Repentance, *New Blackfriars*, Nov. 1990.
7 For example, Jacques Maritain, 1940, *Christianity and Democracy*, Geoffrey Bles, London.
8 The most recent example of this is the membership of the Movement for Christian Democracy (MCD). For an account of its policies and strategy see Christopher Graffius, A Value-Vacuum in British Politics, *The Month*, August 1991.

References

Periodicals

The Christian Democrat
The Catholic Worker
The People and Freedom News Sheet
The Tablet

Books and Theses

Brittain, Vera, 1971, *Testament of experience*, Cedric Chivers, London.
Catlin, George, 1972, *For God sake's go!*, Colin Smythe, Gerrards Cross.
Cleary, J. M., 1960, *Catholic social action in Britain, 1909–1959: a history of the Catholic Social Guild*, CSG, Oxford.
Craig, Mary, 1977, *Longford*, Hodder and Stoughton, London.
Cripps, Stafford, 1970 [1945], *Towards christian democracy*, Greenwood Press, California.
Fielding, S. J., 1988, *The Irish Catholics of Manchester and Salford: aspects of their religious and social history 1890–1939*, PhD thesis, University of Warwick.
Fogarty, Michael, 1957, *Christian democracy in western Europe 1820–1953*, Routledge and Kegan Paul, London.
Foote, Geoffrey, 1985, *The Labour Party's political thought*, Croom Helm, London.
Gallagher, Tom, 1987, *Glasgow: the uneasy peace*, Manchester University Press, Manchester.

Hanson, Eric O., 1987, *The Catholic church in world politics*, Princeton University Press, Princeton.

Molony, J. N., 1977. *The emergence of political Catholicism in Italy: Partito Popolare 1919–26*, Croom Helm, London.

Ormrod, David, 1987, The Christian left and the beginnings of Christian-marxist dialogue, 1935–45, in Jim Obelkevich, Lyndal Roper and Raphael Samuel (eds), *Disciplines of faith*, Routledge and Kegan Paul, London, pp. 435–5.

People and Freedom Group, 1939, *For democracy*, Burns, Oates and Washbourne, London.

Rauch, R. William, 1972, *Politics and belief in contemporary France: Emmanuel Mounier and christian democracy 1932–50*, Martinus Nijhoff, The Hague.

Schneer, Jonathon, 1988, *Labour's conscience: the labour left 1945–51*, Unwin Hyman, London.

Sturzo, Luigi, 1938, *Politics and morality*, Burns, Oates and Washbourne, London.

Watkins, Alan, 1966, *The Liberal dilemma*, MacGibbon and Kee, London.

Whyte, J. H., 1981, *Catholics in western democracies: a study in political behaviour*, Gill and MacMillan, Dublin.

PART IV
THE INTERNATIONAL DIMENSION

11

THE EUROPEAN PEOPLE'S PARTY: TOWARDS A NEW PARTY FORM?

David Hanley

The movement towards European integration has clearly affected parties within the states of the European Community (EC) in many ways. One dimension which has not received perhaps as much study as it deserves is the organisational dimension. Increasingly, parties are being forced via the processes of the European Parliament (EP) and other transnational arenas to address the problem of supra-national collaboration, and to design structures and procedures for furthering such collaboration. Probably the most obvious manifestation of this trend is the growing cohesion of groups within the EP, which often seems to reach the point where national parliamentarians within such groups feel more solidarity with the group than with their original party which sent them into the EP in the first place.[1] EP groups vary in their cohesion from the *ad hoc* arrangements of the Rainbow Group or the European Democratic Group through the conflictual but increasingly tight collaboration of the Socialist Confederation to the apparently seamless mesh of the Christian Democrats in their European People's Party (EPP) (Jacobs and Corbett, 1991, pp. 55–83).

The EPP is however, to borrow a phrase, *un parti pas comme les autres*. Alone of the EP groups, it claimed for sixteen years to have gone beyond the status of a confederation or union and to have become a veritable supra-national party, of which the original national parties that comprise it are now mere sections. Only recently has it been joined in this aspiration by the socialist group, which mutated at the end of 1992, belatedly and somewhat enviously, into a European Socialist Party (Confederation of European Socialist Parties, 1991; Woltjers, 1991).

Clearly the implications of such a claim are considerable for the analysis of parties. This chapter will aim first to trace the development of the EPP as a transnational organisation. It will then seek to analyse the nature and functions of the EPP, and thereafter to explore the effects of the EPP on its actual constituent parties. Finally, it will attempt to see if there are any wider lessons for the development of parties and party systems in general.

Christian Democrats and the problem of transnational organisation

Unlike their communist or social democratic rivals, CD parties have had, surprisingly perhaps, considerable difficulty in elaborating forms of transnational collaboration (Mayeur, 1980, pp. 151ff). No such organisations existed prior to 1914, and the interwar period saw Christian Democrats unable to develop anything more than a secretariat for international collaboration (the International Secretariat for Democratic Parties of Christian Inspiration), with its seat in Paris. This body organised a number of international congresses but was never able to overcome the disagreement between the French and German parties over the Versailles Treaty; with the triumph of fascism in the two countries with the strongest CD parties, the organisation was soon doomed anyway and had collapsed by 1939. More serious attempts at international co-operation came after 1945, with the foundation of the Nouvelles Equipes Internationales (NEI) (Mayeur, 1980, p. 229; Papini, 1986). Even these meetings of leading CD activists did not take place at party level, however, but were purely an initiative of internationally minded elites, often undertaken against the advice of the party apparatus. From 1965 a new impulse was given by the leading party in power the Italian DC, which helped the NEI (by now based in Rome) to launch a European Christian Democrat Union, with Leo Tindemans as secretary general. Already national parties which had joined the new organisation *qua* parties were divided as to its nature and scope, with Southern Europeans opposing attempts to include British and Scandinavian Conservatives, whereas the German CDU was in favour. Plus ça change . . . It was the formation of the EC and the development of a new style of parliamentary life within its Assembly (following on similar developments within the Assemblies of the Coal and Steel Community and Council of Europe) that brought the next move forward, with the formation of party groups and the slow development of cross-frontier solidarity within them. Finally, the advent of direct elections for 1979 triggered in July 1976 the actual birth of the EPP–Federation of Christian Democrat Parties of the EC, to give the full title. Appropriately Tindemans was its first president and it began with twelve parties from seven states (Jansen, 1986).[2] Subsequent enlargements in 1980 and 1986 plus the merger of the three Dutch parties into the CDA have brought it up to its present total of fourteen full member parties from ten states (plus three associate members and two permanent observers).

The rise of the EPP is of course inseparable from that of the *European Christian Democratic Union* (ECDU) which is itself a section of the *Christian Democrat International* (CDI) (A 1). It is necessary at this point to consider rapidly the transnational structures of Christian Democracy.

The ECDU was originally simply the direct successor to the NEI (its congresses continued the numerical sequence of those of the NEI with the first one being number 17) (Letamendia, 1986). Fourteen parties from nine states joined, but there were some significant absences, notably the French, engaged at this time in trying to play down the Christian element of their identity for electoral reasons (Hanley, 1991). Commentators seem agreed that the new organism was lethargic; congresses (annual events in the NEI) were now held only every three or four years. The main political activity took place in the political bureau, itself dominated by party leaderships from the national parties and the EP. Resentful tongues spoke of Italian-German domination. Satellite organisations for youth, women, small businesses and even trade unionists were set up, but seem to have enjoyed the fate of their less than prominent counterparts in the Socialist International (SI).

Since 1961 the ECDU had joined with its Latin-American sister Organisation of Christian Democrats in America (OCDA) to form the World Union of Christian Democrats, which in turn decided in 1982 to reinforce its structures and its identity and become the CDI (Palmer, 1986). Although this was an organisation built from the bottom upwards and to some extent a partnership between (relative) equals, unlike the Socialist International with its total European domination, relations between the two halves have not always been easy. The Latin Americans have frequently suspected the Europeans of being at best complacent Eurocentrists and at worst social and economic conservatives, if not allies of imperialism. Recently, a third element has re-emerged in the shape of the Central European Union of Christian Democrats (CEUCD). Long a US-based émigré organisation, but admitted to membership of the CDI so as to bear witness to the continuing existence of the CD tradition even after communist takeovers (again there is a similar organisation within the SI), it has, since the collapse of communism and the electoral success of revamped or new CD parties in the East, acquired considerable weight under its current secretary-general, the charismatic Slovak leader Jan Carnogursky. It is clear that its parties will have an important role in the future within a redefined ECDU (Sinienewicz, 1986).

The ECDU and within it the EPP is, then, one of the three major poles on which the CDI is built. Christian Democrats have, like their Social Democrat rivals, invested enormously in these transnational links. It seems fair to say that whereas the conservative and liberal Internationals have yet to take off, the CDI and the SI are thus far the major players in this type of politics. With this in mind, we will now examine more closely the structures of the EPP and its place within the ECDU.

The nature of the EPP

The EPP has put out two sets of modifications to the original 1976 statutes, one in 1979 and one more recently after its Dublin congress of November 1990 (European People's Party (EPP), 1984, 1990a, 1990b). As party structures go, they are complex, as seen in A 2, which also tries to chart the relationship to the ECDU. A number of points can be made to help clarification.

First, we should note the virtual non-existence of EPP direct members (those who do not belong to a constituent party) (EPP, 1990a). Such people exist (indeed one or two MEPs must fall into this category such as the Ulster Unionist Jim Nicolson or refugees from other groups like the liberal Giscard d'Estaing and a handful of ex-Gaullists); but their numbers are not to our knowledge revealed and in any case their membership can only be approved with the agreement of their own national party. They may attend congress, but have no voting rights. This example (which reminds students of French politics of Giscard d'Estaing's UDF) suggests that the weight of the constituent national parties must still be very important.

A second feature is the wish to go beyond normal types of membership by offering what can only be described as corporate membership. Thus (unspecified) institutions may, by virtue of Article 6 of the statutes, acquire the status of sponsors (*mécènes*) and be invited to meetings. But such bodies may be expelled by the presidency (as indeed may individual members) on the request of their respective national party. It is thus hard to see in this new type of corporate membership anything more than the most limited gesture towards supranationality.

Third, it is hard to avoid the impression of a deputy-driven party. It may be true, as Brouwer, a former official of the EPP parliamentary group, claims, that MEPs do not hold the majority on the bureau or the presidency, which are clearly the main powerhouses of the EPP (Brouwer, 1991, pp. 34–5). None the less key positions such as president are invariably held by senior parliamentarians with experience of the EP as well as of their own parliament (and usually government); and mechanisms such as presidential power to co-opt make it easier to fill such bodies with parliamentary notables (EPP, 1990b, Article E).

Reinforcing this is a fourth feature, namely an institution which only made its appearance in the rules in 1990, but whose real existence preceded its juridical one by many years. This is the conference of party and government leaders, which brings together the president and secretary-general of the EPP, the leader of the EPP MEPs, the president of the ECDU (if his party is in the EPP), all CD party leaders and all CD heads of government within the EC, plus a representative of those EC commissioners who belong to a CD party (EPP, 1990a, Article 10). The president takes the conclusions of such meetings back to the next bureau. Jansen points out also that there are regular shadow meetings of CD ministers from member states in advance of Council of Ministers sessions, even though such events do not figure in EPP statutes (Jansen, 1986, p. 281). Clearly the significance of such institutions is immense, permitting access to the very heart of the EC decision-making process; it hardly seems an exaggeration to say that these gatherings of national party leaderships are effectively setting much of the EPP agenda.

The EPP is financed by member parties but also by its group of MEPs. This major input, logistical as well as financial, gives the parliamentarians and party leaders further leverage.

Thus far then, the picture is one of a party in which parliamentarians and national party leaders seem extremely powerful. It is these features which partially explain the ascendancy of the EPP within the wider ECDU.

Once the EPP was launched with the onset of direct elections to the EP and the consequent boost in legitimacy (and resources) it was inevitable that it would dominate within the ECDU. Critics soon complained about the loss of dynamism by the latter in terms of publications, conferences and general energy in spreading CD ideas (Letamendia, 1986, p. 62). In 1984 the decision was taken to replace Jean Seitlinger, the part-time secretary-general (he was also an MEP) with a full-timer, Thomas Jansen, who would take over the running of both ECDU and EPP. The two organisations were also to have the same treasurer. This reinforced the feeling that the EPP was the dominant partner, and in fact it made sense to see it thus. The CD operation in Europe had a strong core (the EC states) which were covered by the EPP; the remaining states were until recently mainly Nordic ones, where the CD parties were weak and Protestant. It was felt that it was enough to have a looser structure like ECDU to look after these, especially as there were possibilities for involving them anyway in some EPP activities.[3] But with the recent re-emergence of Christian Democracy in Eastern Europe and its modest upsurge in Scandinavia, the ECDU may not now be quite the poor relation it had become. We shall return to this question later; but for the moment we may note the presence of a powerful EPP within a weaker ECDU.

The functions of the EPP

The EPP's functions may be considered under two headings. On the one hand it performs a number of roles within European institutions; on the other it has a relationship to the different parties which make it up.

With regard to its institutional role, it performs much as does any national party within the structures of its own nation state. Thus within the EC it campaigns for a federal Europe. This action takes place on both the electoral and the parliamentary level and most of it can be seen as essentially a pedagogic or propagandistic exercise, whereby the party tries to relay to a wider audience the themes espoused by its constituent parties within their own states. These are so well known as to need but the briefest of recapitulation; and one of the tidiest recent statements is probably still the electoral manifesto for the 1989 election to the EP (EPP, 1989). The foreword recapitulates the explicitly Christian Democrat identity of the party and its doctrinal commitment to personalism. It is unambiguous about the desire to create a federal Europe:

only a united Europe can determine its own future in freedom, security and solidarity. Therefore our most important task is the further development of the EC to a political union, to a socially responsible economic and monetary union and to a security union. (EPP, 1989, pp. 7, 15)

All the rest of the document is subsumed here. The usual precautions are taken to reassure those worried about erosion of national sovereignty by invoking the magic word of subsidiarity, and the standard demands for institutional change are set out: reinforcement of the EP towards a position of 'codecision' on legislation with the Council of Ministers; increase of the EC's own resources; strengthening of the Commission to the point where it becomes the 'real government' of the EC and downgrading of the Council of Ministers to the status of a Senate; strengthening of EC legal institutions at the expense of national jurisdictions; and finally in foreign policy, a firm Atlanticism tempered by the wish to strengthen European defence co-operation (as 'second pillar' of the Atlantic Alliance) and place it firmly under EC aegis.

Outside election campaigns the main forum where the EPP can carry out its task of ideological (or as CD activists prefer to call it, doctrinal) education is clearly the EP. The party's day to day strategy here probably deserves a separate detailed study, but we may identify two features in particular. One is the taking of intiatives designed to force the pace of integration and to have maximum impact on public opinion. The most spectacular example of this type is the convocation of the Rome assises in November 1990 which brought together MEPs and national MPs from EC states and which gave rise to a document calling for increased federalism and increased power for the EP (EPP, 1991). The EPP played a major role in getting this venture started and in so doing underlined a second feature of its action. This is cross-party collaboration, particularly with Social Democrats (who were well represented at the Rome gathering). Increasingly within the EP there is extensive collaboration between the EPP group and the Confederation (now ESP), with a view to securing the majorities for (or against) a favourable EP opinion so as to influence the Council or Commission in the decision-making process of the Community (Jacobs and Corbett, 1991, pp. 80–83). Indeed both groups often enlarge the consensus beyond their own ranks, sometimes pulling in Liberals or Communists for key votes. In other words the EPP is helping create a highly federalist elite which will have effects beyond the confines of the Strasbourg assembly. Clearly there are extensive party political implications here and we shall return to this question.

Arguably more significant in the long run, albeit less visible, is the action of the EPP outside formal EC institutions particularly regarding CD parties. We may say here that it fulfils the classic roles of party Internationals in that it acts as a legitimator and a gatherer, the two tasks in fact being inseparable. Since 1976 the EPP has brought into the CD fold parties such as the Irish Fine Gael (FG) and the Greek Nea Demokratia (ND). Clearly such operations can be to the advantage of both sides. The party applying successfully for membership can use its acceptance to enhance its credibilty as an international actor within its own domestic arena. Equally the International can claim that its representativity and prestige are increased by the addition of yet another member. This two-way process has certainly been a feature of the SI and probably helps to explain the continuing viability of party Internationals (Portelli, 1983). But it is usually not without problems, and this has certainly been true of the EPP.

The main problems would seem to be: first, the criteria for accepting parties, and second, the institutional methods for so doing. This latter aspect really impinges on the relationship between the EPP and the ECDU.

Theoretically the criterion for acceptance by the EPP is willingness on the part of candidate parties to accept the programme and statutes of the party. Anyone can sign a programme, however, and CD activists and external analysts alike have wondered about some of the members. Why was Fine Gael recruited as the Irish member and not Fianna Fail? It has as many (or as few) Christian Democratic features as the latter.[4] Why was the Spanish PP let in if, as Brouwer claims, 80 per cent of its members are much further to the right than the thus far rejected UK Tories? Why was ND allowed to switch over from the conservative group in the EP? And whereas individual Danish members belong to the EPP group, why does their party as a whole not do so? Such anomalies go to the heart of the question of CD identity: what actually constitutes a CD party?

The whole of the ECDU and the EPP's history has been dogged by this debate, which has been all the more intense because of various attempts to downplay its significance (Portelli, 1986). But it is fair to say that there have always been two tendencies within the CD movement as a whole.

Particularly strong within the Benelux parties and in parts of the Italian DC (and *a fortiori* in Latin America generally) has been the very principled reading of CD politics, with a willingness to engage in ideological debate. Based on fidelity to *Rerum Novarum* it has stressed themes of social and economic justice; it is no accident that this tendency seems stronger in those states where ancillary organisations (unions, youth, media, etc.) are still vigorous. Alongside this has coexisted the other pole, of which the German-speaking states are seen as the core. Laying more stress on market values and individualistic liberalism, but generally striving to avoid commitment to tightly drawn ideology, it has often seemed more concerned with blocking socialism or communism than anything else; as such it has drawn increasingly close to the classic liberal-conservative right in the various forms which the latter takes across Europe. Seiler saw this polarity as central to modern CD parties (Seiler, 1980, p. 332). Indeed in his view those that took the first route (i.e. clung to a principled and demanding concept of Christian Democracy) were probably doomed to electoral decline, given the growth of secularisation. The second variety, which were becoming *Volksparteien* or catch-all parties, with the potential for spanning the ground from the centre across most of the right, had the best potential for the future. The living symbol of this tension is the double membership of a certain number of parties, which are in the conservative International Democratic Union (IDU) and its European wing the EDU (European Democratic Union), while retaining membership of the EPP/ECDU.[5] Needless to say the tension also runs across individual parties (the French CDS is a classic example).

Overlapping with this tension is another. It may be no accident that the most pragmatic CD party is one which is the least Catholic, the German CDU. Admittedly it is supported in this pragmatism by the CSU and the Austrian ÖVP, of whom the same observation could obviously not be made. But it is also true that none of the Danish CD forces belongs to the EPP and few of the other Scandinavian parties until very recently had joined the ECDU.[6] Taken together these facts suggest that it is necessary to ask the question: how far does adherence to CD positions in Europe assume not just a Christian but a *Catholic* culture? To ask this is not to deny the fact that many Protestants vote for and are active in CD parties. But it seems hard to deny that the more principled tendency within the CD movement described above rests on specifically Catholic assumptions. It is beyond the scope of this chapter to assess to what extent some or all of these assumptions may be difficult for non-Catholics; but there is an underlying tension and it is not one which CD politicians seem willing to bring out into the open. (It hardly seems for instance to have surfaced in the case of the British Conservatives; perhaps EPP leaders are not impressed by the joke about the Church of England being the 'Tory party at prayer').

Tensions among Christian Democrats have been given new urgency by the actual mechanisms for legitimising or co-opting new parties. Two cases are relevant here, the Spanish Partido Popular (PP) and the British Conservatives. Spanish Christian Democracy under Franco had difficulty in finding suitable political forms, except of course for its peripheral varieties in Catalonia and the Basque country: the Basque PNV and the Catalan Unio Democratica were members of the NEI. After some false starts a PDP (Partido Democratico Popular) was put together out of the original fragments known as Democracia Cristiana; this small formation was let into the ECDU in 1984 and the EPP in 1986. Shortly before the EP elections of 1989, however, this group merged with a large fraction of the old Spanish right (previously called the Allianza Popular and led by M. Fraga Iribarne, the former minister of Franco) to form the PP. The Spanish Christian Democrats felt that their presence and programmatic input into the new party was such as to render it Christian Democratic almost overnight; they wanted the soon-to-be-elected MEPs of the PP to be taken into the EPP group.

Clearly this was a test case. If a strongly conservative party, many of whose elites had a *franquista* past, could be whitewashed in this way, then it boded ill for tenants of the principled view of Christian Democracy. Certainly the chairman of the CDI F. Piccoli and the Catalan party leader Duran Lleida objected vehemently, the former speaking of 'people who are clearly on the right and whose presence condemns the Social-Christian movement (*sic*) to death' (Brouwer, 1991, p. 32). Eventually the fourteen MEPs (only two of whom had been previously known as Christian Democrats) were let into the EPP group despite the protests (and resignation) of the Basque member. Clearly the operation could be seen as the thin end of a wedge. In effect the EPP group had had its hand forced (fairly willingly, some suspected) by a last-minute, well-timed manoeuvre: a set of local elites, already legitimised, had co-opted another group further to the right and was using its own legitimacy to smuggle the new group into the EPP. Clearly the EPP MEPs were prepared to go along with this strategy. And equally clearly membership of their group could be seen as the antechamber of full admission to the EPP and ECDU. It looked like an operation driven by the CD parliamentary elites, keen to maximise numbers at all costs.

The same could be said of the UK Tories, though here the problem is one of integrating northern Protestant Conservatives rather than Mediterranean Catholics with authoritarian proclivities. The saga of the Tories and international Christian Democracy is older than is often realised and goes back to the beginnings of the Council of Europe (Brouwer, 1991, pp. 14–17). Before British membership of the EC, the CD youth movement was working to incorporate the Young Conservatives, and the latter were actually members of the European Union of Young Christian Democrats in 1972–3, then leaving to join a rival body the Conservative and Christian Democrat Youth Community; within this, according to Brouwer, they were particularly close to the CD parties of the German-speaking states (who had membership of both bodies). The 'adult' Tories were, of course, founder members of the EDU in 1978 and the IDU in 1983. Some believe that it was the surge of the Social Democratic group in the 1980s that led the EPP to try to expand its membership towards the Tories; whatever the reason we can see that there was some kind of precedent. Clearly both sides have had to tread carefully, given the stranglehold until recently of the Thatcher tendency on the Conservative Party on one hand, and the mistrust of many European CD activists on the other hand.

Nevertheless the outline is clear. Essentially as a result of negotiations at the level of the EP groups (and behind them to some extent of national party leaderships) a compromise formula was developed. This envisages co-operation between the conservative group (British and Danes) and the EPP in the short term, giving rise to a special two-year partnership between the groups. This two-year *Fraktionsgemeinschaft* was to run for two years from 1 May 1992 (Jansen, 1993). During this time the Tories were to answer a series of questions about their identity and their policies in the context of their claims to be valid CD members. An inter-party summit of April 1991 had already found that they were in agreement with the political principles of the EPP as defined at its Dublin congress. But before forming a combined group with the EPP, Conservative MEPs had to answer a series of questions relating to: the Christian image of mankind and its political implications; family, social and environmental policy; agricultural policy; monetary policy; defence and security and, last but not least, a federal Europe. Assuming that they pass this examination, the way should be in theory clear for them to join the EPP group (maybe not as full members initially?). In this way two other parties could be eased in to the CD family. It is hard not to believe that all possible will be done to ease the Conservatives' passage, despite solemn warnings that the EPP cannot compromise on its Christian Democratic identity or its federalism (Jansen, 1993).

The EPP parliamentary group enjoys a leading role in this legitimation process, not least because of the number of options available to it. Whole parties can of course be admitted. But members can also be admitted as individuals, thus paving the way for groups or whole parties to follow. They can be admitted to full status, or if this is felt to be too drastic a step, as *apparentés*. All these modes of integration are supple and play an assimilative role, offering as many routes as possible for MEPs and groups to enter the wider family. Similar structures operate within the PPE *per se*, where parties can be full members, associates or observers.

This prominence of the parliamentary group has only recently begun to be challenged, relatively speaking, by developments within Europe. On the one hand the collapse of communist rule and on the other the movement of EFTA nations towards the EC have opened up new possibilities for the CD movement. But by definition any aspirant parties from EFTA or ex-communist states can only pass through the ECDU not the EPP. Hence the former has been extremely busy over the past two years, co-opting and legitimising a number of CD parties (A 1). In the case of the parties from ex-communist states the ECDU has played a role in helping to decant the claims of various rivals and on occasion to help bring about fusions of competing parties into a more viable whole (clearly in Hungary and Poland this is very much an ongoing process). One unavoidable aspect of this is that the purist wing of Christian Democracy is likely to be further disappointed. For while some parties often have an authentic pedigree (e.g. the Slovaks), others fit much more easily into the centre-right *Volkspartei* mould. In certain cases (Poland?), even this formulation would probably be a polite one (Ost, 1991).

The fact is that the CD leadership of both EPP and ECDU are thinking in the long term. In the medium term they envisage an EC of nearly twenty (adding in the EFTA states and small states like Malta and Cyprus), hence the need to recruit allies there. To this end it is now possible for parties in countries seeking EC membership to join not just ECDU (which they mostly have) but also to have associate membership of the EPP – an option taken up thus far by the Austrian ÖVP, the Finnish KDS and the Maltese PN. But there is also the longer term prospect of a European Community of twenty-plus including ex-communist states, especially those that have split up into their various parts, usually allowing strong CD parties to emerge (such as Croatia, Slovenia and the Ukraine). Here the ECDU has been straining to recruit allies at speed, conscious that if it is too fussy about the credentials of newcomers, then it might simply increase the space available to national/populist and other more muscular variants of right-wing politics.[7] Clearly in the medium term new members must be welcomed through the ECDU; but in a sense this is only a halfway house, especially when new candidates have first to accept the very loose status of observer, which gives them no rights but simply the opportunity to learn the rules of good Christian Democratic behaviour. If it is successful in welding these new members into its ranks, then the EPP in twenty years' time could look forward to a future as the biggest grouping in any European institutions, certainly bigger than the rival Social Democrats. So the ECDU has a role to play in the long-term strengthening of the EPP, which remains the centre of gravity of the whole operation.

Transnationalism and party form: the nature of the EPP

It is now possible to attempt some overall classification of the EPP as a party. It is an organisation which unites national parties of similar style into a loose framework for political co-operation within European institutions for the pursuit of broad goals (economic and political integration). Despite its provisions for individual or corporate membership it is not a mass party nor ever likely to become one in the foreseeable future. On the contrary its motor is its elites, first the deputies in its EP group and behind them (in some cases it is the same persons) the leaderships of the national CD parties. This is entirely logical because its role is not to mobilise so as to capture power (such is the task of national parties) but to co-ordinate.

Co-ordination is a more useful concept for understanding the EPP than supra-nationalism. It seems to us idle to refer to the EPP as a 'superparty' on transnational lines. Brouwer's claims for supra-national status for the EPP rested on its new features: majority voting in the bureau; representation of groups in the bureau and also the activity of 'working groups' at lower levels; and above all individual membership. Unfortunately none of this amounts to very much. Group representation has nothing necessarily to do with supra-nationalism, but it does hark back to a much older tradition in Catholic thought, namely corporatism. Moreover the groups seem to play hardly any role. The only one Brouwer cites is, unsurprisingly, that of EC employees in Brussels; and even this seems to have ceased existence. Individual members are a more promising claim for supra-nationality, but they are hardly legion. Even majority voting in the bureau is reduced in value by the fact that CD leaders in EC states have long since been in very strong agreement about European policy anyway. In short it seems more sensible to agree with Duverger that what is required in Europe is 'a permanent coordination structure' between what are still essentially national actors, even if the eminent MEP believes that superparties will figure on the agenda in the (very distant) future (Duverger, 1992).

The EPP's role of co-ordination is enhanced by its position within the wider ECDU, into which it fits like the proverbial Russian doll. This flexible structure enables a wider grouping of parties to be kept in the CD fold, with the prospect of graduating eventually to the inner sanctum of the EPP. The EPP operates on the basis of consensus, like any International has done historically (with the exception of the Comintern). This consensus is facilitated by the nature of its elites; we are dealing with a highly cultivated, multilingual set of professional Europeans, buttressed by a common set of religious values. It is reasonable to suppose that such an elite, which lives out in its daily life the reality of an integrated Europe, is far ahead, ideologically, of its national party activists, let alone voters. The main area in which this elite does its work, the EP, is not a place where two sides contest power. In this assembly there is precious little power to contest, compared with the Council of Ministers, the Commission or *a fortiori* national politics. Essentially the EP is about struggling to obtain influence on other more powerful bodies and broadcasting the message of European integration; its function has more to do with pedagogy than with decision-making.

Despite the need to take its supra-national claims with a pinch of salt, the EPP has nevertheless some effect beyond the sum of its mere parts, on national party politics. This seems mainly to concern parties that are not yet fully integrated into it. To take the British case, it seems fair to say that contacts with the EPP have helped the majority of Tory MEPs to 'go native' to the point where most of them (unlike their Westminster colleagues) could honestly sign the EPP programmes, federalism and all. Equally in Spain, EPP influence could be said to have forced part of the Spanish right to rethink its whole strategy after its repeated failures to break through against the PSOE. Much doubt was shed on the sincerity of its conversion, as we saw, but none the less movement occurred and the EPP must be given some credit for this. Similar remarks could be made for Central and Eastern Europe where instruments such as the party's parliamentary committees for different countries and in particular Wim van Velzen's working party on Central and Eastern Europe have helped ECDU sort out the emergent party map. It is also useful to draw attention to the role of bodies such as the Adenauer foundation in this context. Scenarios like those of Brouwer which speculate on the break-up of the EPP seem unfounded. He envisages the party being lost in a big grouping with the conservative (and liberal?) Internationals or on the other hand shedding its more right-wing members and linking up with selected regionalists and mainstream Social Democrats (Brouwer, 1991, p. 44). The party will clearly continue to try and play the *Volkspartei* strategy in a big way, but hope to keep the principled Christian Democrats on board. It has managed thus far.

All in all the EPP seems to have established itself well. It is not a transnational party in any meaningful sense, but it is an effective and flexible co-ordinating mechanism. We need to try to assess why it has been so successful in this guise and whether there are any wider implications for other parties. In particular were those Social Democrats correct who wanted the Confederation to become a European Socialist Party (and who at last persuaded their leaders)?.

There are a number of factors favourable to the type of evolution enjoyed by the EPP. The first is the nature of its doctrine, especially its federalist thrust. This is something on which all the national parties were agreed before the EPP was ever founded; unlike their Social Democratic colleagues, CD groupings have never had to contend with an awkward squad of British or Danish Labourites. Another set of factors is more cultural/institutional. In most states CD leaders knew they could never be in the majority; accustomed as most of them were to coalition politics in their own countries, they were always likely to be predisposed in favour of a more permanent type of coalition beyond their own frontiers, but this time within their own family. Many of them must indeed have felt more comfortable here than in the company of other parties, left or right, in their own states which were often inspired by memories of earlier Church – State struggles; at bottom many Catholic politicians have never felt totally at home in the modern republican state with its instinctively secularist bias. At the same time, the profound anti-communism of CD politicians furthered another dimension with transnational implications, namely Atlanticism. On security questions, they have mostly been the firmest champions of the 'European pillar' of the alliance. All in all then, there was considerable doctrinal homogeneity at the beginning of the transnational project.

It was reinforced by institutional practice. Christian Democrats have enjoyed lengthy periods in government within EC states and this has led to extensive consultation at ministerial level and above. Such practices nourished a willingness to think in a less national way. Mention has already been made of the EP and its relatively non-adversarial culture. Here too habits of group concertation (extending from collaboration with Social Democrats on policy issues to work in intergroups) have helped this mentality to flourish.

A final feature has been the attitude of CD elites towards the image of their movement. It might have been possible to envisage a much stricter definition of Christian Democracy, hence a less numerous albeit ideologically clearer EPP. But the tendency has been towards the looser *Volkspartei* approach. This has advantages in that it has enabled the EPP to grow and it is likely to prove easier when dealing with Scandinavians or East Europeans. But it is clear too that it has set limits to the degree of cohesiveness that the EPP can except. It is a party which can only operate with a lowest common denominator of agreement (though some would say that its federalist choices represent in fact quite a high common denominator).

The implications for parties in general are limited. The essentials of political power still remain largely at national level. In a recent commentary on Christian Democracy, Hartmann reminds us that:

political parties are first and foremost national institutions. Their *raison d'être* is to be found in their national political systems; if constitutional texts mention parties, they ascribe national functions to them. (Hartmann, 1986, p. 71)

What is special about the EPP is that it is dominated by a group of national leaders (party and governmental) who happen to agree about very fundamental aspects of policy. Nevertheless there are some things on which these leaders do have differences (and which would merit a separate study). Also, even though they consult regularly within and outside the EPP, these leaders remain first and foremost national politicians, responsible to national electorates. There is nothing thus far to suggest that voters in EC states are willing to see the end of their national parties or to see themselves no longer as French or German, etc., but simply as Europeans. To that extent the experience of the EPP would suggest that one cannot hope to create a supra-national structure from the top, based on genuinely transnational elites. The experience of previous Internationals suggests this also; national priorities win out. Even the one apparent historic exception to this rule, the Comintern, gave way to this imperative in the end. It may come about that one day the essential locus of decision-making power within Europe will lie solely in Brussels; if and when that happens, then it will be paralleled by the emergence of genuinely transnational parties. Such an outcome is, however, at present pure speculation. Today the EPP is a useful co-ordinating structure between national actors who already see eye to eye on many essentials, and a useful means of developing some friendships with forces that may be much less close, in view of a future that is still very open. Whether such an organisation gains anything by being called a party is a moot point; but the Social Democrat leaders whose first instinct was to refuse such a tag for their own organisation might have done better to follow that instinct.

Notes

1 See the allegation that most British Conservative MEPs had become closest federalists (*The Guardian*, 21 November 1992).
2 The twelve initial parties were: CVP and PSC (*Belgium*); CDU and CSU (*Germany*); CDS (*France*); PSC (*Luxemburg*); KVP, ARP and CHU (merged into CDA as from 1977) (*Netherlands*); DC and Südtiroler Volkspartei (*Italy*); FG (*Ireland*).
3 EPP statutes (art. 4) allow full membership to parties from EC states which accept the EPP programme and statutes. But ECDU parties from states that have applied for EC membership can be admitted to the EPP as associate members. Observer status is available to *équipes nationales* (i.e. embryonic parties or groups thereof) from non-EC states which are ECDU members or, more widely, to 'any democratic party from EC member states which shares the basic political conceptions of the EPP or feels linked to the CD movement'. These more generous provisions were added on to the 1990 rules revision.
4 De Brouwer claims (1991, p. 13) that to have admitted Fianna Fail with its traditional anti-British bias and its territorial intransigence over Northern Ireland would have upset those wishing to lure the UK Conservatives into the EPP. This seems a strange argument; certainly the governments of Charles Haughey and Margaret Thatcher never let such considerations cloud their very positive relationship.
5 The parties enjoying dual membership of ECDU and EDU are: ÖVP (Austria); CDU and CSU (Germany); ND (Greece); DR (Cyprus); CDS (Portugal). The Swiss CVP and Maltese PN are observers in EDU.
6 The Norwegian KFP joined ECDU and the CDI in 1981; the Swedish KDS joined the CDI in 1984 but ECDU much more recently. The Danish Christian People's Party (KFP) joined ECDU in December 1991. Parties enjoying observer status in ECDU at the start of 1993 included the Finnish SKL; the EPP has given permanent observer status to the Swedish Conservatives (while the Swedish KDS is still only an associate) as well as to the Finnish Kansallinen Kokoomus (which is also a member of the conservative IDU). This practice of encouraging more than one member per country is probably to be read as a pressure on the parties concerned to move towards some kind of merger. If so, it is not a development to gratify the purist wing of the CD movement.
7 Interview with T. Jansen, Brussels, May 1991.

References

Brouwer, A. de, 1991, *Le Parti Populaire Européen: son identité, son nécessaire élargissement*, Insititut de Ciencias Politicas y Socials, Barcelona.

Confederation of European Socialist Parties, 1991, *Towards a European socialist and social democratic party*, Brussels.
Duverger, M., 1992, Vers des partis européens, *Le Monde* 25 January.
European People's Party (EPP), 1984, *Programme et Statuts* (2nd edn), Brussels.
EPP, 1989, *On the people's side*, Brussels.
EPP, 1990a, *Statuts du PPE, adoptés par le congrès de Dublin*, Brussels.
EPP, 1990b, *Règlement intérieur du PPE*, Brussels.
EPP, 1991, *For a democratic Europe*, Brussels.
Hanley, D., 1991, Christian Democracy in France, 1965–1990: death or resurrection? in N. Atkin and F. Tallett (eds), *Religion, Politics and Society in France since 1789*, Hambleden, London, pp. 203–19.
Hartmann, J., 1986, La Démocratie chrétienne et la recomposition des courants modérés, in Portelli and Jansen, pp. 73–84.
Jacobs, F. and Corbett, R., 1991, *The European Parliament*, Longman, Harlow.
Jansen, T., 1986, Le Parti Populaire européen: structures et développement, in Portelli and Jansen, pp. 277–83.
Jansen, T., 1993, *Report of the Secretary General of the EPP/ECDU to joint meeting of EPP political bureau and ECDU council*, EPP, Brussels.
Letamendia, P., 1986, L'Union européenne des démocrates chrétiens, in Portelli and Jansen, pp. 55–62.
Mayeur, J.-M., 1980, *Des Partis catholiques à la démocratie chrétienne*, Colin, Paris.
Ost, D., 1991, The generation of interests in post-communist East Europe: Solidarity, the incipient bourgeoisie and the crisis of liberal democracy in Poland, paper given at XVth congress of IPSA, Buenos Aires.
Palmer, B., 1986, De l'Union mondiale démocrate chrétienne à l'Internationale démocrate chrétienne, in Portelli and Jansen, pp. 41–54.
Papini, R., 1986, Le début des Nouvelles Equipes Internationales, in Portelli and Jansen, pp. 31–40.
Papini, R., 1988, *L'Internationale démocrate chrétienne*, Cerf, Paris.
Portelli, H., 1983, *L'Internationale Socialiste*, Editions Ouvrières, Paris.
Portelli, H., 1986, La Démocratie chrétienne et les Internationales, in Portelli and Jansen, pp. 85–93.
Portelli, H. and Jansen, T., 1986, *La Democratie chrétienne; force internationale*, Institut de Politique Internationale, Nanterre.
Seiler, D.-L., 1980, *Partis et familles politiques*, Presses Universitaires de France, Paris.
Sinienewicz, K., 1986 L'activité internationale des démocrates chrétiens d'Europe centrale, in Portelli and Jansen, pp. 233–43.
Woltjers, T., 1991, *Vers un parti socialiste européen*, Socialist Group of European Parliament, Brussels.

Annex 1 EPP and ECDU, January 1993

The following are full members of EPP:

Belgium	Christelijke Volkspartij
	Parti Social Chrétien
France	Centre des Démocrates Sociaux
Germany	Christlich Demokratische Union
	Christlich Soziale Union
Greece	Nea Demokratia

Ireland	Fine Gael
Italy	Democrazia Cristiana
Luxemburg	Christlich Soziale Volkspartei
Netherlands	Christen Demokratisch Appel
Portugal	Centro Democratico Social (membership temporarily suspended)
Spain	Partido Popular (not in ECDU)
	Unio Democratica de Catalunya
	Partido Nacionalista Vasco

Together with the parties listed below they form ECDU:

Austria	Österreichische Volkspartei*
Cyprus	Democratic Rally
Czech Republic	Czech team (Czech People's Party + CD Party of Bohemia & Moravia)
Denmark	Kristeligt Folkepartiet
Estonia	CD Union (EKL)
Hungary	Hungarian team (Democratic Forum + People's CD Party + Small Farmers' Party)
Lithuania	CD Party (LKDP)
Malta	Partit Nazzjonalista*
Norway	Kristeligt Folkpartei
Poland	CD Labour Party
Romania	National Peasant and CD Party (PNT – cd)
San Marino	Partido Democratico Cristiano
Slovakia	CD Movement of Slovakia
Slovenia	Christian Democrats
Sweden	Kristdemokratiska Samhaells Partiet*
Switzerland	Swiss team (Christlichdemokratische Volkspartei + Evangelische Volkspartei)

* = associate member of EPP

The following have observer status in ECDU:

Bulgaria	Nikola Petkov Peasant Union
	Democratic Party
	United Democratic Centre
	CD Union
Czech Republic	CD Party (KDS)
Croatia	CD Party
	Democratic Union
Finland	Christian Union (SKL)
Lebanon	Union Chrétienne Démocrate Libanaise
Lithuania	CD Party
Poland	Centre Alliance
	CD Congress
Romania	Hungarian Democratic Alliance (RMDSZ)
Slovakia	Hungarian CD Movement (MKDM)

Several applications are pending from Central and Eastern Europe.

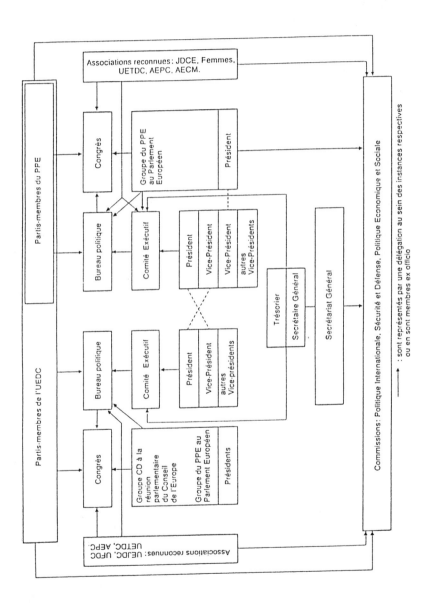

Annex 2 Structures of ECDU and EPP

Source: EPP, 1984.

12

THE SECURITY AND DEFENCE POLICIES OF EUROPEAN CHRISTIAN DEMOCRACY

Patrice Buffotot

Translated from the French by Siân Jones

The study of the security and defence policy of a European family (in this case, the Christian Democrats), provides an insight into how a European political organisation, made up of national political parties, behaves when confronted with an issue affecting state sovereignty, and succeeds in developing a common position.

Questions of security and defence constantly demand the attention of European Christian Democrats. Already members of the ECDU, they decided in July 1976 to group member parties of the European Community within a specific organisation, the European People's Party (EPP). For obvious reasons of effectiveness, the two formations have common secretariats and commissions, which means that the EPP can be considered as representative of the position of the Christian Democrats, and even more so since the Christian Democratic group in the European Parliament plays an important role within the party's structure.

The Christian Democratic group in the European Parliament is undoubtedly the most European group and also the most coherent. Therefore, as far as we are concerned, it is the European political formation that most strongly defends the idea of a common European policy on security and defence. However that does not mean to say that there are no differences of opinion among Christian Democrats. But unlike other European political forces, these differences have not blocked discussion nor prevented the adoption of relevant programmes.

The Christian Democrats make simultaneous use of the concept of defence and above all, security. The concept of defence is an old one and concerns all civil or military activities that can work towards 'military' defence. On the other hand, 'security' is a much wider concept. Let us note their own definition of the term. Security involves the 'political, military, and economic aspects, but also the ecological, technological and psychological aspects of life in society and between states' (Parti Populaire Européen [PPE], 1990, p. 5). The report presented by the deputy H.G. Pöttering and adopted by the Parliament on 10 June 1991, clearly specifies that a common security policy 'must include economic, ecological, demographic and technological factors, including all other elements which form the basis of social life and relationships between States' (PPE, 1991, p. 13).

Initially, the Christian Democrats define their doctrine with reference to Christian social doctrine. Confronted with an increasing Soviet threat, they create a 'global strategy for freedom'. At the same time, this does not prevent them from defining a security and defence policy for Europe nor conceiving within the framework of the process of European political union, a genuinely European security policy.

It is obvious that international events such as the disappearance of communism in the Soviet Union, the fall of the Berlin wall, the unification of Germany, the collapse of the Warsaw pact, and the disintegration of the Soviet Union have all contributed towards changing the geo-strategic landscape in Europe and stimulating the Christian Democrats to intensify the European process.

The ideological roots of security policy

The first texts, resolutions and programmes of the EPP refer explicitly to Christian social doctrine. Thus the motion adopted at the 4th Congress in Paris in 1982 confirms the member parties' adherence to the fundamental principles of Christianity, their faith in moral and spiritual values (PPE, 1982, p. 5).

Peace should not be the 'simple absence of war' or be reduced to simple, more or less precarious, military balance. If a solid and lasting peace is desired, then according to the Christian Democrats, four conditions are necessary (PPE, 1982, pp. 14–15).

In the first place, peace is inextricably linked to freedom and to respect for human rights. One of the causes of conflicts is the violation of human rights. The Christian Democrats conclude that very often it is dictatorships which are the instigators of modern-day conflicts. Therefore they believe that human rights precede all other rights, including that of state sovereignty (Groupe du PPE, 1984, p. 2).

The numerous interventions by EPP deputies in the Parliament confirm the interest that the Christian Democrats accord this subject. They are however aware that the definition of human rights varies from one continent to the other, in spite of the universal declaration. It is for this reason that they are in favour of more precise regional declarations.

The second condition is that peace cannot exist without economic and social justice both within as well as between states. For the Christian Democrats, socio-economic inequalities are sources of disorder and of domestic and foreign conflicts. This explains their active policy of aid to the development of Third World countries.

The third condition has been particularly relevant since 1989 for European countries. In effect, peace supposes the end of 'nationalisms'. The whole process of European unification is based on the abandonment of part of state sovereignty in favour of supra-national institutions (PPE, 1984, p. 19).

The final condition is disarmament. Lasting peace is impossible if there is an accumulation of arms. Christian Democrats suggest simultaneous, progressive disarmament, controlled of course at the lowest possible level, whatever the form of armament (nuclear or conventional). In addition we should remember that we were, at this point, at the beginning of the 1980s at the start of a new arms race between the two superpowers. The theme of disarmament, as we shall see, will constantly command the attention of the Christian Democrats; which does not mean that they are in favour of unilateral disarmament.

Since 1985 the EPP has stopped referring to Christian social doctrine. Many hypotheses can be formulated about this absence of ideology. Is it because the theoretical principles are so well established and it is no longer useful to return to them or because the end of the ideological rivalry with the Soviet Union means that recourse to ideology is no longer necessary? It is also perhaps for political reasons. The EPP's willingness to expose itself to political forces that are not explicitly Christian in both Western and Central Europe, prompts Christian Democrats to be more silent on the subject.

The last battles of the Cold War

The new tension between East and West at the end of the 1970s, notably with the invasion of Afghanistan and the deployment of Euromissiles in Europe worried Europeans. The threats were not new, but they had become more diverse, becoming multiform. They involved military threats (the deployment of the SS20 rocket was the latest example). They also included conflicts provoked and exacerbated by the Soviet Union in Third World countries, and economic threats that could strike European countries as well as those in the Third World. Faced with these multiform threats, Europeans must provide a global answer. Christian Democrats believed that military solutions, although necessary, were insufficient. Only a global political solution to the Soviet challenge would enable the West to win in the long term.

It is for this reason that the EPP suggested a 'global strategy for freedom', that could provide a solution that is at once political, economic, social and ideological (PPE, 1982, p. 3). It is evident that during this period of a new Cold War, the security policy of the EPP consisted mainly of strengthening interdependence within the Atlantic Alliance. For the Christian Democrats, American presence in Europe was absolutely necessary since it alone maintained a balance with the forces of the Warsaw pact. It is obvious that this balance was still based on 'the alliance between Europe and the United States'. It is for this fundamental reason that 'the EPP is firmly committed to balanced solutions, based on understanding and agreement' in order to solve the disputes and conflicting interests between the United States and Europe in the fields of economic, monetary and security policy, that could endanger this alliance (PPE, 1987).

The so-called 'Star Wars' project (Strategic Defense Initiative [SDI]), launched by the United States President Ronald Reagan on the 23 March 1983, prompted a re-evaluation within the EPP which led to the creation of a working group on the SDI. The Christian Democrats supported the project but deplored the differing positions of the various European states. They asked that the countries concerned 'consult each other to define together the conditions for co-operating with the SDI'. This would at least allow Europeans to secure better conditions from the Americans. The Christian Democrats wished to examine within the framework of the WEU, and in co-operation with the United States, 'the possibilities of new means of non-nuclear defence against ballistic missiles, cruise missiles, aircraft and conventional weapons'. Finally they asked the WEU to establish a commission to study the problems of creating a European defence initiative (EDI) which would complement the American SDI (Parlement Européen, 1985).

Disarmament

Although the Christian Democrats were in favour of disarmament, they pointed out that they are opposed to unilateral disarmament, which would, they believe, amount to surrendering democracy to dictatorship. It is for this reason that they were opposed to the 'pacifist' attitude during the Euromissiles affair and especially to the attitude of the German Evangelical Church. The Christian Democrats explained that the pacifist approach was in the first place erroneous since the problems did not only develop from the existence of arms, but from men themselves and from situations of injustice in the world (PPE, 1984, p. 13). It was therefore dangerous since it increased the risk of war by provoking an imbalance of power that could cause one participant to wish to profit from his temporary advantage in the strategic domain.

The EPP was in favour of controlled disarmament between East and West. Nevertheless if Europeans wanted to see their interests taken into account, they must defend a common position with regard to disarmament. The EPP's objective was to guarantee security by a balance of forces at the lowest possible level. That called for balanced and controllable disarmament in Europe in order to render a massive attack by the Warsaw pact impossible. That implied an important reduction in conventional forces but also a balanced reduction of the American and Soviet tactical nuclear weapons in Europe. (Groupe du PPE, 1984, pp. 27–8).

Finally the Christian Democrats demanded the signing of a treaty supporting the prohibition of chemical weapons in the world and a 50 per cent reduction in strategic weapons between the two superpowers. (PPE, 1988, pp. 53–4). The Intermediate Range Ballistic Missiles (IRBM) agreement between the United States and the Soviet Union marked the beginning of an interesting process in disarmament for the EPP and a respite in international life. But the absence of Europe from those negotiations must stimulate Europeans to adopt a common policy on disarmament and in consequence in the field of security policy. This treaty must set in motion the process of disarmament in Europe and should be followed with conventional and tactical nuclear weapons.

As far as the conference on Security and Co-operation in Europe (CSCE) was concerned, the Christian Democrats supported these negotiations since they were a stabilising factor in the co-operation between the peoples of Europe and the United States. They asked that the preparations for these negotiations, that were to take place in Paris on the 19–20 November 1990, be undertaken within the framework of European Political Co-operation (EPC) and in co-ordination with the Parliament to ensure that Europe spoke with one voice.

They believed, immediately before the conference met in October 1990, that the CSCE could be the ideal framework to develop a new European structure. After the Paris conference, and the signing of the treaty on Conventional Forces in Europe (CFE-1) (which to a great extent answered the Christian Democrats' concern about avoiding massive surprise attack by the forces of the Warsaw pact), they called for continued negotiation and the involvement of the European Parliament at the conference through a delegation of observers (Groupe du PPE, 1991, p. 43).

Towards a common security and defence policy

A security policy within the Alliance (1976–88)

The United States and the Atlantic Alliance play an important part in Christian Democrat concepts. It is not surprising to see the EPP recognising that the 'United States remains the principal guarantee for Western security, which is also that of Europe' (Groupe du PPE, 1984, p. 13) Consequently the United States is of pivotal importance to European security in spite of the uncertanties of American policy, notably during the presidency of Jimmy Carter when, as the Christian Democrats deplored, 'we had to cope with a somewhat irrational American policy' (p. 14).

In the December 1982 agreement, the EPP recalled the important role played by the Alliance in the maintenance of peace in Europe. The Alliance and its military organisation (NATO) are subsequently indispensable in ensuring the security of Europe (Groupe du PPE, 1984, pp. 19–20; PPE, 1982, p. 2).

The Christian Democrats recognise however that there is a real imbalance between the United States and the European allies. Their whole policy was to consist of giving more power to Europe so that it could negotiate with the United States on an equal standing. Consequently a united Europe was necessary to restore this balance and lead to a collaboration based on 'equality of rights and responsibilities' within the Alliance (PPE, 1982, pp. 3–4). The EPP suggested that the Europeans reinforce their participation in the field of conventional weapons in order to raise the nuclear threshold in Europe, although they recognised on the other hand, that 'deterrence' had contributed towards avoiding conflict in Europe (p. 5).

The cooling in relations between the United States and the Soviet Union at the end of the 1970s only encouraged the European Democrats to 'confirm their attachment to the Alliance . . . which is the political expression in foreign policy of our choice in favour of democracy' (PPE, 1988, p. 49). That did not prevent them from recognising that the Alliance remains in spite of imbalances and that Europe could deal on an equal basis with the Americans if it spoke with one voice. It did not mean replacing the Alliance but building a 'European block' within the Alliance.

During a conference organised by the EPP and the ECDU on relations between Europe and the United States in 1986, the leaders of these two political organisations recognised the existence of different opinions and approaches which corresponded to the divergent interests of the United States and Europe. 'A permanent dialogue between Europe and the United States is therefore clearly indispensable on all levels' (PPE, 1986, p. 11). The Christian Democrats envisaged in particular meetings with the two biggest American political parties, the Democrats and the Republicans, for further discussions on these matters.

The Christian Democrats therefore wished to fight to ensure that security policy is integrated into European Political Co-operation. But 'the primordial objective is the development of a concept of European security within the framework of the Atlantic Alliance' (p. 15). However the Christian Democrats were aware that 'in the long term only a United Europe (European Union), can respond to the challenge of an "equal partnership" with the United States of America'. It is also for this reason that the Christian Democrats wish to orientate the Community towards a federal union. The report submitted by P. J. Teunissen of the EPP/EUCD on 15 January 1987 specifies that a political union would therefore imply a 'joint action in arms production and defence'. But to reassure the Americans and Europeans attached to the Alliance it states that 'this Western European military identity should be established within the framework of the Atlantic Alliance, and in agreement with the United States. Military co-operation with the United States within the Alliance remains indispensable' (UECD/PPE, 1987 p. 2).

The 'joint agreements on military strategy' between the Europeans and the United States would be linked to maintaining a discussion on the lowest possible level, the presence of American forces in Europe, the need to give credibility to the doctrine of 'flexible response', increasing the Europeans' contribution within the Alliance, and the necessity for the Europeans to speak with one voice at the NATO council, whether through the president or a representative of the EPC (p. 3).

One idea particularly expressed by the EPP during its 7th Congress was the constitution of a European bloc within the Atlantic Alliance: 'the Europeans would therefore be partners in a better position to defend their interests on an equal basis with the United States' (PPE, 1988, p. 49). The only framework for the development of this policy was European Political Co-operation.

The institutional battle (1985–9)

The Christian Democrats called for the institutionalisation of EPC. In its 1984 programme, the EPP suggested establishing a European security council, a premature project perhaps, but one that set a long-term objective. In the short term the Christian Democrats were fighting to ensure that the political and economic aspects of security be taken into account in the draft project of the Single European Act. This Single Act, signed on 26 February 1986, foresees in article thirty (section three), paragraph six, 'that a stricter co-operation on questions of European security will obviously be indispensable to the development of a European identity in foreign policy'. It is therefore anticipated that different countries must 'further coordinate their positions on the political and economic aspects of security'. It is clearly specified that this co-operation does not impede those already in place within the WEU and the Atlantic Alliance.

Although this document does not go as far as the Christian Democrats might wish, they did however call for its application. Therefore the President of the Security and Disarmament commission in the European Parliament, Hans-Gert Pöttering, raised a question on 22 January 1988 asking the council to undertake to apply the measures of the Single Act concerning security policy. This question was supported by socialist, conservative and communist deputies (Groupe du PPE, 1988, p. 14).

The EPP's 7th Congress in November 1988 established the creation of a European Union as an objective for the end of the century, which would 'dispose of the attributes of political and diplomatic sovereignty'. In the immediate future, it requested that European Political Co-operation 'become a common foreign and security policy, with appropriate operational instruments' (PPE, 1988, pp. 50–51). The idea of a European Security Council was again considered. This would be composed of members of the European Council and defence ministers of the WEU member states. This council would meet at least once a year, immediately before the Atlantic summit in order to define a common European policy. One of the Christian Democrats' concerns was to resolve the co-operation between the diverse institutions (EPC, Parliament, the Western European Union, the Atlantic Alliance and the CSCE). Meetings with the representatives of these various institutions took place in an attempt to resolve this delicate question (Groupe du PPE, 1989, pp. 25–6).

EPC tested by international crises

The Gulf war followed by the crisis in Yugoslavia was to shatter these common policy projects in foreign and security policy. The European countries were in effect incapable of defining a common policy at the time of the Gulf war and during the Yugoslav crisis. Diverging interests and assessments emerged and became obstacles to the creation of a common policy. Hans-Gert Pöttering, in his report adopted by the European Parliament on 10 June 1991, recorded an 'incapacity to act jointly' on the part of the Europeans during the Gulf war, and he deplored the fact that 'certain members aligned themselves with other powers, some members attempted in vain to take independent community action and some preferred not to express themselves' (PPE, 1991, p. 11).

This ineptitude on the part of Europe only confirmed the Christian Democrats' will to fight for the establishment of a common policy and even more so now that Europe was likely to be confronted in future years 'with dangers particularly on the Southern flank'. In order that Europe could react, 'joint action by the EC and its member states becomes clearly necessary'. The EPP's Security and Defence Commission proposed a 'Union for European Security', meaning a collective system of security and assistance (PPE, 1990, p. 4).

The speaker regretted the fact that the Single Act is not restricting enough. There is no obligation to joint action in foreign policy. He made a bitter assessment of the working of the present day institutions: 'The current structures and mechanisms of the EPC are not sufficient when the Community has real need to conduct independent foreign and security policies which are influential and efficient' (p. 5). In future, since the political, economic and military aspects intersect, they must consequently be treated as a whole (PPE, 1991, p. 13).

The Christian Democrats suggest a series of institutional measures. It is necessary to confer powers similar to other common policies, including foreign and security policies, upon Community institutions. Therefore, the EPP recommends the creation of:

(a) a defence council drawing together defence ministers of the member states;
(b) a security council drawing together foreign affairs ministers and defence ministers;
(c) the adoption of decision-making procedures, notably the principle of the three-quarters majority to facilitate the elaboration of common positions;
(d) the integration of the EPC secretariat into the Council of Ministers.

As far as the Commission is concerned, a Commissioner should be appointed with responsibility for foreign and security policy and for establishing an agency for observing and controlling arms productions and sales.

Finally, the European Parliament should be able to discuss questions of security fully, and be kept regularly informed by the Council as well as by the Commission. It is understood that all fundamental decisions shall be approved by the Parliament. What remains is the difficult question of co-operation with the other European institutions involved with security; the Atlantic Alliance, the WEU and the CSCE.

In the strictly military field, the Christian Democrats are calling for the establishment of a common policy on arms exports, harmonisation of the legal bases of national service in all the member states and finally the establishment of multinational European units so that the Community can intervene if the case arises, 'to guarantee the peace and security of all the members of the Community'. The Christian Democrats want defence doctrines to be orientated towards 'defensive' strategies and states to reduce their military budgets and arms production (PPE, 1991, pp. 15–31).

The Christian Democrats' battle to secure a common policy on security and defence is a permanent one, in spite of the numerous difficulties that they have encountered in the process. Their attitude is explained by the relative homogeneity of the Christian Democrats. They are all strongly pro-European; the rifts that appear are between the 'ultra-Atlanticists' (especially the Dutch and the Italians) and the 'European Atlanticists', that is to say those in favour of a European bloc within the Atlantic Alliance, such as the Germans, the Turks and the Belgians.

Certainly the cohesion of the Christian Democrats is facilitated by many factors. The first is the existence of a French Christian Democrat party (the CDS), which has always defended a strongly Atlantic position. Even if it accepts the French line on deterrence, it has always had a doctrine similar to the Alliance and moreover does not make great play out of deterrence on a European level. The second factor is the fact that the 'ultra-Atlanticists' will be obliged to make concessions since they contradict themselves: on the one hand they support the Atlantic Alliance but on the other, they are as European as they are federalist.

The Christian Democrats are confronted by important barriers to the creation of a common security and defence policy, since it affects state sovereignty, and certain European political forces are not yet ready to make sacrifices in this domain. So far, the Christian Democrats have been one of the political driving forces behind the construction of Europe. But they should not allow their willingness to expose themselves to new political forces to endanger their coherence, nor force them to abandon their project of European political union.

References

Groupe du PPE, 1984, *Le défi européen: positions de principe, réalisation et objectifs du groupe PPE de 1979 à 1984*, Brussels.

Groupe du PPE, 1987, Debate in EP in *Rapports d'activité, juillet 1986 – juillet 1987*, Luxemburg.

Groupe du PPE, 1988, *Rapport sur les activités, juillet 1987 – juillet 1988*, Luxemburg.

Groupe du PPE, 1989, *Rapport sur les activités, juillet 1988 – juin 1989*, Luxemburg.

Groupe du PPE, 1990, *Rapport sur les activités, juillet 1989 – juillet 1990* Luxemburg.

Groupe du PPE, 1991, *Rapport sur les activités, juillet 1990 – juillet 1991*, Luxemburg.

Parlement Européen, 1985, Rapport de P. Bernard-Reymond (PE 102.125/rev), Brussels.

PPE (Parti Populaire Européen), 1982, La paix dans la sécurité et la liberté (motion du 5ème Congrès), Brussels, Documentation 5.

PPE, 1984, Liberté, justice, paix: la responsabilité des Européens dans le monde, Brussels, Documentation 5.

PPE, 1986, Colloque du PPE/UEDC groupe PPE sur les relations Europe/Etats-Unis, *Bulletin du PPE* 6, Brussels.

PPE, 1987, Résolution du bureau politique du PPE 13 janvier 1987, *Bulletin du PPE* 7, Brussels.

PPE, 1988, Programme d'action du PPE, 1989–94 in *Aux cotés des citoyens*, Brussels, Documentation 8.

PPE, 1990, Projet de la commission Sécurité et Défense adopté le 26 octobre 1990 à Strasbourg, Brussels.

PPE, 1991, *Europe: Sécurité et Défense*, Brussels, Textes et Documents 4.

UECD/PPE (Union Européenne Démocrate Chrétienne/Parti Populaire Européen), 1987, Rapport de P. J. Teunissen à la commission Sécurité et Défense: 'Concept européen de sécurité – identité européenne', Brussels.

CONCLUSION: THE FUTURE OF CHRISTIAN DEMOCRACY IN EUROPE

David Hanley

The future of Christian Democracy presents a number of challenges, all of them linked. There are questions of strategy and tactics. There are also a number of policy questions. Finally, there are ideological questions, inseparable to some extent from organisational questions. All of these questions highlight in their different ways the central preoccupation of this book, namely the identification of Christian Democracy as a distinct political species.

Beginning with the strategic dimension, it is clear that the CD movement must decide quickly on new recruits and partners. The case of the UK Conservatives will be crucial here; if they join the EPP as full partners, it will suggest that the looser, less principled version of Christian Democracy has prevailed. This might well have implications for alliances, with parties of liberal or conservative hue being preferred to the Social Democrats who, as this volume suggests more than once, are often the natural partners.

The evolution of the EC will also obviously be crucial. If, as seems likely, integrationist pressures give way in the wake of Maastricht to a more intergovernmental phase, it will be interesting to see how far progress can be made on issues such as foreign policy or defence. At the same time, if the EC expands rapidly, it will be important to analyse what effect the new Nordic members will have on CD prospects within EC institutions. In particular, how far will relations with Eastern and Central Europe, where CD prospects are undoubtedly stronger, be affected?

The potential for growth of the CD movement in these regions is not to be underestimated. It starts out with an advantage over the main competitor in international terms, Social Democracy. This movement is being eclipsed in the West, as one party after another loses office. Further East, the remains of Social Democratic parties are bound to suffer for a while yet from association with the mistakes of the recently demolished command economies, even though Social Democrats were always among the earliest, firmest and most persecuted opponents of the Communists. The Christian Democrats have an advantage over Liberal and Conservative rivals also in that in many parts of ex-Communist Europe the CD movement had a fair degree of organisation before 1939. This base can be built upon, for the

electoral history of countries which emerge from long periods of dictator-
ship (Iberia, Greece) tends to show that old party loyalties do have
remarkable subterranean longevity. But the reconsolidation of Christian
Democracy east of the Elbe is not a simple task; much will depend on the
quality and commitment of CD elites and the support given to them by the
international bodies of the CD movement. Uncritical recruitment of
groups on the basis that anything to the right of Social Democracy is an
acceptable addition to the family will serve only to dilute further the
specificity of the movement. This whole area is in constant flux.

Whatever their alliance choices, CD parties are clearly bound to play a
major role in the governance of most of Europe. They will thus have to
confront a number of policy choices, some of which will test fully the
resources of the CD political family. It can safely be assumed that as
national economies become ever more subject to international competitive
pressures, the number of jobless throughout Europe will increase. At the
same time, the differentials between those in work and the jobless will
probably rise. We may assume that the wider problems of advanced
industrial societies will become no easier to manage: urban decay, home-
lessness, increasing crime, drugs, racial tension. All these problems are
likely to result in increased demands on the public purse in a period when
sources of revenue are under great pressure. Hard choices will have to be
made, and the CD commitment to social justice will be tested fully. It is in
this arena of social expenditure that the two versions of the Christian
Democrat world view, the principled and the minimalist, will contend for
influence.

In addition, there is one set of problems which affect the Christian
Democrats even more than other political families. They are to be found at
the interface of public welfare policy and private morality and include such
issues as euthanasia and abortion, as well as issues related to the repro-
duction or maintenance of life (in vitro fertilisation or the transplanting of
human organs). Related as they are to the question of the family and its
social role, such issues invariably link up with wider moral questions such
as pornography and sexual permissiveness generally. All political parties
have to confront these issues of course, but because of their very nature
they go to the heart of CD politics. No other party has such an explicit
commitment to a specifically Christian world view, in which the sanctity of
life and the pivotal role of the family are paramount. At a time when
advances in science and changes in social attitudes raise questions about
these assumptions, CD parties may well find themselves internally divided
and at odds with some of their partners, especially those with a Liberal
outlook. This whole area of bio-ethics is fraught with difficulty for
Christian Democrats, and the difficulties are likely to become worse as
science increases the possibilities of modifying life and its maintenance.

Finally, with regard to the general ideological context, it must be
assumed that secularisation will grow apace. This means that if voters are
still to be mobilised it cannot be achieved on a purely religious basis. A
solid governmental track record would probably be a better catalyst; but
even this will be insufficient if there is no ideological or cultural humus in

which appeals to generosity might take root. By what means can CD values be propagated nowadays? We can speculate endlessly as to how far religious values of solidarity and caring for one's neighbour have become part of the secular heritage of all modern societies. But it would be unwise to assume that such a heritage is safe; for every good Samaritan who has never read the Bible there is probably at least one Essex man waiting in the wings.

CD politicians will doubtless be confident that their parties can continue to mobilise on the basis of a common culture, as they have done in the past. They would do well however to pay some attention to the infrastructure of their movement. Historically, the CD movement has been buttressed by a whole associative network of women's and youth movements, trade unions and professional associations, mutual insurance societies and credit unions, sport and recreational associations. Some countries have shown much more strength here than others; but most successful CD parties usually owe something to such an infrastructure, if it is only a continuing supply of committed activists and, more important perhaps, the circulation of CD ideas and culture. There has in fact been little serious study of this associational infrastructure and its relationship to CD parties. But there is reason to believe that the infrastructure is ailing, like that of secularist parties; if so, the effects on the future of CD parties will need urgently to be assessed. It would seem to us however that a certain vital minimum of *tissu associatif* is needed if the CD ideas of social generosity and solidarity are to survive amid the growing individualism at the end of this century.

The CD movement goes towards the twenty-first century surrounded by challenges and questions. It has long been used to such pressures, and we may expect it to face them with the same confidence and skill that it has usually exhibited beneath its sometimes bland and paternal discourse. But there will be much work for political scientists to do in charting the movement's adaptation to what will certainly be a difficult period. Christian Democracy will remain a major actor on the European stage for the foreseeable future. Based on past experience that is a justifiable expectation and as safe a prediction as is possible in the radically changed Europe of the 1990s.

INDEX